Also by Brian M. Fagan

Southern Africa during the Iron Age (1966)
Iron Age Cultures in Zambia (1967 and 1969)
In the Beginning (1972)
People of the Earth (1974)
The Rape of the Nile (1975)
Elusive Treasure (1977)
Quest for the Past (1978)
Archaeology (1978)
World Prehistory (1979)
Cruising Guide to the Santa Barbara Channel (1979)

Return to Babylon

RETURN TO

Travelers, Archaeologists, and
Monuments in Mesopotamia

BABYLON

Brian M. Fagan

LITTLE, BROWN AND COMPANY BOSTON, TORONTO

FIRST EDITION

Library of Congress Cataloging in Publication Data

Fagan, Brian M
    Return to Babylon.

    Bibliography: p. 286
    Includes index.
    1. Iraq — Antiquities. 2. Excavations — (Archaeology)
— Iraq. 3. Archaeologists — Iraq — Biography. I. Title.
DS69.6.F33   935   79-18197
ISBN 0-316-27306-6

80-34

MV
Designed by D. Christine Benders

*Published simultaneously in Canada
by Little, Brown & Company (Canada) Limited*

PRINTED IN THE UNITED STATES OF AMERICA

To Paul

with gratitude for friendship
and much research

When I approached the earth, there was a high flood,
When I approached its green meadows,
The heaps and mounds were pi[led] up at my word.
— PRONOUNCEMENT OF THE GOD ENKI, FROM THE
SUMERIAN POEM "ENKI AND THE WORLD ORDER,"
TRANSLATED BY SAMUEL KRAMER

Acknowledgments

MY GREATEST ACADEMIC and personal debt is to Paul Friedman, without whose support and willing assistance this book would never have been completed. I can but dedicate it to him. Richard McDonough and Henriette Neatrour provided sage advice throughout the project. Professor Seton Lloyd gave me valuable insights into Mesopotamian archaeology from the 1930s onward, while Drs. David and Joan Oates kindly criticized a draft of Chapter 21. I owe a particular debt to Marge Mahoney who typed the manuscript and to Rodney Searight of London for his help with illustrations. Jean Whitnack provided detailed criticism during production which was simply invaluable. The assistance of the libraries of the University of California at Berkeley, Los Angeles, and Santa Barbara is gratefully acknowledged. The staffs of the Royal Geographical Society and the Society of Antiquaries of London were most helpful. I am also grateful for facilities given to me at the British Museum and Library, at the Public Record Office, and in the Santa Barbara Public Library.

Author's Note

FOR THE PURPOSES of this book, the terms Iraq and Mesopotamia have been used interchangeably except in specific and self-evident contexts where a more precise meaning is intended. Arab names are spelled in their modern mode and I have used the *Times Atlas of the World* (1977), as a basic yardstick for geographical place names. Archaeological sites are spelled according to the most common and widely adopted usage in the academic literature; for instance, Assur instead of Asshur, which is used in many atlases.

Contents

V. Science and Nationalism

MAPS

Chronology: 7000 B.C. to A.D. 571

	Mesopotamia	Developments Elsewhere
Early Settlement		
By 8000 B.C.	Early farming in the Zagros foothills	Earliest settlement at Jericho
By 7000 B.C.	Early farmers in northern Mesopotamia	Early development of agriculture in Egypt (?)
5800 B.C.	Hassuna	
5500 B.C.	Choga Mami and Samarra	
5300 B.C.	First settlement of the Mesopotamian delta and beginning of 'Ubaid period; emergence of Eridu as a city	Pre-Dynastic farmers in the Nile valley
3600 B.C.	Uruk period of Mesopotamian prehistory begins (named after the city of that name)	
3100 B.C.	Jemdet Nasr period begins; emergence of writing	
2900 B.C.	Emergence of the Sumerian civilization in southern Mesopotamia	Unification of Egypt and the emergence of ancient Egyptian civilization
Sumerians and Akkadians		
2500–2000 B.C.	Royal cemetery at Ur of the Chaldees. Emergence of Sumerian city states, among them Kish, Lagash, and Umma. Beginnings of systematic historical records, mainly known from Lagash	Pyramids built in Egypt
2380 B.C.	Lugalzaggesi of Umma overthrows Lagash and sets up a Sumerian empire, describing himself as "king of Erech" and ruler of territory that extended from the "Lower Sea along the Tigris and Euphrates Rivers to the Upper Sea"	

2370 B.C.	Sargon I of Agade (the Great) overthrows Lugalzaggesi, founds the Akkadian Dynasty, and forms a vast empire that rules not only Sumer but extends far into Asia and to the Mediterranean	Emergence of Harappan civilization in the Indus Valley
c. 2200 B.C.	Overthrow of the Akkadians by mountain peoples and the renewed prosperity of Lagash under Gudea and other Sumerian governors	
2140–1945 B.C.	The Third Dynasty of Ur. The surviving ziggurat at the site is built	Middle Kingdom in Egypt
1750 B.C.	Final decline of the Sumerians as the Babylonians assume power in Mesopotamia	

Babylonians and Assyrians

1790 B.C.	Hammurabi of Babylon establishes rule over the Sumerian domains and a wide area of the Near East	Minoan civilization in Crete/ Egyptian New Kingdom
1307–1275 B.C.	Adad-Nariri assumes the leadership of the emerging Assyrian empire based at Assur	Hittite civilization/Mycenaean civilization in Greece
1115–1077 B.C.	Tiglath-Pileser I	
883–859 B.C.	Ashur-nasir-pal II (Assyrian capital at Nimrud)	
858–824 B.C.	Shalmaneser III (Nimrud)	Phoenician merchants in the Mediterranean
744–727 B.C.	Tiglath-Pileser III (Nimrud)	
721–705 B.C.	Sargon II (Khorsabad)	
704–681 B.C.	Sennacherib (Nineveh)	
680–669 B.C.	Esarhaddon (Nimrud)	
668–627 B.C.	Ashur-bani-pal (Nineveh)	Etruscan civilization in Italy/Darius at Behistun
612 B.C.	Collapse of the Assyrian Empire after the sack of Nineveh by the Scythians, Medes, and Babylonians	

*Babylon
and Later
Events*

604–562 B.C.	Nebuchadnezzar's empire based at Babylon; he builds the major public buildings of the city	
538 B.C.	Cyrus of Persia overthrows Babylon and establishes Persian supremacy in Mesopotamia	Classical Greece
323 B.C.	Alexander the Great conquers the Persian Empire and Babylon	
322–280 B.C.	Seleucus rules Mesopotamia	Rome controls Italy
250 B.C.	Parthian period begins	
A.D. 226	Sassanian kings control Mesopotamia	Roman Empire
A.D. 571	Birth of Mohammed and the emergence of Islam	
C. A.D. 750–1230	Baghdad at the height of its prosperity under the caliphs	The Crusades
A.D. 1515	Mesopotamia becomes al-ʿIraq, a province of the Ottoman Empire	

NOTE: This chronology makes no pretensions to being complete, and many sites and rulers' names are omitted. Dates, especially those earlier than 2000 B.C., are highly provisional.

Binbirkilise △

Birecik
Carchemish
Jerablus

Iskenderun
Antakya
Orontes R.

Amik Golu

Aleppo

AR

K

Khorsab
(Dur
Sharruk

Khabur R.

Hatr

Euphrates River

CYPRUS

Tripolis

Palmyra

Beirut

Is-Geria

Mediterranean
Sea

Damascus

SYRIAN
DESERT

H

Jerusalem
Lachish △

Amman
△ Jericho

Petra

SINAI

MESOPOTAMIA

-N-

SCALE:

| 0 | 100 | 200 | 300 KMS |

| 0 | 100 | 200 MILES |

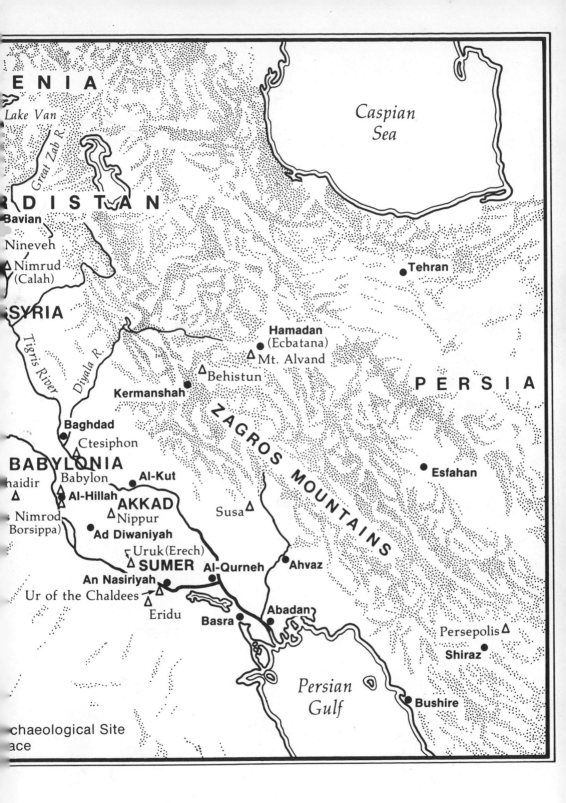

ENIA

Lake Van

Great Zab R.

RDISTAN

Bavian

Nineveh

△ Nimrud
(Calah)

SYRIA

Tigris River

Diyala R.

Hamadan
(Ecbatana)
△ Mt. Alvand

△ Behistun

Kermanshah

Baghdad
Ctesiphon

BABYLONIA

haidir   Babylon   Al-Kut
△   △ Al-Hillah

 Nimrod   AKKAD
Borsippa)   △ Nippur
               Ad Diwaniyah

             ⌐ Uruk(Erech)
             △ SUMER   Al-Qurneh

     An Nasiriyah
Ur of the Chaldees △ △
          Eridu   Basra

*Caspian
Sea*

● Tehran

PERSIA

● Esfahan

ZAGROS MOUNTAINS

Susa △

● Ahvaz

Abadan

Persepolis △

Shiraz ●

*Persian
Gulf*

● Bushire

chaeological Site
ace

I

LOST KINGDOMS AND BIBLICAL LANDS

1

A Legacy of Civilizations

Thy shepherds are asleep, O King of Assyria.

"D ESOLATION MEETS DESOLATION: a feeling of awe succeeds to wonder; for there is nothing to relieve the mind, to lead to hope, or to tell of what has gone by," wrote the famous archaeologist Austen Henry Layard about Mesopotamia in 1853. The age-old lands of the Biblical Garden of Eden, of Old Testament cities like Babylon, Erech, Nineveh, and Ur of the Chaldees, were no more than dusty, forgotten mounds of debris and mud brick. A year later, another English archaeologist, William Kennet Loftus, similarly described the landscape at Erech in southern Mesopotamia: "There is no life for miles around. No river glides in grandeur at the base of its mounds, no green dates flourish near its rivers . . . a blade of grass, or an insect, finds no existence there. The shriveled lichen alone, clinging to the weathered surface of the broken brick, seems to glory in its dominion over these barren walls." The desolation of Mesopotamia struck every nineteenth-century European traveler to the region. The fertile and prosperous lands of the Old Testament had become little more than a harsh wilderness inhabited by nomadic tribes.

To devout Westerners who believed implicitly in the historical truth of the Scriptures, as most of them did, the blasted landscape of

Mesopotamia was dramatic confirmation of the dire predictions of the Old Testament prophets. "He will stretch out his hand against the north, and destroy Assyria; and he will make Nineveh a desolation, a dry waste like the desert," thundered the prophet Zephaniah. Armed with prophecies like this, the early travelers and archaeologists wandered over the mounds of long-abandoned Nineveh in pardonable confusion. What had become of the glorious cities of the Scriptures? Could any sense be made of the chaotic jumble that lay before them? Fortunately for science, Mesopotamia held a strange fascination for many of these travelers and archaeologists. Gradually they replaced the mystery of centuries with a glorious palimpsest of civilizations and cities, of great kings and laboring serfs, of remarkable religious, literary, and artistic achievements.

This book is a story of high adventure and laborious excavation, of brilliant intellectual insights and patient investigation, of high-minded scholarship and blatant chicanery. It is also the story of the Mesopotamians themselves, for centuries exploited and ruled by Macedonians and Persians, Arabs, Turks, and British. The early archaeologists had to pursue their work in the midst of constant political change, of emerging Iraqi nationalism and eventual political independence. Today, Mesopotamian archaeology is the province of specialists and scholars: experts in cuneiform writing, esoteric art styles, mound excavation, and temple architecture. Their conclusions are more cautious than those of their adventurous predecessors, who lacked both professional training and academic rigor. The Iraqis themselves now run their own antiquities service and museum. Foreign archaeologists are closely supervised and can no longer help themselves to priceless antiquities with impunity. The heroic days of Mesopotamian archaeology are gone forever, but their passing, however nostalgically regarded, only benefited serious scholarship: the pioneers often did irrevocable damage with their picks and huge gangs of workmen. Even so, their achievements were staggering: the recovery of the long-lost Assyrian, Babylonian, and Sumerian civilizations, which had been crumbling literally to dust; the discovery of new art traditions that rivaled those of Egypt, Greece, and Rome. The early archaeologists wrote of Biblical legends come true, of clay tablets, conquering kings, and great lion hunts. They showed that the Biblical Flood had a solid basis in Babylonian and Sumerian literature thousands of years older than the Scriptures. They provided the Victorians with startling vignettes of ancient human societies, often almost as fresh as the day they were recorded by sculptor or scribe. The modern science of archaeology flourishes in Mesopotamia because these early discoveries fired the popular imagination, thereby stimulating the flow of money for training, sound excavation, and further scholarship. Without question, the discovery of the Sumerians and the Assyrians ranks among the greatest archaeological achievements of the nineteenth and twentieth centuries.

The adventures narrated in these pages are even more remarkable because Mesopotamia had always been off the beaten track for European travelers, and after 1515 was an impoverished and decaying province of the Ottoman Empire, ruled by the sultan of Turkey. As for the provincial capital, Baghdad, such was its magical and legendary reputation that European visitors expected to enter a magnificent oriental city of romantic splendor and fabulous wealth. They were invariably disappointed. Baghdad had become a shadow of its former self.

The beginnings of Baghdad were modest. It had been little more than a village until 762, when the great caliph al-Mansur chose it as his new capital. "It is excellent as a military camp," he rationalized. "Beside here is the Tigris to put us in touch with lands as far as China and bring us all that the seas yield." In four short years al-Mansur turned Baghdad into a circular city with double brick walls and four gates from which major highways led to the outposts of the empire. The caliph's palace and the Great Mosque stood at the center of the circle. Within a few generations an Arab author was able to write that Baghdad was "a city with no peer throughout the whole world." And he was probably right. The Abbasid caliphs made their capital into a great commercial city and a center of sophisticated learning at a time when few European kings could even write their names. Its wealth was staggering. When Caliph al-Muqtadir received the ambassadors of Emperor Constantine VII from Constantinople in 917, one hundred lions and sixteen thousand cavalrymen marched in the ceremonial parade. The wealth, exotic tastes, and luxury of the Abbasid court caused such wonder in their own time that they passed into history as an Arabian Nights fantasy preserved by generations of Arab and Western writers. Small wonder that romantic visitors of the eighteenth and nineteenth centuries were disappointed to find only crumbling palaces and breached walls. Baghdad, like the rest of Mesopotamia, lived on its former glories.

A variety of motives took European travelers to this obscure part of the world before the nineteenth century. Some went to visit Christian communities or to search for trading opportunities. These heroes braved the hazards of caravan and desert travel to reach the land between the rivers. Traditionally, caravans approached Mesopotamia across the Syrian Desert. Some travelers, like the Elizabethan merchant John Eldred, joined a caravan disguised as Moslem merchants and rode from Syria to the Euphrates near Babylon. They were harassed and robbed and were often lucky to escape with their lives. Others reached the Tigris at the town of Mosul and floated downstream on

The great ziggurat of the Third Dynasty at Ur of the Chaldees,
as seen from the northeast

a *kellek*, a wooden raft supported by inflated goatskins which were strengthened with wooden crosspieces and fastened together with strong reeds. The goatskins were reinflated every day and were continuously soaked to prevent them from bursting. Two large oars of split cane served to steer the raft. The passengers perched themselves on the bales of merchandise. Wealthier people bought a wooden bedstead and covered it with a felt awning. The bed was placed in the middle of the *kellek* and served as a couch by day and as a bed at night. These rafts had been in use in Mesopotamia since Assyrian times.

Once in Mesopotamia, few travelers stayed long enough to acquire a detailed knowledge of the country. They would visit Mosul or Baghdad, pause to examine ancient Nineveh or Babylon, and then go about their business.

The first Christian travelers were astounded at the sight of Nineveh and Babylon. Their tales of desolate ruins circulated so widely that the celebrated guidebook of Sir John Mandeville, written in about 1357, included "Babylone the Grete." This endearing work, which begins with a chapter entitled "To teche you the weye out of England to Constantinope," described the "grete tour of Babel . . . of which the walles weren lxiii furlonges of heighte." Generations of European travelers visited Egypt and the Holy Land with Mandeville in hand. The few that crossed the desert to Mesopotamia found no reason to doubt the existence of the "grete tour of Babel." Certainly no European traveler could have done better than the eminent Arab geographer al-Mas'udi, who visited Nineveh in 943. He found it to be "no more than a complex of ruins in the middle of which are several villages and farms. It is to these settlements that God sent Jonah." He added: "One finds stone statues covered with inscriptions."

The dramatic story of Mesopotamian archaeology begins not with casual travelers but with the European consuls who served their countries faithfully in remote outposts at Baghdad and Mosul. Today the British embassy in Baghdad prizes the portraits of its early incumbents. Few diplomatic posts can have been blessed with such talented and dedicated occupants. The calm and authoritative Claudius James Rich, who arrived to take up his post in 1808 at the age of twenty-two, is the first to gaze down at us. A brilliant linguist and an accomplished orientalist, Rich made the first dispassionate surveys of Nineveh and Babylon, and took archaeology from the realm of travelers' tales into that of scientific fact. He also combined his antiquarian studies with skillful diplomacy. He and his wife literally held court in Baghdad. His formula for dealing with the local pasha was simple, and emulated by his successors: "Nothing but the most decisive conduct will do." When

Rich left Baghdad in 1821, the entire city turned out to bid him farewell. The antiquities he had collected were among the first Assyrian finds to reach European soil.

Rich's successor, Colonel James Taylor, survived a plague that killed more than two thirds of Baghdad's 150,000 residents in 1831. He was such an eminent Arabist that the local Arab scholars were said to consult him on the nuances of manuscript transcription. Taylor was the first European to examine Sumerian mounds in the desolate wastes of the delta. He was the man who introduced his successor, the Indian Army officer Henry Creswicke Rawlinson, to the complexities of cuneiform script.

Rawlinson's portrait conveys an air of forthright authority, an impression of a formidable personality. British prestige was never higher than in Rawlinson's day. Even his dogs were said to be greeted with deference in the bazaars. He turned the British residency into a veritable menagerie of leopards, lions, and dozens of smaller animals. Yet this superb diplomat found time to copy and decipher the inaccessible cuneiform inscriptions at Behistun in Persia that were to serve as the Rosetta Stone of Mesopotamian archaeology. A tradition of diplomacy and scholarship combined survived at the residency into this century. Baghdad was a prized post for the type of Englishman who relished oriental life and comparative solitude.

The British diplomats were normally obliged to stay close to their offices in Baghdad. While they aided and encouraged the pioneer excavators, they did little digging themselves. But the French government encouraged its consular officials to excavate. Paul Emile Botta, a quiet, introspective man, was sent to Mosul to find and excavate ancient Nineveh. After an abortive dig into the mound of Kuyunjik across the Tigris from Mosul, Botta was lucky enough to discover the palace of the Assyrian king Sargon II at Khorsabad, fourteen miles to the north. The French were so impressed with his finds that they supported a year of excavation with public funds. Later, Victor Place was to continue the digs at Khorsabad until the whole of Sargon's palace had been uncovered.

The spell of Mesopotamia fell most intensively on one of the most remarkable Englishmen of the nineteenth century, Austen Henry Layard. Layard came to the Tigris by accident while riding from Europe to India. He stayed to excavate the mounds of Nimrud and Nineveh and to write two immortal books on his excavations. A tempestuous, enthusiastic visionary, he was befriended by Rawlinson, lionized by the public, and gave up archaeology at the age of thirty-six. His descriptions of ancient Mesopotamia fired the imagination of thousands of readers. "The great tide of civilization has long since ebbed," he wrote. "We wanderers were seeking what they had left, as children gather up the colored shells on the deserted sands."

The magnificent Assyrian bas-reliefs in the halls of the British Museum and the Louvre still electrify the visitor today, as they did for the first time over a century ago. But the surge of public interest caused by the early Assyrian excavations was nothing compared to the sensation when George Smith found the greater part of the story of the Flood on some clay tablets from Nineveh. His discovery of the missing lines after only a few days of excavation is one of the great coincidences of archaeology. It is difficult for us to understand the impact of this extraordinary revelation on a public nurtured on the firm conviction that the Old Testament represented recorded history.

The picture gallery of Mesopotamian archaeologists includes many heroes and villains. There are excavators like Hórmuzd Rassam, who literally dug up the landscape in a frenzied search for tablets and antiquities. He was alternately praised as a great digger and condemned as a robber. There are museum officials like Wallis Budge, who resorted to downright trickery to save tablets for the British Museum. Sober and experienced German scholars like Robert Koldewey and Walter Andrae are seen spending season after season reconstructing Babylon and Assur from the most inconspicuous of mud-brick foundations. The heroic gallery of Mesopotamian archaeology closes with the English archaeologist Leonard Woolley, excavator and raconteur extraordinary, who dug at Ur of the Chaldees in the 1920s and made discoveries that rivaled the spectacular treasures of Tutankhamun's tomb. Woolley was in the heroic mold, a brilliant improviser who was never at a loss. Like all the early archaeologists, he was a prodigious worker.

The story of Mesopotamian archaeology bristles with lesser figures, too: Robert Ker Porter, an aristocratic romantic whose fine paintings of Mesopotamia influenced the courts of Europe; William Kennet Loftus (quoted earlier on), an unsuccessful digger who never quite found the Sumerians; Gertrude Bell, whose idealism and archaeological acumen created the Iraq Museum in the 1920s. Most of the major and minor characters in our story were remarkable people deeply in love with the East. They had a gift for languages and for getting on with the local people, who helped them on their way or dug in their trenches. It was this ability to thrive in an alien environment that was the key to their ultimate success. In their times a foreigner's word was law; decisive behavior and a revolver could win the day. If our heroes seem larger than life, it is hardly surprising. They needed extraordinary personal qualities to achieve what they did. Certainly, we shall never see their like again: the cautious and inflationary world of today cannot afford their enormous enterprises.

The heroic age of Mesopotamian archaeological discovery left us with a spectacular legacy of early civilization that extends back over six thousand years. Subsequent researches have added at least two thousand more years to this span, which is summarized in the chronology (pages xv–xvii). The sequence of cultures and civilizations provide the background for the narrative of archaeological discovery in this book. More recent, much more meticulous excavations have added many details to the pioneers' original framework of villages, towns, and long abandoned cities. The early excavations revealed some startlingly vivid vignettes of early Mesopotamia that flash on the screen of history with dramatic brilliance.

"And as men migrated in the east, they found a plain in the land of Shinar and settled there. And they said to one another, 'Come, let us make bricks, and burn them thoroughly.' And they had bricks for stone, and bitumen for mortar. Then they said, 'Come, let us build ourselves a city, and a tower with its top in the heavens, and let us make a name for ourselves, lest we be scattered abroad upon the face of the whole earth.' " The eleventh chapter of Genesis recounts the legend of the founding of early civilization, and of the mythical Tower of Babel. In the course of their search for the earliest Mesopotamians, the pioneers unearthed humble villages of reed-and-mud huts that clustered by the Tigris and Euphrates five thousand years before Christ.

Our second archaeological scene comes from fifteen hundred years later. By that time the Sumerian towns of Eridu and Uruk (the Biblical Erech) in the southern delta were already revered and ancient settlements. The walls of Uruk were almost six miles around and enclosed an area of three and a half square miles. A vast, high temple dominated the city, gleaming white in the brilliant sunshine. Uruk's architects had designed elaborate mosaics of glazed clay cones to adorn acres of imposing ceremonial buildings in the center of the city. Traders from all over Mesopotamia congregated in the city's markets, one of the founding centers of Sumerian civilization.

The kaleidoscope of villages and rapidly growing cities gives way to a picture of the world's first urban civilization, resurrected from years of excavation in desolate mounds, at Telloh, Nippur, Uruk, and elsewhere. The Sumerians were a remarkable people by any standards, brilliant technological innovators who developed the wheel, and the sailboat, and cuneiform writing with which to record their religious beliefs and myriad commercial transactions. Their tablets reveal them to be a contentious and pragmatic people who prized wealth, power,

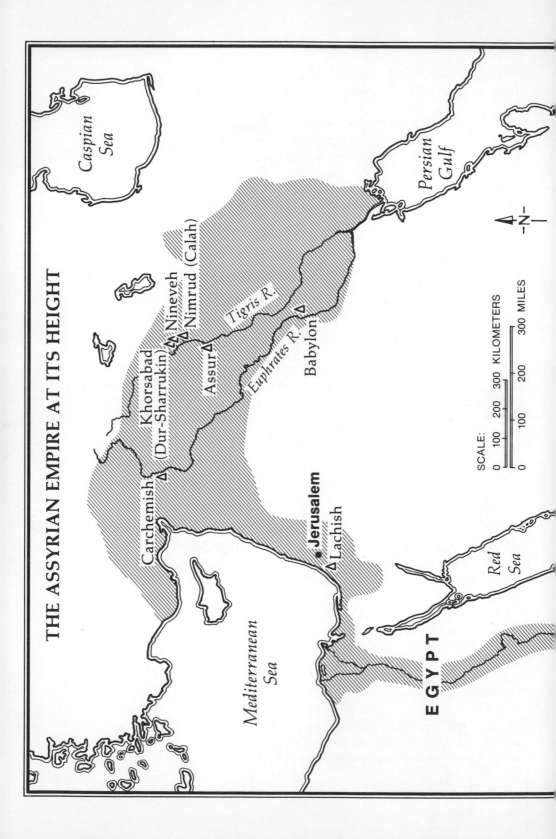

THE ASSYRIAN EMPIRE AT ITS HEIGHT

Caspian Sea

Persian Gulf

Khorsabad
(Dur-Sharrukin)

Nineveh
Nimrud (Calah)

Carchemish

Assur

Tigris R.

Euphrates R.

Babylon

Jerusalem
Lachish

Mediterranean Sea

Red Sea

E G Y P T

-N-

SCALE:

0   100   200   300 KILOMETERS

0   100   200   300 MILES

and personal freedom. Sumerian literature abounds with apt proverbs and practical advice. "The traveler from distant places is a liar," reads one example. "Keep a sharp eye on your work," admonishes a farmer's almanac. The Sumerians developed philosophical tenets and religious beliefs that were to survive throughout the long history of Mesopotamian civilization. They defined the fundamental relationships of Mesopotamian life in clear terms — those between humanity and its environment, and between humanity and the gods. The elements themselves were the ultimate enemies: the vast heavens from which the sun shone pitilessly all summer, and from which violent rains poured in winter, causing floods, suffering, and loss of crops and homesteads. Sumerian civilization lasted, we know, for a thousand years, but its teachings lasted far longer, and have influenced both Christianity and Islam.

Perhaps our most vivid archaeological scenes come from the Botta and Layard excavations at Khorsabad, Nimrud, and Nineveh, digs which unearthed yard after yard of the palace bas-reliefs that were subsequently shipped to London and Paris. We can admire strutting, hirsute kings, conquering armies, platoons of deities, and laboring hosts. Line after line of cuneiform praises the king in extravagant terms. "People from enemy towns and men from remote mountain regions which I have conquered, worked with iron picks and sledgehammers, and quarried limestone . . . for the construction of my palace," boasted King Sennacherib on the walls of his Nineveh palace. He called his royal residence "the Palace without a Rival." This enormous structure contained over seventy halls, chambers, and passages, almost all with finely sculptured reliefs that depicted Sennacherib's military campaigns and hundreds of unfortunate prisoners. "I deported them and made them carry the headpad and mold bricks," the great king trumpeted.

The Assyrian kings come down to us as militant and bombastic imperialists, who thought nothing of deporting entire cities or torturing prisoners of war. They created the most efficient army the world had ever seen, a fighting machine that relied heavily on horse-drawn chariots. Neighboring states lived in constant dread of Ashur-bani-pal and Shalmaneser III, Sargon II, and Tiglath-Pileser III, monarchs whose slightest word could unleash horrifying vengeance. Truly, in the words of Lord Byron, "The Assyrian came down like the wolf on the fold."

Our bloodthirsty impressions of Assyrian life are muted by one of the pioneers' greatest discoveries: the library of the last world-renowned Assyrian monarch — Ashur-bani-pal. The king was not only a successful conqueror but no mean scholar as well. It was Austen

Henry Layard who stumbled over Ashur-bani-pal's library and archives, a magnificent collection of cuneiform tablets that give unique insights into Mesopotamian literature and religion, law, and commercial life. We owe to Ashur-bani-pal the preservation of two literary master-pieces of ancient Mesopotamia — the *Epic of Gilgamesh* and the *Epic of the Creation*. One can imagine the "Great King, King of the World," listening with delight to stanzas that had been first committed to tablet at least two thousand years before. "I have solved complicated problems of multiplication and division, which were far from easy," Ashur-bani-pal claimed. "I have read the ancient script of Sumer, and the obscure Akkadian, hard to master." We can be grateful for his devotion to learning.

Whatever their scholarly predilections, the Assyrian monarchs lived grandiloquently. When King Ashur-nasir-pal II celebrated the completion of his huge new palace at Nimrud, he threw a ten-day banquet to which all the 17,500 inhabitants of the city were invited, as well as 52,000 other people from all over his empire. The guests consumed fourteen thousand sheep, ten thousand skins of wine, and enormous quantities of nuts and dates. Everyone, we are told, went on their way satisfied.

Our final scene comes from the meticulous German excavations of King Nebuchadnezzar's Babylon. Nebuchadnezzar was determined to make his capital the greatest city in the world. His architects and builders labored for years to lay out a vast royal precinct and a long processional way decorated with long lines of glazed-brick bulls and dragons. The Greek chronicler Herodotus tells how it was possible to drive a four-horse chariot along the double defense walls. And Nebuchadnezzar's Hanging Gardens rose tier upon tier to the roof of his palace. The luxuriant displays of flowers and vines that draped the towering walls of his residence were one of the Seven Wonders of the World. Every detail of this astounding city comes to us from lengthy and highly complex excavations of dry brick heaps.

Nebuchadnezzar's dazzling capital was doomed almost before it was completed. A short time after his death, it was captured by Cyrus of Persia, and survived only as a minor provincial capital. The brightly colored palaces and temples soon crumbled to shapeless heaps of rubble as the ancient city slowly vanished into oblivion. Mesopotamia itself passed under the domination of successive foreign leaders, whose hold on the country was not to loosen until the twentieth century. But the landscape and people remained unchanged, a kaleidoscope of desert nomads and settled farmers, of harsh, hot summers, and biting winter cold, of placid rivers and violent storms. It is hard to believe that this strange and neglected land had once witnessed the world's first urban civilizations. Small wonder the first European visitors believed that the words of the prophet Nahum had come to pass: "Your shepherds are asleep, O King of Assyria; your nobles slumber. Your people are scattered on the mountains with none to gather them." It appeared that Divine Vengeance had descended on the Garden of Eden.

2

Early Travelers

The olde tower of Babel

"Assyria possesses a vast number of great cities," wrote Herodotus in 460 B.C. Sketchy at best, his description of Mesopotamia was a compilation of information based on the campaigns of King Cyrus of Persia and on local folklore. Babylon, he said, lay in a broad plain, was heavily fortified, and a hundred and twenty furlongs in length each way. It was to be centuries before more accurate accounts of the land between the rivers were available to Western scholars, except to the few expert linguists who had a command of Arabic and a knowledge of Islamic literature. And those who studied Islam were cautious about broadcasting their knowledge. Heresy was a serious crime in medieval Europe.

Between the mid-eighth and the early thirteenth centuries the Arabic-speaking peoples possessed the most cultured civilization in the world. Baghdad, and its favored province, al-ʿIraq, lay at the hub of Islam. Its scholars were engaged in all manner of scientific inquiry: into astronomy and alchemy, mathematics and geography. Generations of illustrious Arab geographers traveled through the province and described its roads and towns. They collected legends and factual information, and admired ancient Persian palaces. Their place-name catalogues and essays on manners and customs were so thorough that modern scholars have been able to use them to identify archaeological sites and long-abandoned Abbasid towns. The geographer Muqaddasi, who wrote about A.D. 985, compiled such eloquent summaries of each province of Islam that they have been described as "some of the best-written pages to be found in all the range of medieval Arab literature." To learned Arabs geography was more than a science, it was an art.

The ancient Biblical cities came under careful Arab scrutiny. Each learned visitor collected local legends and walked over the ruins of Nineveh and Babylon. Al-Mas'udi included Nineveh in his *Golden Meadows and Mines of Gems* and we have already quoted his observations in Chapter 1. Four hundred years later the celebrated Berber geographer ibn-Battuta, whose worldwide travels rivaled those of the Venetian Marco Polo, his contemporary, wrote the definitive Arab account of Nineveh. He admired the imposing buildings of Mosul and its "very fine" bazaar with iron gates surrounded by shops. "There too is the hill of Yunus (upon whom be peace)* and at about a mile from it the spring called by his name. It is said that he commanded his followers to purify themselves at it, after which they ascended the hill and he prayed, and they with him, whereupon God averted the chastisement [of the city] from them." He added: "In its vicinity is a large village, near which is a ruined site said to be the site of the city known as Nineveh, the city of Yunus (upon whom be peace). The remains of the encircling walls are still visible, and the positions of the gates that were in it are clearly seen." Ibn-Battuta admired the Mosque of Jonah; he described the Christian convent that had preceded it, and also the place where Jonah was said to have prayed and performed his devotions. A small village lay on the summit of the Nebi Yunus mound. Its buildings proved to be a major obstacle for early archaeologists wanting to delve into the ancient levels underneath the modern houses.

The encyclopedic writings of ibn-Battuta and his predecessors threw no new light on the ruined cities of al-'Iraq, being little more than compilations of local folklore fully as vague as the legends bequeathed to posterity by Herodotus and his contemporaries. But the first European visitors to Mesopotamia had no Islamic scholarship to guide them. Ibn-Battuta and Mas'udi were not translated into English or French until the eighteenth and nineteenth centuries. Although many medieval pilgrims and crusaders visited the Holy Land and often settled there more or less permanently, few of them dared venture eastward across the lawless Syrian Desert to the Euphrates. No one knew much about al-'Iraq, except for tales of fabulous and exotic

* Yunus is the Arabic form of Jonah. The mound is today called Nebi Yunus.

Baghdad and of the horrible fate that could await unprepared for-eigners. They had but the Old Testament and Herodotus to guide them. It was believed that the ruins of the Tower of Babel might be found near the Euphrates, tangible proof of the terrifying fury of Divine Vengeance.

We are fortunate that some of the few Europeans to visit al-'Iraq were intelligent and observant men accustomed to recording their travels. One such man was a Jewish rabbi named Benjamin of Tudela, who set off from his hometown in northern Spain on a long, circuitous journey through the Near East in 1166. It was a time of great prosperity for Islam, the period of the immortal Saladin and the later crusades. Benjamin made his leisurely way through the south of France, visited Rome and southern Italy, then Corfu, Greece, and Constantinople. From there, he passed some time in the Greek islands, visited Rhodes and Cyprus, and reached Damascus via the Christian-controlled cities of southern Turkey and the Holy Land. Everywhere Benjamin went he stayed with local Jewish leaders, with whom he enjoyed the com-mon bonds of language, religion, and culture. His writings record their names and details of their trading activities. No one knows why he embarked on his extraordinary journey. Perhaps he was looking for an asylum for Jews who were being persecuted in Spain, Germany, and elsewhere. But whatever his motives, Rabbi Benjamin traveled thou-sands of miles on a trip that took him into al-'Iraq when it was pros-pering under the Abbasid caliphs.

From Damascus, Benjamin went north to Aleppo, then east to the Euphrates and the upper reaches of the Tigris at Mosul. He found seven thousand Jews living in the "very large and ancient city" of Mosul, which was "connected with Nineveh by means of a bridge. Nineveh is in ruins, but amid the ruins there are villages and hamlets. The extent of the city may be determined by the walls, which extend forty parasangs."

But Rabbi Benjamin, very much a man of the contemporary world, was more interested in Baghdad and the great palace of the caliph than in Nineveh. He admired the extensive park with its fruit-bearing trees and animals. There, "whenever the caliph desires to indulge in recrea-tion and to rejoice and feast, his servants catch all manner of birds, game, and fish." Benjamin marveled at the opulence of the palace, and at "great buildings of marble and columns of silver and gold, and carvings on rare stones . . . fixed in the walls." He also described the caliph's hospitals for the sick and mentally ill — people became insane, it seems, "in the great heat of the summer." As for the caliph himself, Benjamin had only praise: "The caliph is a righteous man, and all his actions are for good." At Ramadan he emerged from his palace and rode in state to the Mosque of Mansur, where he mounted a "wooden pulpit" and expounded the law of the land. Pilgrims came from far and wide to visit the palace and kiss his sleeve, a scarf of black velvet from the hangings of the mosque in Mecca. The large Jewish community of Baghdad lived under his benevolent protection. The twenty-eight synagogues included famous scholars who were in close touch with Moslem intellectuals.

From Baghdad, Benjamin traveled south for a day to the "ruins of Babylon which is the Babel of old. The ruins of the palace of Nebuchadnezzar are still to be seen there, but people are afraid to enter them on account of the serpents and scorpions." From Babylon, he journeyed to Al-Hillah and visited the Jewish community, ten thousand strong. "Thence it is four miles to the Tower of Babel," he wrote. He gazed up at the enormous mass of Birs Nimrod and was duly impressed. "The length of its foundation is about two miles, the breadth of the tower is about forty cubits, and the length thereof two hundred cubits. At every ten cubits' distance there are slopes which go round the tower by which one can ascend to the top." Benjamin scrambled to the summit and admired the twenty-mile view. "There fell fire from heaven into the midst of the tower which split it to its very depth," he remembered. The words of the Scriptures seemed to come alive as Benjamin gazed on this extraordinary manifestation of Divine Power.

Benjamin traveled on from Mesopotamia to Yemen and Egypt. He described the Arab trade with India, Ceylon, and even China. In Egypt, he wondered at people "who, like animals, eat of the herbs that grow on the banks of the Nile. They go about naked and have not the intelligence of ordinary men. They cohabit with their sisters and anyone they find." But he admired the celebrated Nilometer, used to measure the floodwaters of the river. Everywhere he went, the rabbi kept notes on his experiences. Later, he compiled them into a book, his now famous *Itinerary of Benjamin of Tudela*, which was printed in Constantinople in 1543. The book was largely ignored until 1840, when it was translated into English and subjected to scholarly commentary. By that time, other Christian travelers had already published accounts of the celebrated ruined cities that lay by the Tigris and the Euphrates.

The educated European of the fifteenth century was largely dependent on Mandeville for information on Mesopotamia: *The Voyage of Travaile of Sir John Mandeville, Knight.* Purportedly an accurate guidebook for pilgrims to the Holy Land, this entertaining volume titillated and entertained the prospective traveler with a wealth of detail about Mandeville's journey to the East in 1322, culled from classi-

Birs Nimrod, as sketched by the Euphrates Expedition. From Chesney's Survey (1850)

cal sources, fables, folklore, and highly unreliable crusaders' and travelers' tales. The *Voyage* was soon accepted as gospel truth, the work of an inveterate traveler of vast experience. Alas, Sir John Mandeville never existed, and the author, a Frenchman named Jean d'Outremeuse, had never set foot in the Near East. The entire book was a complete fabrication, a total literary fraud.

Whatever d'Outremeuse's motives, the reader was at least assured of a compilation of available information that the author had culled from many, though unidentified, sources. It was in this spirit that he sat in his comfortable study and wrote of ancient Babylon in the "grete Desotes of Arabye." It had been, he said, "fulle long sithe that any Man durst [go] neyhe to the Tour; for it is alle deserte and fulle of Dragonns and grete serpentes, and fulle of dyverse venymouse Bestes." The walls of Babylon, twenty-five "myles" in circumference, contained not only the Tower of Babel, but many "Mansions and many grete duellynge places." The "Ryvere of Euphrate" ran through the city, set in a "fair Contree and a Playn." (Actually, of course, King Cyrus of Persia had diverted the river and destroyed Babylon in the sixth century B.C.)

From the twelfth through fifteenth centuries a few other visitors followed in Benjamin of Tudela's footsteps. Pethahiah of Ratisbon covered the same ground in the twelfth century, and visited the same Jewish communities. A few other clerics ventured into the distant land of the rivers to visit Christian minorities, men like Vincenzo Mario di Santa Caterina di Siena, the procurator-general of the Carmelite Order, and Emmanuel de St. Albert, a Dominican. Their reports add little to our knowledge of al-'Iraq. A Bavarian traveler, Johann Schiltberger, journeyed widely in the East between 1396 and 1427 while a slave in the service of various Moslem leaders. "I have also been in the kingdom of Babilonien," he boasted. Then follows the familiar litany: of a great city surrounded by long walls, of the Euphrates flowing through the ruins. "The Tower of Babilonien" lay fifty-four stades away, protected by "dragons and serpents, and other hurtful reptiles." His account, dictated upon his return to Bavaria in 1427, reads suspiciously like Mandeville's. No one knows if he really visited the ruins.

By Schiltberger's time Baghdad's fortunes had declined. The Abbasid dynasty had lost its grip on its vast empire in the tenth century as the internal structure of society decayed. Floods and devastating plagues further weakened Abbasid political and economic power. In 1258, Mongol armies descended on al-'Iraq, sacked Baghdad, and slaughtered the caliph. The Abbasid capital now became a provincial capital of the Mongol kingdom of Persia. The Mongols, in turn, were replaced by the Ottoman Turks, one of many Turkish tribes displaced from the steppes by the Mongol invasions of the thirteenth century. In 1453, they captured Constantinople, which became the center of their enormous empire.

The Ottoman sultan Selim I, known as the Conqueror, expanded his realms into Persia and Armenia and added Mesopotamia to the empire in 1515. Baghdad, though still the capital of the province of al-'Iraq, became a frontier town against the hostile Persians. The zenith of Ottoman power was in 1566, when the Turks controlled not only the Near East but part of the Balkans, Greece, and much of North Africa. Thereafter, the empire embarked on a long period of decline, fostered both by internal weaknesses and external political forces. The Ottoman sultans ruled their domains from Constantinople, where they lived in splendor. Each sultan appointed a grand vizier, who ran the day-to-day affairs of state and headed the imperial bureaucracy, known as Bab al-Aali (the Sublime Porte). The provincial governors, one of whom was based in Baghdad, another in Mosul, enjoyed some autonomy, but personal initiative was discouraged. A combination of unduly centralized bureaucracy, harsh taxation, and endemic corruption led to gradual impoverishment throughout the empire.

Al-'Iraq's remoteness and fierce climate made communication difficult for a faraway governing power. Its people were sharply divided into several Islamic sects, all of them different from the one the Turks subscribed to. Baghdad never regained its former status and decayed quietly, becoming an obscure backwater suffering under harsh and despotic governance. Except for a half century of Persian rule, from 1580 to 1638, Baghdad was to stagnate in an atmosphere of weak government, and in constant fear of desert Arab raids, until the late nineteenth century. From 1704 to 1831 Mameluke governors ruled Baghdad with virtual autonomy.

The Ottoman sultans were careful in their dealings with Western nations. Trading connections evolved gradually. The French and Venetians were first in the field, trading for silks, "muskadels and Turkie carpets." But Europeans were wary of the Turks and their alleged atrocities, and held back from greater involvement in the Ottoman trade until the late sixteenth century. In 1581 the sultan granted the English "Turkey merchants" a seven-year monopoly, which resulted in the formation of the Levant Company. For four centuries the company prospered by trading English wool and cotton goods for spices, silk, dyes, and other Eastern luxuries. Their coffee imports were behind the coffee-shop boom in London in the seventeenth century. The Levant merchants opened factories in Aleppo and Smyrna (Izmir) through which much of the trade with remoter areas was channeled. Aleppo was an important caravan terminus that enabled English merchants to trade in Persian markets and with Mesopotamia.

The more enterprising merchants spent a great deal of time investigating new markets and looking for overland trade routes that would link the Mediterranean with Persia, the Persian Gulf, and India. We know little of these tentative explorations, nor of the occasional scientists who donned local dress and accompanied caravans into remote Iraq. The German botanist Leonard Rauwolff ventured to the Tigris and Euphrates in the 1570s. He was amazed at the ruins of Babylon, by the "ancient and delicate antiquities that still are standing about in great desolation." Rauwolff described brick arches and fortifications, and the Tower of Babel, "which the children of Noah began to build up to heaven." So many vermin infested the tower that one could not approach closer than half a mile except in winter. Rauwolff went to Nineveh, too, and walked over the Nebi Yunus mound. "It was entirely honeycombed, being inhabited by poor people, whom I often saw crawling out and in large numbers like ants in their heap," he wrote. Like most visitors, he was satisfied that the extensive mounds and ruins near Mosul were the site of Biblical Nineveh.

English merchants were especially interested in the caravan routes to Mesopotamia, for they had begun what became a centuries-long quest, a search for a safe, prosperous overland trading route to India. The famous chronicler Richard Hakluyt published the report of a London merchant named John Eldred, who traveled "to Trypolis in Syria by sea and from there by land and river to Babylon and Balsara, 1583." Eldred left London on a ship called *Tiger* in the company of John Newbery, Ralph Fitch, "and six or seven other honest merchants." They arrived at Tripoli on May 1, 1583, and reached Aleppo three weeks later. Newbery had passed this way two years before and was able to make the necessary contacts to get them on a desert caravan. Dressed in Arab costume, the merchants left Aleppo on May 31 and reached the Euphrates in three days. They then hired flat-bottomed boats and floated downstream in very hot weather, trading with the desert people, "of whom we bought milke, butter, eggs, and lambs, and gave them in barter . . . glasses, combes, corall, amber, to hang about their armes and necks." Eldred added: "These people are very thievish," a complaint echoed by many later travelers. Once opposite "New Babylon," actually Baghdad, the merchants tried to hire camels. But the weather being too hot, the camels' owners did not want to risk their animals' lives. The Englishmen were forced to do with one hundred asses to carry their merchandise on a hazardous nighttime journey across the desert. It was during this journey that Eldred stumbled on ancient Babylon, "many olde ruins whereof are easily to be seene by day-light." Eldred made the journey between Aleppo and the Tigris three times, so he had ample opportunity to look at the site. "Here also are yet standing the ruines of the olde tower of Babel, which being upon a plaine ground seemeth a farre off very great," he wrote. The tower was "above a quarter of a mile in compasse, and almost as high as the stone worke of Paul's steeple in London." He commented on the courses of sun-dried brick and layers of matting in the ruins. Baghdad, he observed, "joineth on to aforesayed small desert where the olde city was."

John Eldred was above all a merchant. He expressed no surprise at finding the Tower of Babel in the desert and was far more interested in the modern city of Baghdad, "a very great thorowfare from the East Indies to Aleppo." He bought food from "rafts borne upon goat skins blowen up full of wind in maner of bladders" that came from "Mosul which was called Ninivie in olde time" upstream. Eldred's journey ended in Basra and he returned to England (his companions went on to India, where they were imprisoned by the suspicious Portuguese).

Eldred, Newbery, and Fitch had accomplished their mission: they had explored an established caravan route that Europeans could utilize. It became relatively well known to foreigners by 1600. Eldred was followed by the Shirley brothers, who visited Mosul and Baghdad in 1598. Sir Anthony Shirley was among many who compared ancient Nineveh to modern Mosul, to the latter's disadvantage. Mosul, he reported, was "a small thing, rather to be a witness of the other's mightiness and God's judgment, than of any fashion of magnificence in itselfe."

John Eldred went on to be one of the founders of the East India Company in 1600, an organization that was formed to develop new overseas markets for English cloth, which could be exported instead of valuable bullion. The company prospered, so much so that it came to depend with increasing frequency on the overland route from Basra to Baghdad and Aleppo. The company agent in Basra used Arab and Turkish caravans to send travelers and merchandise across the desert in about thirty-eight days. Basra became so important that the sultan recognized a British consul there in 1767. Most people avoided Baghdad, which was politically volatile and liable to devastating plagues.

The merchants brought back travelers' tales with them, stories of the exotic East that no doubt gained much in the telling. These superficial travelers were castigated for returning with "foppish fancies, foolish guises and disguises, the vanities of Neighbor Nations." Were, for example, the Turks as barbarous as everyone made out? Perhaps,

PIETRO DELLA VALLE
IL PELLEGRINO
Hic peragro peregrinus adhuc: tellus, tamen ulla
Hic peregrina mihi, Sed domus, et patria est.

Pietro della Valle, from the frontispiece of his Travels *(1657)*

wrote Sir Anthony Blount in the sixteenth century, they were ruled "by another kinde of civilitie, different from ours, but no less pretending." The fables and fantasies of Sir John Mandeville were replaced by guides to the "most uncouth countries of the world," compiled, as was Samuel Purchas's *Purchas his Pilgrims* (1625), from actual travelers' reports. As travel off the beaten track became more commonplace, people tried to satisfy their curiosity about Turks, Arabs, and Islam. No less a personage than Archbishop Laud established a professorship of Arabic at Oxford University in the seventeenth century. Richard Pococke was the first holder of the chair. He traveled widely in the Near East, studied the Pyramids, and collected Arabic manuscripts. Thomas Roe, the British ambassador in Constantinople from 1621 to 1628, employed agents throughout the Levant to collect on his behalf. Many of the manuscripts described Arab proverbs, fables, and fairy tales. The *Arabian Nights* was translated into French in 1712. Within a century, Arab fairy tales were firmly entrenched in European fiction. Pococke, Roe, and their contemporaries were the first scholars to recognize that the East had played a leading role in the early development of European civilization.

Scholars whose attention was focused on the East were fascinated with the discoveries of an Italian traveler named Pietro della Valle, who returned to Europe in 1626 with a remarkable collection of curiosities. Valle was born in Rome in April 1586. He received a good education and spent some time in military service and on an expedition to North Africa. In June 1614 he set off on a long journey to the East, a trip undertaken, we are told, "owing to a disappointment in love." He sailed to Constantinople, then proceeded to Asia Minor and Egypt, where he visited Mount Sinai. From Sinai, he journeyed to the Holy Land, Damascus, and Aleppo. His wanderings then took him across the desert to Babylon. He was one of the first scholarly European travelers to visit the ancient city.

Valle wandered over the desolate ruins many times. He found it difficult to describe them, for the mass of crumbling bricks and mounds was highly confusing. It was difficult for him to believe that a mighty city had ever existed in this dry and flat country. By far the most conspicuous ruin was a huge mass of decaying brickwork in the form of a tower, about half a mile in circumference. The four sides of the tower "faced the four corners of the world." Finding no signs of stairs or doors, he thought the building to be the tomb of King Belus, its legendary builder. It was, he reported, about the size of some of the great palaces of Naples. Mystified by the unfamiliar architecture, Valle walked over piles of baked and unbaked brick, some with reeds and bitumen still adhering to them. Absently, he picked up some strangely inscribed bricks for his collection of curiosities.

Romance found Valle in Mesopotamia. His researches at Babylon were interrupted by frequent visits to Baghdad, where he had fallen in love with a Christian lady named Maani. It took months for him to persuade her family to let him marry her. But in 1616 he succeeded, and the couple left to travel through northern Mesopotamia and Persia. There Valle spent several days copying ancient rock inscriptions and inscribed bricks. Eventually, he and his wife traveled as far as the Caspian Sea, where they took part in Persian skirmishes against the Turks. Apparently Maani was fearless, "a warrior who fears neither to see blows, nor to hear the sound of firing." They saw Shiraz and Persepolis, where Valle copied more cuneiform inscriptions. Then Maani died of fever. Her grief-stricken husband had her corpse embalmed and carried it with him as far afield as India and Goa. It was not until March 28, 1626, that Valle returned to Rome and finally buried his wife.

Valle spent the rest of his life writing of his travels, siring fourteen children by his second wife, and receiving the many visitors who came to see his collections of antiquities and curiosities from the distant East. The Valle collections were justly famous for their two Egyptian mummies, which now reside in the Dresden Museum. But the artifacts that raised the greatest interest were "some square bricks on which were writings in certain unknown characters." Most of these specimens came from the ruined city of Persepolis. Valle himself pored over the bricks for hours, but failed to decipher the wedge-shaped characters. He did observe that the thicker ends of the horizontal characters were always on the left, which led him to conclude that the writing was set down from left to right. Some of the scholars who flocked to Valle's house were familiar with Egyptian hieroglyphs. Already baffled by the complexities of ancient Egyptian, the experts shook their heads in puzzlement. The wedge-shaped writing was quite unlike any known script, even Chinese. As of April 1652, when Valle died in Rome, no one had been able to decipher even a syllable of cuneiform. Valle himself had left a priceless legacy for his successors, the first specimens of ancient Mesopotamian script to reach Europe. He also bequeathed a long narrative of his travels, and, we are informed, some pleasing musical compositions.

Valle's cuneiform bricks caused such interest that later travelers began to copy inscriptions and collect additional specimens. But their efforts at copying were fragmentary at best, one of the most widely circulated being a mere two lines of cuneiform copied by an East India Company agent named Flower, who visited Persepolis. Flower's work appeared in the *Philosophical Transactions* of the Royal Society of London in 1693. The sporadic explorations and inquiries of the five hundred years since Benjamin of Tudela made his circuitous journey had done nothing but compound the profound mystery that surrounded the ancient cities of Mesopotamia.

3

Cuneiform Recorder

Come, let us build ourselves a city, and a tower with its top in the heavens, and let us make a name for ourselves, lest we be scattered abroad on the face of the whole earth.

So FAR, THE EUROPEAN visitors to distant Mesopotamia had done so without official sponsorship, mostly for commercial motives. But the eighteenth century saw a new phenomenon, that of the government expedition. The Renaissance had motivated many governments to support knowledge, learning, and the arts. Many European monarchs now sought lasting fame by sponsoring the arts and sciences. When King Frederick V of Denmark decided that he would emulate his royal neighbors and embark on a bold cultural program, he thought in terms of botanical gardens and natural history museums. He also decided to send an expedition to Arabia. The idea for the expedition had come from the German theologian and orientalist Johann Michaelis of Göttingen University. Michaelis was unusual for his time in that he refused to believe that the Scriptures were strict historical truth, to be taken as *the* account of early history. He thought of them as historical texts to be examined critically. What better way to do this than to send an expedition to Arabia? The scientists could study geography, collect plants and animals, and gain insights into Old Testament society by studying the Arabs. Frederick V seized on the idea with alacrity. The expedition was out of the ordinary, of political importance, and potentially a good investment. Contemporary scholarship was passionately interested in science, the Scriptures, foreign countries, and, increasingly, the Orient. The king provided funds for a five-man expedition, charged "to make new discoveries and observations for the benefit of scholarship," as well as to collect "valuable oriental manuscripts." Among the five scientists chosen for the expedition was a young man named Carsten Niebuhr.

Niebuhr was born in Friesland on March 17, 1733. His father was a poverty-stricken farmer, who only reluctantly agreed to Carsten's attending school. By the time Carsten was sixteen his parents were dead and he was working as a farmhand on a neighbor's farm. Four years later, however, he used a small legacy from his father to obtain training as a surveyor. He attended school in Hamburg and was admitted to the University of Göttingen in 1757, where he studied mathematics under the famous Professor Kastner. Kastner soon recognized Niebuhr's intelligence and obtained a scholarship for him to study astronomy. The young man realized he had found his calling and studied with great enthusiasm.

When the Danish government cast around for a fifth member for the Arabia expedition, Kastner promptly recommended his young protégé. Niebuhr spent the next two years learning history, geographical surveying, and astronomy. He learned how to repair his instruments in the field, and attempted to learn Arabic, a project he soon gave up in disgust. In October 1760 he found himself in Copenhagen, having been appointed engineer-lieutenant of the expedition.

Niebuhr's colleagues were a varied group: the Swedish scientist Peter Forskål, a botanist and a theologian with forthright and controversial views; Friedrich Christian von Haven, a Danish oriental philologist; Georg Wilhelm Baurenfeind, an artist; and Christian Karl Kramer, appointed as expedition doctor. It was a tragic combination of personalities. The five explorers did not get along well together. At one point one member of the team tried to poison the others. Invariably the quiet and self-effacing Niebuhr tried to remain aloof from the personal intrigues of his colleagues.

The expedition was to go to Constantinople and Cairo, then through the Sinai and into the Arabian interior. The return journey was to be through Basra, Aleppo, and Smyrna. All the members of the party were to learn Arabic and keep diaries, which they were to send home as frequently as possible. They were to purchase manuscripts, "particularly the most ancient which employ an alphabet differing from that used in the present day." And manuscripts that Haven was unable to decipher were to be "copied with care." The scientists were urged to behave circumspectly toward Moslems, "and not to behave towards [the Moslem] women with European freedom."

The expedition left Copenhagen in January 1761. After a stormy voyage and several brushes with British warships, the expedition reached Malta, then sailed on to Constantinople. There, Niebuhr recuperated from a bad dose of fever and the scientists donned Turkish dress. A Turkish vessel carrying a cargo of slave girls carried the party to Alexandria. Forskål and Niebuhr found themselves occupying a cabin immediately below the women. "Eventually," wrote Niebuhr, "the girls took to tapping on the window as a sign to us that they were now alone; and in this way we both had great fun during the trip."

At Alexandria the slave girls vanished silently. The explorers had their first taste of the Arab world when they saw some Bedouin robbers beaten to death in the street. After taking a boat upstream to Cairo the scientists threw themselves into an orgy of botanizing and mapping. They spent almost a year in Egypt awaiting official dispatches from Copenhagen. Niebuhr compiled a detailed map of the city, studied irrigation methods, and measured the Pyramids, which he described as "surrounded by people who must be regarded as potential robbers." He copied hieroglyphs while his colleagues quarreled among themselves about the leadership of the expedition. There was time for Niebuhr, Forskål, and Baurenfeind to visit a "rather distinguished Arab of Cairo," who allowed them to draw the anatomy of a circumcised peasant girl in the flesh.

In August 1762 the dispatches finally arrived, and after a final party complete with dancing girls, the scientists joined a caravan crossing the Sinai. They rode in its middle section, where the chances of survival in the event of an attack were best. There were at least four hundred camels in the caravan, which reached Suez in thirty-two hours. From there the scientists took ship down the Red Sea to Jiddah and Loheia. For almost a year they vanished into the deserts of Yemen. Finally, three members of the party reached an English ship at Mocha in August 1763. They reported that Haven and Forskål were dead of malaria. Six months later, only Niebuhr was still alive, being cared for by an English doctor in Bombay. But his efforts had yielded the first definitive map of Yemen and a wealth of information about a hitherto-unknown wilderness.

The original plan had called for the expedition to return overland to Copenhagen via Mesopotamia. Niebuhr spent the next fifteen months in India, where he learned English, packed up the surviving expedition notes for dispatch to Denmark, and studied Hindu customs. On December 8, 1764, he boarded a British warship for the

Persian Gulf. They stopped in Muscat and Bushire. Niebuhr drew a fine map of the gulf, described the island of Bahrain, and bemoaned the unpredictable weather. At Bushire, he disembarked and joined a mule caravan for Shiraz. The trip took eighteen days of arduous travel through the mountains. Rain fell nearly every day and the travelers slept in the open. Fortunately, Niebuhr received hospitality from the only English merchant in Shiraz, who smoothed his way with the governor. This official assured Niebuhr that anyone annoying him would be beheaded immediately. A week later he left on the two-day trip to Persepolis, traveling on a mule and accompanied by a Moslem servant and a guide.

Niebuhr was agog with excitement at seeing Persepolis, whose royal palace had been burned by Alexander the Great. He had read the accounts written by Valle and other previous European visitors and had reviewed all the scattered copies of the inscriptions that had caused such interest in Europe. Unlike his predecessors, Niebuhr came to Persepolis with the objective of reconstructing the great palace and recording as many inscriptions as possible.

The sun was setting as he gazed down on the valley of ruins for the first time. The columns were bathed in a rosy glow. Enchanted, he wandered among the columns until darkness fell, whereupon he left to find lodgings in the nearby village of Merdast. Every morning he rode out by donkey to Persepolis. He surveyed the ground plan of the palace, studied the architecture, and copied cuneiform inscriptions. Forty-three pages of notes and descriptions, and thirty-nine pages of plans, drawings, and copies resulted from his labors. He worked absolutely alone, apparently in complete harmony with the local people. These lonely weeks among the ruins gave him a unique place in scientific history, for he provided scholars in faraway Europe with the first relatively accurate raw material for the decipherment of cuneiform.

The task of copying was impossibly demanding. Many of the inscriptions were placed high on smooth marble walls, brightly lit with harsh sunlight. Without sunglasses, he suffered from constant attacks of blindness from the white glare. By March of 1765 he was near the end of his tether. His Moslem servant became delirious with fever and died in a few days. Niebuhr himself was so debilitated by the exertion and repeated attacks of shivering that he decided to retreat to Shiraz and the blistering heat of Bushire, where he rested for three months.

In studying the inscriptions, Niebuhr saw that they were arranged in three separate columns, each written in what appeared to be a different language. He designated the columns Class I, II, and III respectively, noting that Class I had fewer symbols than the other two. He then attempted to separate out the individual letters of the cuneiform alphabet, and eventually managed to puzzle out forty-two of the dozens of symbols. There he had to stop.

He now embarked on the most difficult part of his journey, a return trip up the Persian Gulf and overland from Basra to Aleppo. It took him months to reach the humid filth of Basra, where he waited four months for a desert caravan. He now decided to travel as an Arab, and assumed the name Abdullah. His disguise gave him not only security but a pleasing anonymity, something the modest Niebuhr always craved. So many robbers were preying on the desert caravans that he further decided to travel up the Tigris by boat as far as Baghdad. The trip began in November 1765. Niebuhr shared a cabin with a sick Turk and scared off would-be robbers with a rifle. After a month he tired of river travel and mounted a donkey to visit Al-Hillah. There he paused briefly at the silent mounds of Babylon and Birs Nimrod. By now most of the city had been quarried away by brick diggers, who were still active among the ruins. Like Rabbi Benjamin, Niebuhr was afraid to wander over the site because of the thousands of snakes in the long grass. So he contented himself with imagining the city in its days of Biblical glory. He thought that the palace and the Hanging Gardens lay on the east bank of the river. But Abdullah did not tarry long. On January 6, 1766, he rode into Baghdad, where he stayed for two months, sufficient time to record the names and dates of the last forty-eight pashas. Neither Babylon nor Baghdad made a lasting impression on Carsten Niebuhr.

Desert travel being still out of the question, Niebuhr joined a Jewish caravan on its way up the Tigris to Mosul. The journey took three arduous weeks at the height of the rainy season. Niebuhr was rarely dry, but he still found time to use his precious astrolabe and to sketch some villages. One of them lay opposite Mosul among the ancient ruins of Nineveh. But the weary traveler added nothing to the outside world's knowledge of the site. Many thousands of miles of traveling still lay ahead of him. On June 6, 1766, he rode into Aleppo and was feted by the European community. From there he journeyed to Cyprus, Jerusalem, and Constantinople. It was not until November 20, 1767, that he rode into Copenhagen. He was greeted by complete indifference.

Times had changed. Frederick V had died while Niebuhr was in Baghdad; his successor was bored by scientific research. Niebuhr found himself politely ignored, the sole survivor of a long-forgotten government venture. So he retired to his study on a small government stipend and started to write of his travels and his colleagues' results. His books were put out by a Copenhagen publisher but were largely ignored by his contemporaries. Even the account of his travels was

Carsten Niebuhr in Arab dress

set aside as uninteresting. After ten years of solid writing, Niebuhr turned down a chance to head a prestigious survey of Norway and became clerk to the council in Meldorf, a small village in western Denmark. He lived happily there in total obscurity with his wife and two children until his death in 1815. By that time the geographical contributions of this blind, eighty-two-year-old traveler were used by leading geographers as a basis for new maps of the Near East. In this, and in the study of cuneiform, humble Carsten Niebuhr had laid the foundations for a new generation of travelers and archaeologists. Tragically, only a few people had the vision to recognize his genius. Among them was Napoleon no less, who carried Niebuhr's *Description of Travels in Arabia* with him to Egypt in 1798.

While Niebuhr added nothing to contemporary information about Babylon, a later French traveler spent a considerable time delving into the desolate landscape that Niebuhr had shunned. Abbé Jean de Beauchamp was vicar-general of Babylon. Between 1781 and 1785, he traveled extensively in Mesopotamia, visiting Christian residents and exploring the countryside. In 1784 he descended the Euphrates to Al-Hillah and Basra, pausing for a leisured inspection of Babylon. He described the mounds there and spent many hours talking to the brick diggers. They showed him clay idols, statues, and inscribed, glazed bricks that they had found. One digger led Beauchamp deep into his trenches to look at thick walls and a subterranean canal made of sandstone blocks. Beauchamp was so excited that he hired two men to clear the debris from a "stone idol." It turned out to be a huge basalt lion that was to be reexcavated again and again by later visitors to Babylon. Beauchamp made copious notes and collected a number of inscribed bricks. He also described "solid cylinders, three inches in diameter, of a white substance, covered with very small writing, resembling the inscriptions of Persepolis." But he failed to buy any of these cylinder seals because the brick diggers never bothered to collect them.

Once Carsten Niebuhr's achievements were recognized, a new era of scientific interest in Mesopotamia began. His Persepolis inscriptions were widely disseminated throughout Europe and provided a new impetus for the study of cuneiform. A steady trickle of Mesopotamian antiquities began to reach Europe. André Michaux, a French botanist, sent a cylinder seal from Babylon to Paris in 1782. By this time the British East India Company had ordered their resident in Basra to obtain some Babylonian inscribed bricks like those reported by Abbé Beauchamp. A small case of Mesopotamian antiquities soon arrived in London, the forerunner of thousands of tons of statuary and other specimens that were to make their way to Europe in the nineteenth century. But this increased interest in Mesopotamia was not entirely academic. Some European powers had realized the potential strategic importance of the Near East. The East India Company was trying to foster trading opportunities and better communications in the land between the rivers. In 1783 the company appointed a permanent British agent in Baghdad. Fifteen years later, Napoleon's activities in Egypt caused the company to upgrade the Baghdad agent to British resident. In 1802 the resident received consular powers. Fortunately for science, one of the first holders of this residency was to transform scholarly knowledge of Mesopotamia.

II

CONSULS AND CUNEIFORM

4

Claudius James Rich

Claudius Rich, Esquire, some bricks has got . . .

THE NEWLY APPOINTED, twenty-two-year-old British resident in Baghdad already had a remarkable career behind him. Claudius James Rich was born in Dijon, France, on March 28, 1787, the illegitimate son of a Colonel James Cockburn. Rich spent much of his childhood in Bristol. When a relation started to teach young Claudius the rudiments of the classics, Rich displayed a precocious ability for languages. He learned several modern languages without formal instruction. At the age of eight or nine he was taken to see the fine oriental library of Charles Fox, a well-known Quaker. Rich was captivated by the exotic scripts, quite unlike anything he had seen before. Fox encouraged him to learn Arabic, and lent him grammars and dictionaries. Soon Rich "had made no mean progress" in Hebrew, Syrian, Persian, Turkish, and Arabic, under the tutelage of Fox and a schoolteacher who also taught him mathematics. He can, perhaps, be compared to Sir Richard Burton, the famous African explorer, who mastered forty languages, and to Heinrich Schliemann, who excavated ancient Troy, another polyglot. One summer's evening Rich met a Turkish gentleman on the hills behind Bristol. The visitor was electrified to be greeted in his native tongue. One can imagine Rich's excitement at being able to use a language he studied from books for so long.

At the age of seventeen, Rich applied for a military cadetship in the East India Company, an application that received powerful support from influential friends in Bristol. When he went to India House in London to fill out the necessary appointment forms, he found himself a minor celebrity. The military people introduced him to Charles Wilkins, the company librarian and an expert linguist high in the councils of the company. Wilkins was deeply impressed by Rich's abilities, so much so that he recommended to the board of directors that Rich be given a civil post where his talents could be used to maximum advantage. Rich was appointed a "writer on the Bombay establishment." His fame even reached the august columns of *The Times,* which, in reporting his appointment, called him a "literary wonder."

Since there was temporarily no vacancy at Bombay, Rich was to serve as secretary to Charles Lock, the newly appointed consul general of Egypt. The appointment would give Rich the opportunity to polish his Arabic and Turkish. In early 1804 he accordingly embarked on the storeship *Hindustan* for Malta, where he was to join Lock. But the *Hindustan* caught fire off Barcelona and was beached. Rich walked ashore with nothing but the clothes he stood up in. A British merchant befriended him and helped him reach Naples. There Rich lived for three months, waiting for Lock to return to Malta from a trip to Turkey. The three months passed quickly as Rich became fluent in Italian and acquired a passion for music and Italian opera. He arrived in Malta just in time to be present at Lock's deathbed. The consul had contracted fever while traveling "in the Plain of Troy."

The board of directors now allowed Rich to travel to Constantinople to improve his languages. He spent several weeks on a leisurely voyage through the Greek islands, in those days infested with pirates. One day a suspicious vessel hove in sight. The captain prepared for a desperate defense. But the ship turned out to be a Turkish merchant-man. When Rich and some of the other passengers visited the vessel, he was accosted by a richly dressed Turk who greeted him warmly. Rich was delighted to recognize his old acquaintance of the Bristol hills!

Rich donned Turkish dress and wandered through Asia Minor for fifteen months, mostly on his own. He visited Constantinople and Smyrna, where he enrolled in a school for young Moslem gentlemen. His journeys took him into Syria, as far as Aleppo and Antakya, perhaps on confidential official business. In May of 1806, he reached Alexandria, where he found a congenial companion in Colonel James Missett, the consul general. He spent his time perfecting his Arabic and learning to ride horses. A Mameluke taught him "the management of the scimitar and the lance."

This pleasant interlude did not last long. Rich was ordered to take up his appointment in Bombay late in 1806. Although he had a choice of several routes, he chose the least direct, going overland through Syria and Mesopotamia to the Persian Gulf. Dressed as a Mameluke, he visited Damascus in the company of thousands of devout pilgrims on their way to Mecca. His Turkish host was so taken with him that he offered Rich his daughter's hand in marriage. Rich pressed on to Aleppo, across the Euphrates through the Turkish foothills to the Tigris. He probably entered Mesopotamia on a *kellek* that carried him downstream to Baghdad and Basra. Rich did not tarry in Basra. He sailed for Bombay on the next ship.

While on his travels, Rich had corresponded with Sir James Mackintosh, at that time the recorder of Bombay. This important official took an instant liking to him — they shared an interest in philosophy, languages, and oriental studies. Soon Rich was part of the family, teaching Mackintosh's daughters drawing and painting. James Mackintosh went off on a cruise with his wife, only to return and find that Rich wanted to marry his eldest daughter, Mary. "He has no fortune, nor had he then even an appointment," wrote Mackintosh, "but you will not doubt that I willingly consented to his marriage."

Rich must have made quite an impression on the authorities in Bombay as well as on his father-in-law. Four months after his arrival, the company began to look for a suitable man to send as British resident to Baghdad, a man with experience of the Ottoman Turks and Mesopotamia, and with command of the requisite languages. Rich, despite his youth, was the only logical choice. He was appointed resident two months before his twenty-second birthday and married Mary Mackintosh six days later. The young couple — Mary was only eighteen — arrived in Baghdad at the head of a mounted Indian sepoy guard in May 1808.

Baghdad was so isolated that British and French policy makers of the time knew very little about the city. The sultan of Turkey was afraid of Napoleon and well aware that the province of al-'Iraq lay on any overland route he would take on his way to British India. The decaying city of Baghdad occupied the most strategic position in the province, at the junction of caravan routes and major river highways. Its bazaars swarmed with spies and secret agents surreptitiously gathering information about the region. The pasha of Baghdad paid only nominal allegiance to Constantinople, for he was a member of the Georgian Mameluke slave dynasties who ruled the affairs of much of the outlying areas of the Ottoman Empire at that time. The countryside groaned under his heavy rule. Lawlessness was endemic, the traveler harassed by every village sheikh. Al-ʿIraq suffered in silence, its people suspicious of foreigners and alien visitors. British prestige was at a low point.

The day after Rich arrived to take up his post, he called on the pasha and was received politely. Privately, he was unimpressed by the ruler and in public he faced up to him boldly. Rich had a great advantage over other foreigners, for besides his knowledge of Arabic and Turkish he had a considerable experience of Eastern psychology. He also possessed an almost oriental patience. Within a few months he had become the most influential foreigner in al-ʿIraq. His extreme youth made his dealings with the pasha a constant tightrope. In 1809, matters came to a head when the pasha challenged Rich's diplomatic credentials. He was refused entry into the city after a country excursion. With sheer patience and force of personality, Rich quietly turned the tables on the pasha. He refused to leave. Eventually, the pasha's own body-guard escorted him into the city. The pasha never challenged his authority again.

Life in the residency centered around "a large and handsome house perfectly in the Turkish style." The heat, unmitigated by air conditioning, fans, or refrigerators, was a constant hardship. The Riches only left the house between five and seven in the morning. "The weather is now so warm, we dine on the terrace," wrote Mary Rich. "In less than a month the heat will become so intolerable that we shall be obliged to sleep in the open air." They lived in public during the hot weather. The roof of the residency was divided into open-air compartments that looked down on the city roofs below. One of the Riches' first guests described how at dawn he could look down on "all the families of Baghdad, with their sleeping apartments unroofed, and those near our own abode often in sufficiently interesting situations."

Rich insisted that the British resident live in considerable style, that his wife dress formally for dinner, even when they were on their own. Their letters to Bombay were filled with requests for more and more clothes, for gloves and "trowsers," for books, "a chess board and men, and also a new flute for Claudius." Thirty Indian sepoys under a subadar guarded the residency, and Rich himself raised a small troop of sixteen European hussars. The residency teemed with servants; there was even a Slavic butler. The household lived and occasionally entertained in style. "If I did not come down as well dressed as I should be in Bombay at a party of fifteen or twenty persons, Mr. Rich would be extremely angry," wrote Mary Rich to one of her sisters. Though the East India Company was unsympathetic toward Rich's insistence on a stylish establishment and paid him inadequate living allowances all the time he lived in Baghdad, he was determined to maintain a conspicuous presence. Anything else, he argued rightly, would lower Britain in Turkish eyes. "If you allow a Turk to gain a point over you, it is next to an impossibility to recover your authority," he wrote to Bombay. He always called on the pasha in full-dress uniform, accompanied by his guard, drums, and fifes.

Baghdad was no paradise for the Riches, even though they entertained a stream of visitors, both distinguished and not so distinguished. Mary Rich looked out over the dingy landscape with resigned dislike. "The view I have of the renowned city is not the most beautiful," she wrote. "The streets are extremely narrow and the whole town is built of sun-baked bricks which give it a very dirty appearance. There is nothing at all splendid about Baghdad."

The first three years of Rich's term of office were difficult politically. He found himself involved in disputes between company officials; he had to intercede with the sultan on the pasha's behalf — he even offered the pasha's ministers sanctuary when Constantinople arranged for the pasha to be deposed and beheaded. Rich had a reputation for fair dealing and incorruptibility, which enabled him to act boldly. On one occasion a residency official was robbed by Arab raiders on the road to Baghdad. Rick calmly invited some visiting British officers to join him and galloped ten miles after the robbers with his mounted guard. The money was recovered forthwith.

Despite the pressures of diplomacy, Rich devoted considerable time to collecting coins and manuscripts as well as other antiquities. During his thirteen years in Baghdad he accumulated a vast collection. His linguistic abilities ensured that he acquire only the best manuscripts, mainly in Chaldee, Armenian, and Syrian. He planned to write a history of western Asia from his collections (a project he never completed).

In December of 1811, he managed to visit Babylon. Diplomatic protocol demanded that he travel in some state, accompanied "by my own troops of Hussars, with a galloper gun, a havildar, and twelve Sepoys; [and] about seventy baggage mules." Rich believed that local customs should be respected and attributed his diplomatic success to his sensitivity to the Turks' liking for "state and show." He wrote: "Above all, they have a horror of women being seen or heard. I am inclined to believe that a Turk who overcomes his dislike to this has lost some of his best feelings." Poor Mary Rich! She was obliged to behave like a piece of the resident's baggage. Her litter swung between two shafts transported by mules. Mary's maids fared even worse. They traveled in *mohaffas*, cagelike seats that were slung in pairs across a mule's back. The two cages were supposed to balance one another. But one of the attendants was slender, the other very stout. So the lighter woman had to sit on a pile of stones to equalize the weight.

The fifty-mile journey took two days, across numerous dried-up canals and abandoned mounds. The governor of Al-Hillah greeted the Riches effusively with his official band, who helped clear away the crowds. Al-Hillah lay two miles from the mounds of the ancient city. Rich found it almost impossible to get a general impression of the site so he set his hussars to work as surveyors. He himself rode the length and breadth of the ruins, a somewhat hazardous undertaking as the mounds were composed of loose earth and were full of large holes dug by brick diggers. "These ruins consist of mounds of earth, formed by the decomposition of buildings, channelled and furrowed by the weather, and the surfaces of them are strewed with pieces of brick, bitumen, and pottery," he reported.

Most of the Riches' ten-day stay was devoted to the huge mounds of brick and earth that lay on the left bank of the Euphrates. He noted the northern mound, which he called Babil. A mile to the south lay another mound he labeled El Qasr. A third he named Omran ibn Ali. He paced out measurements, sketched the mounds, and tried to survey the architectural features of what we now know to be the inner city. He explored the larger ruins and compiled a survey plan that was the first systematic map of Babylon. The brick diggers of Al-Hillah were hard at work extracting fired bricks from the ruins, many of which bore inscriptions. Some well-placed baksheesh ensured him a steady supply of these inscribed bricks for his collection. When he came across some gaping holes in the ruins, he employed some work-men on his own account to dig deeper. To his delight, they disinterred a skeleton in a coffin, which was removed piece by piece in a thoroughly nonarchaeological fashion.

On December 19, 1811, the party rode out six miles from their camp southwest of Babylon to the vast mass of Birs Nimrod. "The morning was at first stormy," wrote Rich, "but as we approached the object of our journey, the heavy clouds separating, discovered the Birs frowning over the plain, and presenting the appearance of a circular hill, crowned by a tower, with a high ridge extending along the foot of it." He felt somewhat disappointed, for the clouds prevented him "acquir-ing the gradual idea," as he approached from afar, as he had done with the Pyramids. But there were consolations, as Rich tells us at his romantic best: "Just as we were within the proper distance, it burst at once about our sight, in the midst of rolling masses of black clouds partially obscured by that kind of haze whose indistinctness is one great cause of sublimity, while a few strong catches of stormy light, thrown upon the desert in the background, served to give some idea of the immense and dreary solitude of the wastes in which this venerable ruin stands." Hastily he measured and sketched the Birs, which he estimated to be 235 feet high, an enormous, oblong mound of decaying and vitrified brickwork.

He returned from Babylon with sufficient sketches and notes to write his "Memoir on the Ruins of Babylon," which appeared in a Viennese journal, *Les Mines de l'Orient*, 1812. The article contained his plan of the ancient city, and a description of its major features. Rich kept his Biblical speculations to a minimum and concentrated on straightforward exposition. The article was soon reprinted in England, where it caused great interest on account of Babylon's Biblical associations. The reviewers praised Rich's "classical and oriental learning" and his "natural fruits of knowledge." He found himself an authority on ancient Mesopotamia, so much so that when a Major Rennell published a critique of the memoir in 1816, Rich felt obliged to return to the site to double-check his original work. His "Second Memoir on Babylon" appeared in 1818, and was to remain the definitive survey of the site until the 1890s. Rich did little to untangle the confusion of ruins at Babylon — indeed, the task was beyond the archaeological skill of the day — but he provided generations of travelers with a map that gave at least some reliable information on the legendary city. He had no time for a truly comprehensive survey, nor did he do any excavation except for cleaning Abbé Beauchamp's celebrated lion. The few finds he did bring back formed the nucleus of the Mesopotamian collections in the British Museum.

So great was the stir caused by Rich's memoirs that Lord Byron immortalized them in his poem *Don Juan,* a tribute paid to few academic authors:

> . . . *Claudius Rich, Esquire, some bricks has got*
> *And written lately two memoirs upon't.*

5

Diplomacy and Archaeology in Baghdad

*Everything was conducted with great
decorum.*

AFTER FOUR YEARS in Baghdad, Rich's health was badly undermined
by the torrid summers and the constant strain of political intrigue. His
temper was not improved by constant bickering with his superiors in
Bombay who considered him a young upstart. So, at Mary's urgent
pleading, he applied for, and was granted, a three-month overseas
leave.

In October of 1813, they set off for Europe, riding with official
Ottoman *tatars* (couriers) to Constantinople. He found Vienna, Paris,
and London so intoxicating that he dreaded the prospect of returning
to his post. Through the influence of his father-in-law, he managed
to prolong his leave for month after month. He dined with the duke
of Wellington and was astonished by the violinist Paganini's virtuosity
in Milan. He talked archaeology with scholars both in England and
on the Continent, men he had corresponded with for years, and found
that they considered him an orientalist of moment. As he relaxed and
enjoyed himself, Rich gradually recovered his health. Such was his
influential position that an attempt by company officials in India to
dismiss him from Baghdad was overruled imperiously from London.
A week after Napoleon's defeat at Waterloo, the Riches began the

long overland journey to Baghdad. The trip was a slow one, for Rich deliberately tarried two months in Constantinople and a month in Mosul, awaiting exact information from London on his status with the company. Finally, in March 1816, the Riches resumed their sojourn in Baghdad.

Claudius Rich had found himself an orientalist of considerable repute in European circles. He had managed to visit a number of orientalists in England and on the Continent, men with whom he had corresponded for years. One such scholar was Joseph von Hammer, who was associated with the Academy of Oriental Languages in Vienna. Hammer had taken a close interest in a promising student at the academy named Carl Bellino. He now recommended Bellino to Rich as a potential private secretary. Rich took to the young man immediately and engaged him at a salary of seventy-five rupees a month. Bellino arrived in Baghdad with the Riches in early May 1816, with the appointment of official interpreter. He was given a horse, which he hated, and the run of Rich's library. The new private secretary was an immediate success. Mary remarked on his loyalty, industrious character, and passion for oriental languages. He was, she wrote, "wild, uncouth, and dogmatical," but they were very fond of him. Claudius found him a kindred spirit, with a priceless asset — he had an uncanny knack for copying cuneiform inscriptions accurately. Rich had found that his European colleagues were more interested in accurate copies of cuneiform characters than anything else. Bellino could take much of this burdensome task off his hands.

It was just as well that Rich had additional help, for Baghdad was in turmoil. The effendi Daud, the pasha's brother-in-law, succeeded in deposing and executing the pasha and took over the pashalik. The Turks and Persians were at loggerheads and Arab insurrection was in the wind. Baghdad was full of executions, treachery, and warring factions. The resident remained pointedly neutral. Even in troubled weeks, Rich's morning office hours were a formal audience attended by senior government ministers every day. "Everything was conducted with great decorum," wrote an early guest of the Riches. "Nothing could be more evident than the high degree of respect with which these interviews inspired the visitors." No important official decisions were made without Rich's approval and imprimatur.

Any traveler en route to the Persian Gulf made a beeline for the hospitable residency. A steady stream of visitors provided the Riches with welcome social diversion. Fortunately, most of their guests were literate and articulate people who were not only entertained but entertaining. One such visitor arrived at the residency gates in rags in July 1816. The ragged figure turned out to be James Silk Buckingham, a

well-known traveler who enjoyed wandering through the East. Buckingham was a charming and widely read man, one who appreciated the
luxury of the residency to the full. He spent months in Baghdad and
later published his impressions of the city and life at the residency.

Buckingham had traveled overland alone from Aleppo to Mosul and
Baghdad. He had joined a small caravan under the patronage of a
wealthy Mosul merchant, who insisted he dress like an Arab to the
skin, with turban, tarboosh, and red silk sash. He wore a "damascus
sabre, a Turkish musket, small carbine, and pistols." His baggage consisted of "a pipe and tobacco bag, a metal drinking cup, a pocket compass, memorandum books, and ink stand." These filled one saddlebag,
the other held the chain fastening for his horse. A "small Turkey
carpet" served as bed, table, and prayer mat, while a woollen cloak
sufficed for bedding. Buckingham, like all his companions, traveled
light, his money tucked away safely in a cummerbund around his waist,
but these precautions did not prevent him from being stripped of many
of his possessions. He hated caravan travel. The camels ambled along
at two and a half miles an hour; every nomad band extorted a harsh
tax from travelers. At Mosul, he attached himself to two *tatars* who
were carrying official dispatches to Claudius Rich. The *tatars* traveled
at full speed. On one occasion, Buckingham found himself riding fifty
miles in six hours at full gallop. This lightning progress ended when the
tatars ran out of horses. So Buckingham joined a Baghdad mule caravan. He found himself riding an overladen mule in appalling heat, not,
he wrote, "a very cool or agreeable occupation." It was so hot that he
jumped in the river fully clothed and then mounted his slow-moving
animal without drying off. The intense heat blistered his face and lips,
dust inflamed everyone's eyes. The rich carried parasols, while the
poor — like Buckingham — had to be content with the scanty shade
of their cloaks.

On July 16, 1816, the gates of Baghdad appeared five miles ahead.
The city guards stopped Buckingham from entering so they could in-
spect his load. He sat cross-legged in the dust by the gate and tried to
smoke his pipe. A Turkish guard promptly snatched it from his mouth,
asking him how he dared smoke when the pasha was about to pass on
the way back from his morning ride. Soon the pasha and his troop of
gaily dressed Mameluke guards swept past, accompanied by a troop
of foot soldiers dressed in cast-off military coats and muskets purchased
from the British residency. "Their whole deportment exhibited a total
absence of discipline or uniformity," observed Buckingham. But he was
impressed by the awe with which the onlookers greeted the pasha:
everyone rose and made some gesture of respect. The pasha returned
the salutations with great dignity. Two Englishmen — the residency

doctor and Bellino — rode at the back of the procession. Buckingham heard their conversation and was smothered in the dust from their horses' hooves. But he forbore to identify himself in this public place.

Once the pasha was inside Baghdad, Buckingham boldly produced his revolver and pushed his mule past the gate. The onlookers cheered at the embarrassment of the Turkish guards. Buckingham made his way to the *tatars'* headquarters, identified himself as an Englishman, and was escorted to the British residency. There he relaxed for the first time in months, reveling in baths, good food, a comfortable bed, and the welcome company of Claudius and Mary Rich. He found himself the guest of a large and luxurious establishment.

The residency was formed from several houses converted into a single large dwelling with two courtyards. One of them was used as a riding ground, surrounded with numerous rooms and galleries. Vaulted subterranean chambers named *serdabs* served as a daily refuge from the intense summer heat. The Rich establishment rose at the dawn, bathed, and went riding until eight o'clock, when everyone met for breakfast. Rich then received official visitors in audience, after which everyone returned to the *serdabs* until sunset. Dinner was served on one of the terraces, the household gathering in formal evening dress for a leisured meal that lasted until ten o'clock. Beyond John Hine, the surgeon, and Bellino, the residency housed numerous dragomen, janissaries, grooms, and servants, as well as a company of Indian sepoys who acted as bodyguards to the resident. Their drums and horn calls regulated the life of the household. A large yacht lay in constant readiness, fine horses were instantly available for guests. Everything, wrote Buckingham, was calculated to impress the local people with the prestige of the resident and his country. He found a small but entertaining European community in Baghdad, of which Rich was the undisputed leader. The only other diplomat was the new French consul, Monsieur Vigoroux, whose establishment consisted of a single dragoman, a few servants, and a tumbledown abode. The few Christians worshipped at the convent, presided over by a Carmelite monk, Padre Vincenzo.

Buckingham rested and amused himself by recording the temperatures during a typical calm summer's day when the brazen sun shone unmercifully from a dusty sky. His thermometer stood at 112° F at dawn, 119° at noon, 122° at 2 P.M., and 114° at midnight. Many people died from the heat. But Buckingham found time to wander through the narrow streets with local guides. After dark he visited bazaars and coffeehouses, thronged with people clothed in brilliant apparel. He would sit for hours in the middle of the famous Bridge of Boats, contemplating the brilliant stars in the heavens, reflected in the placid waters of the Tigris as they rippled past the boats. Buckingham was always interested in women and discovered that the pasha maintained a harem of Georgian girls. "It is permitted only to the Faithful, however, to possess white slaves . . . so that the Georgians and Circassians fall exclusively to the enjoyment of the unorthodox," observed Buckingham. "Sceptics and heretics must content themselves with the sable beauties of Nigritia, Soudan, and Madagascar." History does not relate whether Buckingham diverted himself in this way.

Except for excursions to Babylon and Ctesiphon, Buckingham spent most of his time laid low with fever and closeted in the residency. He consoled himself with Rich's library and the fine collection of "cylinders, amulets, idols, and intaglios of the most curious kind" in Rich's study. Buckingham admired the clay seals with "inscriptions in the arrow-headed character, such as has been found at the ruins of Persepolis, Babylon, and Nineveh." Unfortunately, Buckingham was obliged to limit his occupations to "such light reading as would beguile the time; for the powers of the mind were so unhinged by the influence of the climate, as to be incapable of close application to any subject requiring much thought."

But Buckingham's greatest pleasure seems to have been in the Riches themselves. Nearly ten years later he published his book on Mesopotamia, in which he praised Rich's "boundless generosity" and "unremitting zeal for the interests of science and general knowledge."

Two years later, in October of 1818, the Riches entertained another well-known visitor, the noted traveler and artist Sir Robert Ker Porter. His introduction to Rich's prestige was dramatic. Eighty-five miles out of Baghdad he stopped to rest at a village inn and sent a messenger on ahead to inform Rich that he would arrive soon and that his travel funds were running low. When the landlord of the inn found out that his guest was short of money, he came in with a large bag of piasters, merely requesting that the money be repaid to a friend of his in Baghdad. Ker Porter gasped at this unheard-of gesture of trust. "Simple," replied the landlord. Claudius Rich had such a high reputation that he knew his money was absolutely safe.

Armed with these unexpected funds, Ker Porter pressed on to Baghdad. His companions were so sick that they rode in basketlike carriers flung on either side of a mule's back. A day later they were met by an imposing Turk guarded by two well-mounted Arab horsemen armed to the teeth. Thinking that he was in the presence of a high government official, Ker Porter prepared to pay his respects. To his astonishment, the Turk salaamed and brought him greetings from the British resident, a letter, and a purse of a thousand piasters. Two days later, Ker Porter was escorted into an airy room overlooking the Tigris and greeted warmly by Claudius and Mary Rich.

In Ker Porter, Rich found a kindred soul. He examined his visitor's sketches, notably those of Persepolis and the great, inscribed rock at Behistun in Persia, which later was to provide so many clues to the decipherment of cuneiform. The two men, and Bellino as well, discussed the problems of copying and translating this mysterious script. Rich had been in poor health for a while. Ker Porter's welcome conversation sent him back to his manuscripts and inscriptions with renewed vigor. These academic debates did not prevent Ker Porter from enjoying the hospitality of the wealthier inhabitants. He attended dinners and entertainments, saw male dancers dressed in linen and coins perform violent dances "by twisting the body into all kinds of odious postures, accompanied by a machine-like dodder of the head, which is duly answered by a wriggle from the back, or hips."

Ker Porter's real objective in coming to Baghdad was to visit ancient Babylon, to sketch one of the great cities of Biblical antiquity. The countryside was so disorderly that Rich not only sent Bellino but an armed escort with him. Ker Porter was in a state of eager anticipation, his mind full of the city walls sixty miles in circumference, the brass gates, and the Hanging Gardens, which Herodotus had described, and the ultimate destruction that had beset the "daughter of the Chaldeans." What he found was a solemn sight, the "majestic stream of the Euphrates wandering in solitude, like a pilgrim monarch through the devastated ruins of his kingdom." He went on to deplore how the scene had changed: "These broken hills were palaces; those long-undulating mounds, streets; this vast solitude, filled with the busy subjects of the proud daughter of the East. Now, *wasted with solitude*, her habitations are not to be found."

More than any traveler, Ker Porter was impressed by the desolation of Babylon, the utter destruction extolled by the Scriptures. Here, indeed, was powerful demonstration of the Lord's Handiwork. He paused at Birs Nimrod to admire that "stupendous work arrested before completion." That this was the Biblical Tower of Babel seemed beyond doubt. "It does not seem improbable," he wrote in wonder, "that the fire-blasted summit of the pile, its rent wall and scattered fragments, with their partially vitrified masses, may be a part of that very stage of the primeval tower which felt the effects of the divine vengeance."

As he and his party approached the silent mass of brickwork on a second visit, they saw several dark figures moving along the summit of the ruin. Their immediate thought was of robbers. But Ker Porter was amazed to see "two or three majestic lions, taking their air upon the heights of the pyramid." He was deeply moved, remembering the utter destruction of Babylon foretold by the prophet Isaiah: "But wild beasts will lie down there, and its houses will be full of howling creatures" (13:21).

Meanwhile, Carl Bellino had been hard at work copying the cuneiform inscriptions in the residency library, including those on "a small earthen vase covered with cuneiform" from Nebi Yunus at Nineveh (the vase is now known as the Bellino cylinder). He had, as well, been corresponding with Grotefend and other European experts, to whom he sent copies of his work. Rich had gotten him elected to the Bombay Literary Society, an honor that delighted Bellino. His "Account of the Progress Made in Deciphering Cuneiform Inscriptions," which had been published in the society's journal in 1818, was widely read and praised. Without question, this hard-working and obscure young man was making a major contribution to the decipherment of cuneiform.

In the spring of 1820, Rich planned an official journey to Kurdistan, to higher ground where he could escape the summer heat. The trip was planned with care, for Kurdistan was a remote and little-visited territory for foreigners in the 1820s. He felt he should travel in official splendor, accompanied by most of his household and a guard of twenty-five sepoys. As usual, Mary Rich had to bounce along in her mule-borne litter until the caravan reached remote country where she could mount a horse.

The Kurdistan trip took the Riches into the Zagros Mountains and Kurdish provinces of Persia, where they held court for tribal rulers and studied local customs. Claudius even slipped away in disguise to witness the dancing in a local Arab wedding. The British cavalcade arrived back on the plains at Mosul in October, so that Rich could examine Nineveh across the Tigris from the town. Difficulties with Pasha Daud in Baghdad caused the Riches to spend five months in Mosul. Their stay was saddened by Bellino's death of fever, a heartfelt loss to both Claudius and Mary. Rich spent many days examining Nineveh. "The area of Nineveh, on a rough guess, is about one and a half to two miles broad, and four miles long," he wrote. "The Mount of Kuyunjik is, except at its west and part of its eastern face, of rather an irregular form. Its sides are very steep, its top nearly flat; its angles are not marked by any lantern or turret." Rich's party measured the height of the mound — forty-three feet. It was 7,691 feet in circumference. "It evidently has had building on it, at least round its edges," reported Rich. "Stones and bricks are dug or ploughed up everywhere. There were also other buildings further in the mount, and at a place where they had been digging into it, we saw the same coarse grey stone, shaped like the capital of a column such as at this day surrounds the wooden pillars or posts of Turkish or rather Persian verandahs."

As the party wandered over the surface of Nineveh, they came across the stone and earth floors of long-abandoned houses, thousands of potsherds and brick fragments. The finds included "a piece of fine brick or pottery covered with exceedingly small and beautiful cuneiform writing." Rich visited the small village of Nebi Yunus which flourished on the summit of one of Nineveh's tells. He delved in kitchens and living rooms in search of inscriptions and artifacts. He found that the inhabitants regularly dug up cuneiform inscriptions. But they were terrified of undermining their dwellings. Rich crouched over cuneiform-covered bricks now part of kitchen walls, and persuaded one woman to allow him to record an inscription set into the modern plaster wall of her small room. Rich was tantalized by these inscriptions, but the labyrinth of houses in the village prevented him from digging into the mound below. "It is only on the repairing or falling down of these that such things are discovered," he lamented. So the Riches contented themselves with visiting the Mosque of Jonah on the north end of the mound, "a rather considerable building." The entire population of the village assembled to gaze at the strange sight of some Europeans admiring the view from the terrace of the mosque, but no one objected to their presence. The spectators were heard to mutter that Rich was working out whether the mosque was a suitable gun emplacement to bring a cannonade to bear on Mosul.

The local people kept on reporting almost forgotten discoveries of fine statues in the mounds. Much of Mosul was built of stone and mud brick quarried from them. In one place Rich was shown a quarry where "some years ago, an immense bas-relief, representing men and animals, covering a grey stone of the height of two men, was dug up from a spot a little above the surface of the ground." Apparently everyone in Mosul trekked out to see it. Then the quarrymen broke it up for building stone. The only way to recover valuable specimens was to buy them from the walls of local houses. One beautifully inscribed slab was literally talked out of the houseowner's wall in Nebi Yunus village. "It is now safely lodged among my other curiosities," wrote Rich happily.

Rich now embarked on an ambitious project to map the entire complex of mounds. He was fortunate in having the services of his military escort, whom he dispatched in all directions to measure mounds and fortifications. Sometimes the sepoys could survey a site without anyone's taking notice, when Rich himself would have been followed by dozens of curious spectators. In the meantime, "Delli Samaan, my curiosity-hunter" was dispatched to hunt out antiquities from the local

Mosul and Nineveh, with the mound of Nebi Yunus in the foreground. From Chesney's Survey (1850)

bazaars and villages. Rich himself ranged widely over the countryside in every direction, trying to establish the boundaries of the ancient city. Time and time again he came across erosion gullies or stream banks where flood waters had cut through ancient midden deposits to expose mud-brick courses or stone walls that lay intact below the surface. Claudius and Mary amused themselves by carving their names into a stone wall by a well. "Some traveler in after times, when our remembrance has long been swept away by the torrent of time . . . may wonder, on reading the name of Mary Rich, who the adventurous female was who had visited the ruins of Nineveh," he wrote. "He will not be aware that, had her name been inscribed at every spot she had visited in the course of her weary pilgrimage, it would be found in places compared with which Mosul is the centre of civilization."

Rich continued to explore the countryside whenever the weather allowed. But heavy rains often confined him to the town, where he watched the locals open Mosul's famous Bridge of Boats to let the Tigris flood unimpeded. He also puzzled over his plans of Nineveh. He was certain that all the mounds he had measured were of the "same age and character." The major buildings were, he felt, confined to the mounds of Nebi Yunus and Kuyunjik, an observation he had formulated on an earlier visit to Nineveh many years before. These mounds, he concluded, were the "citadel or royal precincts, or perhaps both, as the practice of fortifying the residence of the sovereign is of very ancient origin." Later excavations were to prove him right.

Rich also traveled widely in search of ancient manuscripts preserved in local monasteries and convents. He was horrified to learn that the monks of one monastery had destroyed a library of five hundred manuscripts some years before as they had no use for them. "Manuscripts are fast perishing in the East," he wrote, "and it is almost the duty of a traveler to rescue as many as he can from destruction." Rich spared neither time nor money in acquiring as much as he could, wherever he traveled. He found that their owners valued theirs but little until the time came to haggle over the price of a manuscript. Then, "with that avidity for money which is so undisguised in the East, they express unwillingness to part with them, in order, too generally, to secure a large sum being offered for them." Fortunately for science, Claudius Rich's manuscripts ended up in the British Museum. A letter from the museum written in 1836 reveals that they possessed eight hundred volumes of Rich manuscripts, the Syriac and Arabic documents therein representing "probably the most valuable collection ever formed by a European."

On March 3, 1821, the Riches started for Baghdad on a *kellek*. They floated downstream through intensely cultivated country. After thirty miles, they came to the ancient mounds of Nimrud, where Claudius, Mary, and a working party disembarked for a difficult walk to the conspicuous mounds. The ruined ziggurat at the northwest corner of the site could be seen from far away, but Rich found it difficult to trace the edges of the city among the plowed fields. The party wandered over the mounds, saw traces of buildings like those at Nineveh, and collected burned bricks inscribed with cuneiform. Rich was elated to find one brick bearing "writing larger than that at Babylon." The rafts were waiting, so Rich had only enough time to make some simple measurements and to observe that "these ruins singularly illustrate those of Nineveh." They floated on downstream for the next ten days, enjoying the countryside and admiring the skill of the boatmen in navigating through intricate passages, sandbanks, and low islands.

Dispatches awaited Rich at Baghdad, one of which was an offer of a senior job in Bombay. This he accepted, but Pasha Daud rescinded British trading rights in the pashalik and refused to allow Rich to depart. Rich now learned that the pasha planned to take him prisoner, so he fortified the residency and had his sepoys man the barricades. When the pasha's infantry started a surprise advance on the residency, they backed off when they saw Rich's preparations. In any case, their commander and most of the townspeople were firm friends of the Riches'. When the pasha's ministers came to negotiate, Rich demanded the removal of the besieging troops. The ministers refused, whereupon he grabbed a stick and angrily drove them from the residency gates. The pasha soon gave in in the face of this display of force and allowed Rich to depart. The Riches left on the residency yacht to the accompaniment of a tumultuous send-off from their friends. They sailed to Basra and then on to Bushire, where Claudius paused to await instructions. He sent Mary on to Bombay in a passing ship. They were never to see each other again.

Ever restless, Rich decided to escape the heat of Bushire and travel to Shiraz, to visit the tomb of Cyrus, the city of Persepolis, and other archaeological sites. During his stay in Shiraz, cholera descended on the city. Over six thousand people died in a few days. The wealthier inhabitants fled the town, but Rich insisted on staying behind to assist in preventing panic and to aid the sick. On October 14, 1821, he developed symptoms of cholera after a warm bath and died within twenty-four hours. He was thirty-four.

6

The Euphrates Expedition

There is nobody to civilize and nobody to convert.

THE CLOSING YEARS of Rich's residency in Baghdad saw him increasingly preoccupied with what was to become the dominant issue of Eastern politics for decades — the Eastern Question. Napoleon's abortive campaign in Egypt in 1798 had raised the specter of an enemy power blocking British access to India by an overland route. By the end of the Napoleonic Wars, Russia was beginning to examine her eastern frontiers and the Dardanelles with interest. Her more aggressive foreign policies raised another persistent worry, that of a Russian invasion of India with the compliance of Afghanistan and Persia. The French wanted to control the Syrian coast, the Germans were eyeing the Persian Gulf. Everyone expected the Ottoman Empire, with its shrinking economy and cumbersome bureaucracy, to crumble and evaporate, leaving a political and economic vacuum behind it. As successive sultans tried to reform their government, almost invariably without success, a complicated checkerboard of patronage, political and economic manipulation, and espionage ebbed and flowed over the Near East. In the long run, the greatest impact of the Eastern Question was to expose even the remote provinces of the Ottoman Empire to new and alien European ideas. The slow changes that resulted from these ideas led in part to a rising tide of Arab nationalism that culminated about the time of the First World War.

Baghdad lay at the center of the Eastern Question, for its strategic position in Mesopotamia made it an obvious military and administrative center for a potential invader. About one hundred thousand people lived there in Rich's time. He and his successors never forgot the strategic importance of Baghdad, even if the city itself was decaying into ruins and had become a shadow of its former self. "It bears a name, and a certain respectability in the East," reported Ker Porter in 1818, "solely from the circumstance of its situation being a central depot . . . from its lying on the main road of traffic between so many distant counties, to receive, and protect, and set forward on their business, all the merchants and merchandise which pass to and fro from Baghdad." As Constantinople took more and more authority into its own hands, Baghdad and its pashalik sank into greater poverty. Constant grain shortages caused the pasha to force thousands of poorer people from the city. The expelled poor starved in the desert, wandered in the harsh foothills, or more often than not, joined robber bands and supported themselves by pillage and murder. Even large caravans were in constant danger of attack, for the pasha's authority was confined to Baghdad itself. The government taxed peasants so heavily on their crops that they grew as little corn as possible. When revenues fell, the tax collectors resorted to extortion and beatings. So the farmers fled their land and joined the swelling city population. Most serious of all, the government neglected to maintain irrigation works and the embankments that checked the floodwaters of the Tigris. Baghdad was a vulnerable city, its rulers living on borrowed time.

The crisis came in March 1831, while Rich's enemy Pasha Daud was still in power. A few cases of plague appeared in the bazaars that spring, isolated occurrences that mushroomed into an epidemic in a few short weeks. Rich's successor, James Taylor, closed the British residency at once to keep the plague outside the buildings. All supplies for the household were delivered through apertures in the wall and passed through water before being touched. Letters and papers were fumigated before opening. While the Europeans went into quarantine, the locals fled in their thousands to the countryside. But the plague still spread. By April 10, seven thousand people had died in the eastern parts of the city. Then a sepoy in the residency contracted the disease. Taylor immediately packed up his effects and fled to Basra. Fortunately, the residency boats were moored beneath the walls of the house and everyone could get away without contact with the townspeople. The only British resident not to leave was a missionary, the

Reverend Groves, who insisted on staying behind to minister to Christians who had taken shelter in his house.

Between April 16 and 21, about two thousand people a day were dying. So virulent was the disease that people hardly dared bury their dead relatives. Many families bought up stocks of winding sheets before the supply ran out. One of Groves's servants told him she saw fifty bodies being carried off for burial within six hundred yards. To cap this misery, the Tigris rose in flood and inundated much of western Baghdad. Bands of desert Arabs roamed the outskirts of the city and robbed those who fled. Food supplies were depleted, cemeteries were overflowing, corpses were buried in the streets. Many people were completely demoralized and stayed at home waiting for death. Infants were left in the streets to die, the dead stacked on mules to be carried away for burial. Dogs mangled and devoured freshly buried corpses.

By April 26, over four thousand people a day were succumbing to the plague. Over a third of the city's population had left, many more had perished. On April 27, Groves recorded that the Tigris had undermined a long length of the city walls, which had collapsed. The floodwaters had rushed into the Jewish quarter. Within hours, over seven thousand mud-brick houses had literally melted, killing at least fifteen thousand people. The survivors camped on higher ground, while the dead were hastily thrown into the Tigris. The survivors were crowded into smaller and smaller space, so the disease struck even harder. The floodwaters also trapped many people who fled the city. They were either drowned or stripped of their possessions by robbers. Caravans carried the plague with them and were decimated on the road. It was not until the beginning of May that the floods receded and the plague retreated. The death rate fell gradually, and by May 26 no more new cases were being reported.

By the time the floodwaters retreated, over two thirds of Baghdad's population had perished. Only a small cluster of buildings on higher ground and a few mosques with strong foundations still stood. The city walls encompassed a barren wilderness of ruined foundations and stagnant pools. It was months before life returned to a semblance of normalcy. Minor plague epidemics returned in two successive years, carrying off a further five to seven thousand people each time, and the government's administrative grip on Baghdad and the countryside was weakened even more. Several pashas murdered their predecessors; Arab sheikhs living within and near Baghdad did pretty well what they pleased. Matters improved after 1831, when Mameluke power in Baghdad was broken and the sultan was able to appoint his own pashas, starting with Ali Ridda.

Given the conditions in Mesopotamia in those days, travel there took considerable courage and resource. A few bold explorers like Richard Mignan (1826–1828) and James Baillie-Fraser (1834–1835) ventured onto the desolate plains between the rivers in Babylonia, accompanied by only a small party of armed Arabs. Baillie-Fraser was probably the first European to visit Tell Muqayyar, the site of the Biblical Ur of the Chaldees.

Baillie-Fraser found Baghdad a gutted town. The city walls still looked imposing, with their courses of well-worn brick and fortified towers. He enjoyed the narrow streets and brick houses whose projecting windows overhung the streets. The sitting rooms of houses across the street from each other were sometimes joined. Occasionally, Baillie-Fraser found himself "illuminated by a beam from some bright pair of eyes shining through the half-closed lattice." The river frontage boasted of "a long range of imposing, if not absolutely handsome" buildings shaded with palm trees. A constant bustle of boats and rafts carrying horses, camels, and people passed to and fro. The bazaars were dilapidated and in ruins, many of the shops neglected and unoccupied. The largest was near the so-called Mosul Gate, a busy place where the headless trunks of executed criminals were exhibited to the public. Above all, Baghdad was noisy, filled with every imaginable din. As Baillie-Fraser sat on his balcony over the street, he was beset by cocks crowing in a nearby yard, the sepoy's reveille call at the British residency, dogs barking, donkeys braying, and herds of sheep and cattle passing through the streets early in the morning. The Arabs, he complained, "rush along in droves . . . hallooing to each other and to all they pass, often maintaining a conversation at the top of their tremendous voices, with some equally clear-piped brother, at a quarter of a mile's distance." Baghdad was still an obscure corner of the Ottoman world even if strategists in Europe were beginning to think otherwise.

The East India Company and the British government were concerned not only about Russia but about fast and reliable land and sea routes to India as well. Their concern was channeled in two directions, through diplomacy in Constantinople and into exploration of new routes to India that would maximize the benefit of steamship travel up the Red Sea and in the Mediterranean. The diplomatic effort was in the hands of the British ambassador in Constantinople, the formidable and powerful Sir Stratford Canning, known to Englishmen and Turk alike as the Great Elchi (elchi is "envoy" in Turkish). Canning believed that the Ottoman Empire "was rotten at the heart" and spent sixteen years, from 1826 on, trying to institute reform. He fostered a policy that bolstered the Ottoman sultans to protect British trade and communications. His main worry was Russia. Al-'Iraq was of lesser importance except as a possible highway route between Europe and India. Canning's influence with the sultan was enormous. He presided over a glittering embassy with almost military precision. An autocrat and a firm believer in the "doctrine of the divine rights of ambassadors," he was to play a leading part in organizing early excavations in Iraq.

With Canning's diplomatic backing, British officers and embassy officials quietly explored many of the sultan's domains. The search for an overland route to India was pursued on a larger scale, however. In the late 1820s, the East India Company drew up a staff document that asked a number of specific questions about possible overland routes to India via Syria and Mesopotamia. In particular, the document stressed the importance of discovering whether the Euphrates was navigable and for what distance, and above all, whether it could be traversed by steamships. The task of studying the routes fell to Captain Francis Chesney of the Royal Artillery, a rocket expert and surveyor who was based in Constantinople. He started off by visiting Egypt in 1829, where he studied the idea of an isthmus canal and showed that such a waterway was technically feasible as far as sea levels were concerned. "The practical question," he wrote, "appeared to be one of expenditure."

In 1831, Chesney traveled across the Holy Land and Syria to the Euphrates, floated downstream on a *kellek*, and eventually visited Baghdad and Basra. He returned to London in 1832 to find that his preliminary surveys had caused quite a stir. Two years later, he was summoned to an audience with King William IV of England, appointed leader of the Euphrates Expedition, promoted to colonel, and given twenty thousand pounds to spend on the enterprise.

The Euphrates Expedition is a unique and extraordinary chapter in the annals of exploration. Chesney was to transport two prefabricated iron steamers from the Syrian coast to the banks of the Euphrates one hundred and forty miles away, assemble them, and determine whether both that river and the Tigris were navigable. The official charge was "to survey the northern part of Syria, to explore the basins of the rivers Euphrates and Tigris, to test the navigability of the former, and to examine in the countries adjacent to these great rivers the market with which the expedition might be thrown in contact." While a major objective was to open a regular steamer route to India, the organizers were interested in commerce too, in opening Mesopotamia up to external trade on a scale unknown since the days of the caliphs.

Faced with this enormous task, Chesney threw himself into it with characteristic energy. He recruited officers from the navy and the army and from the East India Company, arranged for skilled artisans, marines, and seamen to be posted to the expedition. The equipment included not only the two prefabricated paddle steamers *Tigris* and *Euphrates*, but a diving bell, tools for mining coal, Congreve rockets, and numerous guns, and ammunition. Two years' provisions had to be carried overland as well, including "preserved meats and wine."

The expedition reached the mouth of the Orontes River on the Syrian coast in April 1835. The cumbersome steamer components, especially the keels and boilers, were floated as far up the Orontes as possible, then transferred to stout carriages. Heavy carts carried boilers and hull sections. Some were even rigged with square sails, but these did little to help them over the muddy plains. So Chesney's officers hired pack animals and dozens of laborers, three times more, he reported, than would have been necessary in Britain to do the job. While most of the officers and men were busy moving the steamers to the Euphrates, a small group of surveyors began the laborious task of running levels from the coast to the Euphrates to establish the possible feasibility of a canal from the Mediterranean to the river.

The transportation of the steamers to the Euphrates occupied more than nine months of backbreaking work. Many officers and men were felled by fever, or alternately baked by the sun and drenched by record rains and floods. The worst part of the journey was a steep hill near the lake called Amik Golu. A zigzag track had to be built up the slope. Forty pairs of oxen and a hundred men were needed to move the boilers up the hill. Once over the summit, the heavy loads were floated across the lake and dragged 120 miles to a newly constructed stockade at Birecik on the Euphrates, christened Port William after the expedition's royal patron.

Three months later, on March 16, 1836, the *Euphrates* set off on her first trial trip. A few days later, both steamers sailed in convoy downstream, preceded by a small advance party who sounded the river. The local people were astonished at Chesney's supernatural genius in moving vessels without sails or oars. He cashed in on his magic by employing hundreds of laborers to haul the steamers off uncharted shallows. When some desert Arabs stole a corporal's brass buttons, a small party of officers and men rode out to remonstrate with the marauders. They nearly fell into a trap and would have been cut off had it not been for a "rapid demonstration in light infantry order," which enabled the party to return to the shelter of the steamers' rockets and guns. Later, Chesney invited the sheikhs to dinner, which was preceded by a timely demonstration of rocket fire power that had them hastily proclaiming their peaceful intentions.

The survey went smoothly until May 21, hampered only by coal

The Tigris *and* Euphrates *sailing in company downstream. From*
Chesney's Narrative *(1868)*

shortages. Then tragedy struck. The two steamers were proceeding quietly downstream at midday when dark and ominous clouds blew up from the southwest. The steamers were about to enter the rock passage of Is-Geria when the squall was observed. Since there was no room to turn around, the steamers pressed on, intending to secure alongside the bank as soon as possible. Just as they were making for the bank, the storm struck with winds of hurricane force. To avoid a collision with the *Tigris*, the *Euphrates* had to back-paddle, and only with great difficulty, was she secured to a mooring in waves that were rising up to four feet above the bank. By keeping her engines full ahead, she managed to stay in one place. Not so the *Tigris*, which touched the bank, bounced off, and drifted helplessly in midstream. The wind heeled the steamer on her beam-ends. The boilers were extinguished by water that broke through the skylights and paddle boxes. She foundered and capsized only twenty yards from shore in pitch-darkness and flying dust. The thirty-four crew members, who were clustered at the stern end, jumped for their lives. Chesney found himself swimming in a cornfield accompanied by his sodden Bible. The storm ended as quickly as it had begun. When the survivors assembled at the *Euphrates*, they found fifteen of their party missing, as well as four Arabs.

Chesney was undeterred and continued his survey south to Basra, where the *Euphrates* arrived in June, burning empty casks to cover the last forty-three miles. He now sailed her over the open sea to Bushire, carried out essential repairs, and then ascended the Tigris to Baghdad. The river was so shallow that the Arab pilots had to swim and wade ahead of the steamer to spot the channel. On August 30, 1836, the *Euphrates* steamed triumphantly through the Bridge of Boats at Baghdad to be greeted by the British resident and the entire population. An attempt to ascend the Euphrates ended in failure when the engines suffered a serious breakdown. By this time the funds of the expedition were too low to permit another attempt.

The Euphrates Expedition showed that a regular steamer service up the Euphrates was impracticable on account of the many shallows and rapids. Furthermore, the technology of steam power was not yet advanced enough to stem the rapid current of the Euphrates narrows. There was no advantage to a steamer service anyhow, when letters could reach Baghdad from Damascus by camel in eight or nine days. Chesney's reports noted that the Euphrates flowed through desert country inhabited by nomads. "There is," he wrote, "nobody to civilize and nobody to convert." So the overland route through Mesopotamia was quietly shelved. But the expedition did generate some lasting benefits. The Lynch brothers decided to take advantage of the river surveys, which had been mapped on a scale of two miles to the inch. They had three river steamers shipped out from England via the Cape of Good Hope and put them into service on the Tigris between Basra and Baghdad. For years, the Euphrates Steam Navigation Company carried mail, horses, merchandise, and people up and down the river. The steamships provided a vital link with the outside world that made Baghdad less dependent on the whims of desert sheikhs.

With the end of the Euphrates Expedition, Mesopotamia became much more familiar to the Western world. Every traveler to Baghdad carried Chesney's river maps with him. The archaeologists and adventurers who came after him were traveling in territory that was no longer a remote outpost of the Eastern world. The pace of scientific research increased accordingly.

7

Cuneiform Deciphered

A thorough examination of the fragments would lead to the most curious results.

WHEN SIR ROBERT KER PORTER arrived in Baghdad in October 1818, he was armed with many pages of copies of the cuneiform inscriptions left by the Persian kings at Mount Alvand near Hamadan (the ancient Ecbatana) and on the Great Rock at Behistun, twenty miles east of Kermanshah. Bellino and Rich had urged him to publish his copies from Behistun, where the perpendicular rock faces were carved with inscriptions in three languages. "What a treasure of information doubtless was there to the happy man who could decipher [the scripts]," he wrote in his *Travels* (1821). "It was tantalizing to a painful degree, to look at such a 'sealed book,' in the very spot of mystery, where, probably, its contents would explain all."

The Greak Rock demonstrates vividly the megalomania of the Persian kings. Twelve hundred square feet of rock face were carefully smoothed and the weak portions consolidated with a mixture of rock and lead. Dozens of craftsmen burnished the surface to a high polish, and then artists carved a huge bas-relief surrounded on three sides by inscriptions in Old Persian (414 lines), Elamite (263 lines), and Babylonian (112 lines). The relief is eighteen feet wide and more than three hundred feet above the ground. It depicts King Darius standing in triumph over a rival for the throne, one Gaumata. He is attended by two officers, while the god Ahuramazda hovers overhead. Darius's foot rests on his rival's stomach as he pronounces sentence on nine other rebel leaders. "Eight of my family have been kings," boasts Darius in the inscriptions. They recount how Ahuramazda helped the king put down a rebellion led by Gaumata in 522 B.C.

Ker Porter's drawings of Behistun and its inscriptions excited widespread interest in Europe. He had spent many weeks copying the trilingual Persepolis inscriptions, too. His pictures of flying bulls and columns of cuneiform were compared favorably with those made by Carsten Niebuhr many years before. Though it would be a quarter of a century before Behistun was copied accurately and deciphered, by the time Ker Porter's *Travels* appeared a small international community of scholars had begun to argue and correspond about cuneiform. Each new inscription was passed from hand to hand, for accurate copies were in chronically short supply. The experts had developed a healthy respect for Niebuhr's careful work. Niebuhr himself, it will be recalled, was able to identify forty-two different letters in an alphabetic method of writing, in which words were spelled out by letters.

In 1798, Bishop Friedrich Münter of Copenhagen, a well-known historian, published two papers on Persepolis in which he argued that Niebuhr's Class I script was alphabetic, and that his Classes II and III were syllabic and ideographic respectively. Not only that, but each class was not only a different language but a different type of writing as well. He also proved that the Persepolis inscriptions were the work of the Persian Achaemenid dynasty, and speculated that the Class I script was an Indo-European language, Old Persian. Although Münter himself never worked on cuneiform again, he had provided some of the vital groundwork for its decipherment. So did the French orientalist A. H. Anquetil-Duperron, who learned how to read and interpret Old Persian by comparing it with Indian manuscripts he had collected. His works, published in 1768 and 1771, gave the decipherers the necessary linguistic insights to tackle Niebuhr's Class I script. Another vital breakthrough was accomplished by the French scholar A. I. Silvestre de Sacy, who translated later Persian inscriptions and revealed the stereotyped titles of Persian kings. Each monarch was addressed as "Y, great king, king of kings, king of ———, son of X, great king, king of kings." This information was of incalculable value to the new generation of decipherers, among them Oluf Gerhard Tychsen of Rostock, Germany. In 1798 he correctly identified four characters and the critical symbol that separated individual words from one another. His work was of great benefit to the man who finally was successful: Georg Friedrich Grotefend.

Grotefend was born in 1775 at Münden in Germany and studied philology at Göttingen University. In 1797, he embarked on a long, uneventful career as a schoolteacher and eventually became director of the Hanover Lyceum. But this quiet man was a philological genius. He first became involved with cuneiform at the age of twenty-seven, when some friends casually bet him he could not decipher the script. So Grotefend acquired some copies of the Persepolis inscriptions and sat down to attempt what many people thought was impossible. In 1802, he presented some preliminary conclusions to the Göttingen Academy of Sciences. His contribution, "Commentary on the Persepolitan Cuneiform Writing," took over where Münter and Tychsen had left off.

Grotefend began by confirming Valle's conclusion that the cuneiform script was actually a form of writing, that it was written in a horizontal direction and was read from left to right. When he came to look closely at the inscriptions themselves, Grotefend found an astonishing diversity of cuneiform types. From his detailed knowledge of the history of Persepolis, he knew that the Persian king Cyrus had conquered the Babylonians around 538 B.C. This, he believed, suggested that at least one of the three Persepolis scripts was Old Persian. The columns of cuneiform danced in front of Grotefend's eyes as he patiently compared the lines of characters. The middle column was alphabetical, he felt, and written in Old Persian. And a group of signs and another single sign reappeared time and time again. Grotefend hypothesized that this group stood for "king" and that the isolated character represented a divider between words.

So far so good. Selecting the Old Persian inscriptions for further study, Grotefend recalled Sacy's description of more recent royal inscriptions that gave the Persian king the title "great king, king of kings." Had this formula been used in earlier times, with earlier inscriptions? He selected two short inscriptions that Niebuhr had copied from above the heads of royal figures. When he compared these cuneiform groups with each other, he found that the beginnings and ends of the inscriptions were different, but in between, the texts were basically similar, the minor difference being those, perhaps, of genitive significance. Each final group of characters ended with genitive signs. Perhaps, he thought, they comprised the same formula as Sacy's: "Y, great king, king of kings, king of ———, son of X, great king, king of kings."

After much close reasoning, Grotefend was able to identify not only a group of characters that meant "king," but signs that were the names of rulers, which were repeated again and again. Who were these kings? Grotefend checked through the Persian king lists to see whose names coincided most closely with the Persepolis characters. He eliminated Cyrus, Cambyses, and Artaxerxes, found himself left with Darius and Xerxes. Their names fitted perfectly. When Grotefend came to convert the Greek names of the Persian monarchs into Persian form, he found he could add other letters to those he had already deciphered. He ended up with the names of two kings: "Darius, son of Hystaspes," and "Xerxes, son of Darius."

Grotefend eventually succeeded in identifying ten signs and three proper names by using Anquetil-Duperron's Old Persian studies. Though his translations of Persepolitan inscriptions turned out to be full of errors, they gave the essence of the meaning. In 1805 he published a fuller account, which caused great interest. The discussions generated by his work began a long tradition of close collaboration among experts in several European countries. Unfortunately, he started to overstate his achievements and claimed more for his translations than was justified. He eventually ceased to play a leading part in the pursuit of cuneiform and died in comfortable obscurity in 1853.

Grotefend's results were corroborated in large part by his successors, who kept chipping away at the philological problem. By its very nature, the study of cuneiform tended to attract quiet, scholarly men rather than flamboyant adventurers. These low-keyed scholars wrote to one another constantly, reporting each minor advance or new inscription. They worked in cluttered studies, several of them holding down jobs as teachers or ministers at the same time. Cuneiform studies knew no national boundaries, for Danes, Englishmen, Frenchmen, and Germans shared their results freely. Among them were the French philologist Eugène Burnouf and the Norwegian orientalist Christian Lassen. In 1836 each published a treatise on the Old Persian of the Persepolis inscriptions. Their work attracted the attention of two other men, both of whom were to play a key role in decipherment: Edward Hincks and Jules Oppert.

Hincks was an Anglo-Irish priest who acquired an interest in oriental manuscripts while at Trinity College, Dublin. In 1825, he accepted the living of Killyleagh, thirty miles south of Belfast, a post he held for no less than forty-one years. Hincks devoted his abundant spare time to ancient languages. He published a Hebrew grammar in 1832, an article on hieroglyphs in 1846. In the same year he read a paper containing some observations about cuneiform that led this humble, absent-minded man to devote most of his life to its decipherment, more because of an interest in Biblical chronology than in the script itself. He remained an obscure character, embittered perhaps by his lack of recognition in scholarly circles. In 1853, the British Museum gave him a two-month appointment to work on the Nineveh inscrip-

Henry Creswicke Rawlinson

tions, but except for this, the Church never gave him time off to pursue his lifelong interest. Hincks conducted an enormous correspondence with fellow experts, and followed the early excavations at Nimrud and Nineveh with great interest. He worked closely with Layard on the inscribed bas-reliefs from the Assyrian royal palaces. His cuneiform studies ran closely parallel to those of Henry Rawlinson, with whom he had a close love-hate relationship for years.

Jules Oppert was a German-born, naturalized Frenchman. A short, pugnacious man with deep-set, bright eyes, he became closely involved with the decipherment of the Khorsabad inscriptions found by Paul Emile Botta. Oppert was a student of Lassen's who did most of his important work after cuneiform had been at least provisionally deciphered. He was a brilliant linguist, at home in at least six modern languages and several ancient Semitic dialects. He was a member of the French scientific expedition to Mesopotamia in 1853. Oppert worked closely with Hincks and Henry Rawlinson, and together they put the decipherment of Old Persian on a firm footing and became known as the Holy Triad of cuneiform studies. In later years Oppert was hampered by failing eyesight, so he devoted much time to encouraging young students, whom he then, half jokingly, accused of stealing his ideas. At conferences he would keep up a running commentary on his colleagues' papers in an undertone. At one memorable meeting, a German colleague chose to attack Oppert in what he assumed was Oppert's mother tongue — French. Oppert tried repeatedly to jump to his feet and interrupt but his neighbors held him down by his coattails. Finally, with a sudden jerk, he literally tore himself free and rushed to the platform in the ragged remains of his coat. Shaking his long white hair, he denounced the speaker in vigorous and much-applauded German. Though autocratic and overbearing at times, Oppert was a brilliant raconteur who could recite Persian, Arabic, and Turkish poetry for hours at a time.

By 1835 it had become obvious that the end of the road had been reached with the Persepolis inscriptions. They were too short and of too limited a vocabulary for verification of decipherment. What was needed was an accurate copy of the lengthier Behistun inscriptions. But how to get it? Ker Porter, and others who had made the attempt, had tried using a telescope to defeat distance and lack of visibility, but the results had proved unsatisfactory. At this juncture, Henry Creswicke Rawlinson came on the scene and saved the day.

Soldier, political officer, and orientalist of genius, Rawlinson comes across a little larger than life. He was born into a wealthy English county family on April 11, 1810. He showed a remarkable flair for horsemanship at an early age and became a superb shot as a teenager.

Although an average student, he showed a natural aptitude for languages. With these talents, he was a logical candidate for the Indian army. He sailed for India at seventeen. The voyage lasted four months, a fortunate circumstance, for it brought Rawlinson into close association with Sir John Malcolm, the governor of Bombay and no mean orientalist. Malcolm spent many hours with Rawlinson talking about manuscripts and oriental languages. He gave the young officer a lifelong interest in Persian dialects and ancient languages.

Once in India, Rawlinson spent five years enjoying the fast-moving sporting and social life of his regiment — dinner parties, theatricals, horse racing, and hunting. The officers of the Bombay Grenadiers were a dashing lot, but none could touch Henry Rawlinson. When he took on all comers for a wager of a hundred rupees at any sport, he found no takers. On one memorable occasion, he accepted a bet that he could ride from Poona to Panwell, a distance of seventy-two miles, in four hours. Rawlinson arrived in Panwell in three hours and seven minutes, leaving a trail of exhausted horses behind him. Despite all the parties, Rawlinson spent many hours studying Hindi, Marathi, and other languages, including Persian. He acquired a reputation not only as a dashing young officer, but as a linguist as well.

In 1833, Rawlinson was appointed staff officer of a military mission to Persia. The mission was to train the Persian army, a limited response to official concern about Russian designs on Persia. The first two years of the mission were rather humdrum. Rawlinson found himself saddled with routine drills and political duties, but since he also served as interpreter and middleman between the shah and the British, he had ample opportunity to improve his Persian. He particularly enjoyed Shah Mohammed Mirza's chaotic coronation, enlivened by the sight of the newly crowned king waddling to the throne and then perching the diamond-studded crown on his head with a fat hand. Rawlinson endeared himself to the shah by reciting Persian poems, something no British officer had done in Tehran before. In 1835, the shah sent him to act as adviser to his brother, the governor of Kurdistan. The long ride to Kurdistan took Rawlinson through the ancient Persian city of Hamadan (Ecbatana). He rode out to the foot of the slope where the Persian kings' cuneiform inscriptions lay. Unbeknownst to Rawlinson, Burnouf and Lassen were about to publish their partially deciphered versions of these inscriptions. After only a few hours of study, Henry Rawlinson decided to tackle the formidable task of decipherment. He had no scientific literature or philological experience to guide him, just a tough and well-disciplined mind.

In the intervals of raising and training Kurdish regiments, Rawlinson pondered over the ancient inscriptions of the Persian kings. After a month at his Kermanshah base, he found time to ride out to the Great Rock of Behistun, only twenty miles away. He stared at the trilingual inscriptions and the huge figures over three hundred feet above him. Behistun, he realized, held the key to cuneiform. With single-minded intensity, he spent his free time for the next two years copying the more accessible parts of the inscriptions.

The task would have daunted even an expert mountaineer with sophisticated equipment. Rawlinson had no ropes or ladders. The rock was bare, often precipitous, always slippery. Luckily, he was in excellent physical shape. Using makeshift scaffolding and risking his life every time he perched on one of the narrow, rocky ledges, Rawlinson managed to copy half the Old Persian inscriptions in two years of regular visits. Behistun had to be squeezed in between other duties, for the governor kept Rawlinson busy. He was called to quell mutinies of Kurdish soldiers, to ride enormous distances in the mountains. This hectic life took its toll, and Rawlinson contracted a severe fever that could only be cured by sick leave. He decided to spend a month in Baghdad under the care of the British residency doctor. While there, he became friends with the scholarly Colonel Taylor and sat down to master Arabic in the congenial atmosphere of the residency. Taylor was deeply interested in cuneiform and gave his guest every chance to examine the clay tablets in his collection.

During the winter of 1836–1837, Rawlinson was posted back to Tehran, where he devoted himself seriously to the decipherment of the Behistun inscriptions. By this time he had succeeded in copying almost the entire first column of the Old Persian script, and parts of the remaining columns. He concentrated on the royal titles "Darius the king, son of Hystaspes" and "Xerxes the king, son of Darius." Once the royal titles were identified, Rawlinson proceeded to decipher other proper names. He compiled an alphabet by comparing phonetic values and names with possible Greek equivalents, obtained from classical sources and medieval geographers. By late 1837, he had succeeded in deciphering the first two paragraphs of Old Persian and had published his translation in the *Journal of the Royal Asiatic Society*. This academic contribution gave Rawlinson an international reputation and access to the linguistic work of many colleagues throughout Europe. He found that he had, quite independently, progressed as far as they had.

The Persian mission ended in 1839, so Rawlinson returned to political service in India and served with distinction in the Afghan War. In 1843, he was at a loose end, but a fortunate meeting with the governor general of India, Lord Ellenborough, secured for him the vacant residency in Baghdad, an appointment that would involve light political duties and abundant opportunities to work on cuneiform. To this out-door man, the arduous discipline of hours of scholarship was tiresome, especially in the intense heat. So Rawlinson built a cool summerhouse on the banks of the Tigris. An ingeniously contrived waterwheel turned by the river kept the temperature of his study to a mere ninety degrees. He amused himself by taming wild animals, including a young lion and a leopard named Fahad. Fahad stayed with Rawlinson for many years, eventually finding a permanent home in England in the Bristol Zoo. Rawlinson used to visit Fahad frequently, stepping up to the bars of the cage and calling his friend. Fahad would approach, lie on his back, and let Rawlinson tickle his head and ear. One day a keeper rushed in. "Sir, sir," he cried, "what are you doing? The animal's very savage and will bite you." Rawlinson merely smiled calmly. "No, I don't think he'll bite *me*. Will you, Fahad?" Fahad answered with a loud purr and would not let him stop his caresses.

For all his preoccupation with cuneiform and his pets, Rawlinson was a highly successful and respected diplomat. Like his predecessors, he was a political force for the Turks to reckon with. British prestige never stood so high in Baghdad as in his day. Years later, Wallis Budge of the British Museum met an aged retainer from the residency who confirmed widely circulated rumors that Rawlinson had once knocked two recalcitrant Baghdad ministers' heads together. "Had he taken his dog and put his English hat on his head and sent him to the Serai, all the people in the bazaar would have made way for him, and bowed to him," recalled the servant.

Six months after his arrival in Baghdad, Rawlinson was able to leave on a long trip to Persia and to the Great Rock. He now planned to copy the Old Persian inscription in its entirety, leaving the Elamite and Babylonian texts for later. In the event, he managed to copy both the Persian and the Elamite inscriptions in a relatively short time, using makeshift scaffolding and scrambling all over the rock face in the hot sun. He then decided to come back another time, with more elaborate equipment, to copy the Babylonian sections. Characteristically, he insisted on returning to Baghdad through the Zagros Mountains, country rarely visited by Europeans.

Rawlinson's new Behistun copies gave him access to far more accurate cuneiform material than he had been able to draw upon previously. In 1847 he dispatched his celebrated memoir "Persian Cuneiform Inscriptions at Behistun" to the *Journal of the Royal Asiatic Society*. His paper was an absolutely trustworthy decipherment of Persian cuneiform that was soon accepted by Hincks and many other cuneiform scholars. Like his contemporaries, Rawlinson attacked the problem of decipherment at the point of least resistance, by using the royal titles and their Greek equivalents to reconstruct the alphabet. Then, using recent grammatical studies on Old Persian, he compared cuneiform words with those in known languages of approximately the same date. Such decipherment was relatively simple, for the Persian script was alphabetical, with only thirty-two characters (not forty-two as Niebuhr had originally thought).

To decipher the Elamite columns of inscription was straightforward, but the Babylonian script was another matter. Even a superficial examination of the available Babylonian inscriptions from Mesopotamia confirmed that the script had hundreds of characters. Some signs seemed to represent several different symbols, even words. Alternatively, several characters could be used for the same word. Even worse, none of the experts who were trying to make sense of the inscriptions seemed to agree with each other.

In 1847, Edward Hincks achieved a minor breakthrough when he managed to decipher a number of vowels, syllables, and ideograms. Three years later, he used Paul Botta's minute studies of cuneiform letters and words from the excavations at Khorsabad to prove that the Babylonian script was not alphabetical, but syllabic and ideographic. In other words, the signs represented syllables, which were combined in different ways to make words. Alternatively, each sign might represent a whole word.

While Hincks was working on vowels and syllables, Rawlinson made his third trip to Behistun, in September 1847. This time he brought ladders, ropes, pegs, and nails to the rock face, which were carried by an entourage of expert climbers. Some of them were small wiry boys who were more agile than mountain goats. The ladders enabled Rawlinson to reach the narrow ledge below the lines he had copied previously. He verified his copies, but still could not reach other parts because of the overhangs. The local cragsmen told him it was impossible. Eventually a "wild Kurdish boy," who came from a distant village, offered to have a go. He climbed up a narrow cleft to the left of the inscription and drove in a peg. Hanging ropes from the peg, he tried to swing over to another crevice, but the rock projected too far. So, carrying a rope with him, the boy clawed his way across the precipice, literally hanging in midair. Eventually he rigged up a cradle between pegs in the two clefts. Again hanging in midair, the boy made paper impressions of the inaccessible inscriptions under Rawlinson's anxious supervision.

Rawlinson now had the entire 112 lines of Babylonian text to work with, lines that could be deciphered with the aid of the Persian translation. He soon added another element to Hincks's discoveries, the proof that the same sign could stand for more than one sound or meaning.

Once he understood this polyphonic feature of Babylonian cuneiform, Rawlinson progressed rapidly. Soon he could read about one hundred fifty characters and understand the meaning of some two hundred words of what turned out to be a Semitic language (now known as Akkadian). In 1850 and 1851, he published his copies and his provisional decipherment of much of the inscription. Hincks used Rawlinson's work to add even more values to the cuneiform, ending up with about three hundred fifty readings.

Henry Rawlinson's Behistun study evoked great public enthusiasm. His copies were hailed as the "Rosetta Stone" of cuneiform and displayed at the Royal Asiatic Society's rooms and in the British Museum. The impressions were exhibited on and off for half a century, but were eventually partially eaten by mice. By that time, however, they were of little more than historical interest.

Many of Rawlinson's colleagues, while admitting his remarkable mountaineering exploits, challenged the idea that the Babylonian script was polyphonic. How could such a confusing script be used as a writing system if it meant different things to different people, they wondered? The controversies raged until 1855, when Jules Oppert, the third member of the "triad," published a review of the decipherment problem in which he endorsed the Hincks–Rawlinson readings and added some new signs that did have more than one value. He also had the advantage of a flood of new material from the first excavations in Mesopotamia. These included, no less, actual syllabaries prepared by ancient scribes for their own use.

Much of Oppert's new material had come to him from Henry Rawlinson's good offices. Because of Rawlinson's strategic position in Baghdad, he could examine the latest clay-tablet finds as they passed through Baghdad on their way to London or Paris. His office acted as an informal clearinghouse for new discoveries at the time Austen Henry Layard began his spectacular digs at Nimrud and Nineveh in the late 1840s. Layard's second excavations at Kuyunjik in 1850–1851 came just as Rawlinson had finished with Behistun. The dig turned up part of Ashur-bani-pal's royal library, a veritable treasure-house of cuneiform tablets that threatened to overwhelm the decipherers with new data. The library contained syllabaries, lists of different cuneiform symbols, and a mass of grammatical information. The same excavations even yielded a list of religious and legal terms in both Sumerian and Semitic. Rawlinson was the first to examine a great mass of tablets from Kuyunjik with a knowledgeable eye. He wrote in high excitement that they contained "the system of Assyrian writing, the distinction between phonetic and ideographic signs . . . grammar of the language, classification, and explanation of technical terms." He added, in masterly understatement, "A thorough examination of the fragments would lead to the most curious results."

By 1849, Rawlinson had served for over twenty-two years in the East without a single home leave. He was now exhausted and returned to England to find himself a celebrity. The queen entertained him at dinner, he lectured to many learned societies and to enthusiastic popular audiences as well. Four years later he finally resigned from Baghdad and the company service. He received a knighthood and became a director of the East India Company, devoting the remainder of his career to diplomacy, politics, and Indian affairs. But he never lost interest in cuneiform and spent years working with Jules Oppert and others on the Nineveh tablets in the British Museum.

The supreme test of the "triad" came in 1857, when W. H. Fox Talbot, a mathematician and astronomer who was also a pioneer photographer, attempted to translate some Assyrian texts. He took an unpublished 810-line inscription of King Tiglath-Pileser I (1115–1077 B.C.) from Assur, translated it, and sent his version to the Royal Asiatic Society in a sealed envelope. Then he suggested that they ask Hincks and Rawlinson to do the same, independently. The three sealed translations could then be compared. The society formed a five-man learned committee to supervise the test and invited not only Hincks and Rawlinson but Oppert to take part as well. Two months later the seals on the four envelopes were broken. The committee found that each man had made the same general sense of the inscription and that many paragraphs agreed so closely that no one could doubt that Babylonian cuneiform had been deciphered.

Oppert had annotated his translations with comparisons from six Semitic dialects, part of an ongoing study that led to his most important work, *Déchiffrement des inscriptions cunéiformes*, a lucid and comprehensive survey of cuneiform writing insofar as it was known to that date. From that moment, serious criticism of decipherment ceased.

The decipherment of cuneiform must rank as one of the more remarkable scientific achievements of the nineteenth century. In 1800, not a word of the script could be deciphered. By 1860, several hundred inscriptions had been at least partially translated. Rawlinson's "martial and imposing figure" was to be seen around the Department of Oriental Antiquities at the British Museum for the next twenty years as he patiently worked on the compilation *Cuneiform Inscriptions of Western Asia*, a compendium of accurate copies of cuneiform tablets. Generations of students were to benefit from his encyclopedic knowledge of the East and from Oppert's polemical encouragement. In the decades that followed the Royal Asiatic Society's test, dozens of scholars from all over Europe collaborated to read thousands upon thousands of Assyrian, Babylonian, and, later, Sumerian texts. The credit for this academic triumph belongs to a handful of oriental scholars and part-time enthusiasts who not only pursued cuneiform with an almost single-minded intensity in the study and in the broiling Mesopotamian sun, but trained a new generation of Assyriologists to refine their work. Without their efforts, the great pioneer excavations in Mesopotamia would have been little more than glorified treasure hunts.

III

PALACES OF KINGS

8

Excavations at Khorsabad

Why, you can find these things everywhere!

THE EMPEROR NAPOLEON'S campaign in Egypt had been planned as far more than a military venture. He arrived in quest of knowledge as well — information on antiquities, agriculture, demography, folklore, and many other subjects. The campaign ended in failure, but the investigations of Napoleon's scientists had as lasting an impact on Europe as the Eastern Question did. Napoleon's forty scholars were intoxicated with ancient Egypt and published their findings in an exquisite multivolume work entitled *Description de l'Egypte*. The *Description*'s magnificent folios caused a sensation throughout Europe, for they revealed the glories of ancient Egypt in all their fascinating detail to people who were only dimly aware of early civilization.

The 1820s and 1830s witnessed a surge of interest in Egyptian antiquities. Diplomats and travelers, even professional antiquities collectors, descended on the Nile and removed mummies and other artifacts by the thousands. Much of the plunder was assembled by consuls who combined desultory diplomatic activities with collecting. Upon retirement these part-time acquisitors sold their collections to the highest bidder, often the British Museum, the Louvre, or another public institution. Inevitably the currents of nationalism flowed strongly, as the major museums competed for prize specimens and collections. It was only a matter of time before governments sponsored excavations in the Near East with the objective of adding treasures to national collections.

The French Asiatic Society had several members who were deeply involved in cuneiform studies. Julius Mohl, a much respected orientalist, and other prominent members examined inscribed bricks and read Rich's *Memoirs* on Nineveh and Babylon with great interest. Investigations by other members were limited by a lack of inscriptions to work on, so they urged the government to appoint a suitably qualified consul to represent them in Mosul, one who might dig, in the traditions of the *Description*, in the mounds of ancient Nineveh. Such excavations, they argued persuasively, would not only provide more inscriptions and artifacts for the Louvre, but enhance France's reputation as a leader in the fine arts. The government responded by appointing Paul Emile Botta consul in Mosul. Officially, he was to look after French political interests there. Unofficially, he was to carry out excavations at Nineveh. In making this point, perhaps his superiors remembered the words of an eighteenth-century antiquarian: "Antiquity is a garden which belongs by natural right to those who cultivate and harvest it."

Paul Emile Botta was the ideal candidate for this assignment. The son of a well-known Italian historian, he had traveled widely as a young man and had journeyed around the world before entering the service of Pasha Mohammed Ali of Egypt as a physician. His duties gave him a chance to learn several oriental languages, to study national history, and to travel deep into Nubia. He acquitted himself so well that he was appointed French consul in Alexandria in 1833. For the next seven years Botta became familiar with the monuments of ancient Egypt, although there is no evidence that he excavated any sites. He also found time for a lengthy journey into desolate Yemen, an experience he recorded in a widely read book. Perhaps it was on the strength of this work that the French government transferred Botta to Mosul in 1840.

Mosul was a remote consular assignment, even then, a town rarely visited by Europeans. Few foreigners had much polite to say about it. "There are more pleasant places in the world than the city of Mosul," wrote a visiting nineteenth-century clergyman. He was horrified by the "corruption and confusion" of the bazaars. Strange things did sometimes happen in Mosul. Witness the day when a guard at the north gate of the city sounded the alarm and "like a whirlwind, a large troop of wild boar rushed through the town, scattering everyone they met like chaff before them; they tore through the narrow

E. Champmartin
1840

Paul Emile Botta by E. Champmartin, 1840

bazaars, upsetting sweetsellers and fruit and water vendors, and, as though possessed of the devil, precipitated themselves down the city wall about sixty feet high and were all killed or maimed." Eyewitnesses supposed they had met a pride of lions and fled in confusion. It was in this obscure place that the new consul now found himself.

Botta soon settled in. His fluency in Arabic, gained by years of residence in Egypt and Yemen, rapidly made him well known to Mosul. He spent his ample spare time wandering through the ruins of Nineveh and haunting the bazaars in search of antiquities. He bought everything he could lay his hands on—inscribed bricks, pots, clay tablets. Every time he bought a piece, he tried to track down the place of origin. But the sellers were vague. They were puzzled by his questions. "Why, you can find these things everywhere," they replied. So in December 1842, Botta decided to look for himself, by digging into the large mounds across the river—those purported to be ancient Nineveh.

Botta's first target was the conspicuous mound of Nebi Yunus, where the villagers who lived near the Moslem shrine of Jonah were constantly finding inscribed bricks and other artifacts. A storm of protest descended around his ears from the guardians of the shrine, who accused him of desecrating a holy place. Botta was forced to move his excavations to the mound of Kuyunjik nearby. There he dug for several months, finding many alabaster fragments and some inscribed bricks, but the excavations seemed fruitless and he penetrated no further than the topmost levels.

Then, in March 1843, Botta's luck changed. A villager from Khorsabad, fourteen miles north of Kuyunjik, called on him with some inscribed bricks for sale. Excitedly, he told the consul that there were masses of inscribed bricks and other finds of the sort he was looking for in the mound under the village of Khorsabad. His own stove was built out of ancient bricks. Botta did not believe these exaggerated tales, the like of which he had heard many times before. To get rid of the man, he sent a couple of workmen home with him to dig for a while in the reported mound. A week later, one of the men returned in great excitement. Their first few spadefuls of earth had uncovered richly carved walls adorned with strange animals.

Paul Botta jumped on his horse and rode to Khorsabad posthaste. He gasped at the curious sculptures that were exposed in the walls of the small pit: bearded men in long gowns, winged animals, and other wild beasts. The figures were quite unlike anything he had seen in Egypt and were totally unfamiliar to European eyes. After copying these marvels, the consul moved his diggers to Khorsabad. Within a few days the workmen had exposed a whole frieze of sculptured limestone slabs, surely part of the palace of an ancient king. Botta pondered his new finds for a time, then wrote a dispatch to Julius Mohl in faraway Paris. His letter contained the immortal statement: "I believe myself to be the first who has discovered sculptures which with some reason can be referred to the period when Nineveh was flourishing."

The discoveries at Khorsabad made banner headlines in Paris and caused a great sensation. French intellectuals and clerics were fired with excitement. Consul Botta had discovered a wholly "new" ancient civilization, one at least as old as that of the Egyptians, perhaps even older. And, unlike the Egyptian, this civilization had emerged from an utterly desolate landscape. No traces of its temples and palaces survived above ground. It had vanished completely from the face of the earth as Biblical prophets had said it would. Surely the events in the Old Testament were true historical fact! Faced with these astounding revelations, the French government responded magnificently. In the tradition of research that had brought the Napoleonic savants to the Nile, they provided Botta with three thousand francs to continue his work on an enlarged scale. Botta pressed on with his diggings, but under increasingly difficult conditions.

Among the many Ottoman Empire officials not noted for their saintliness, the pasha of Mosul had a reputation for excessive corruption. Mohammed Keritli Oglu was a highly unpleasant man who used every known device to extort money from his subjects and from visitors to the city. He was a short, fat man with only one ear and a single eye who had suffered from smallpox in his youth. His gestures were uncouth and his voice harsh. Austen Henry Layard, who was to have many dealings with this gentleman, said that "nature had placed hypocrisy beyond his reach." One of the pasha's favorite tricks was to pretend he was dead. Those of his subjects who rejoiced lost all their property. Woe betide those who entertained the pasha! They would often find themselves burdened with a tax to compensate for the wear and tear on his teeth. The pashalik of Mosul groaned under his harsh burden as villagers unable to pay their taxes fled to the countryside and lived by robbing travelers.

Such was the political climate for Botta's excavations. The pasha harried him at every turn. Convinced that the consul was digging for gold and buried treasure, he sent minor officials to watch over the excavations. They checked every small patch of dirt for gold, under strict orders to bring all metal objects back to Mosul. When Botta's workmen were threatened with torture if they did not deliver treasure to the pasha, they threatened to quit.

Next, the pasha gave him permission to build a house on the mound at Khorsabad. When it was finished, he promptly informed the authori-

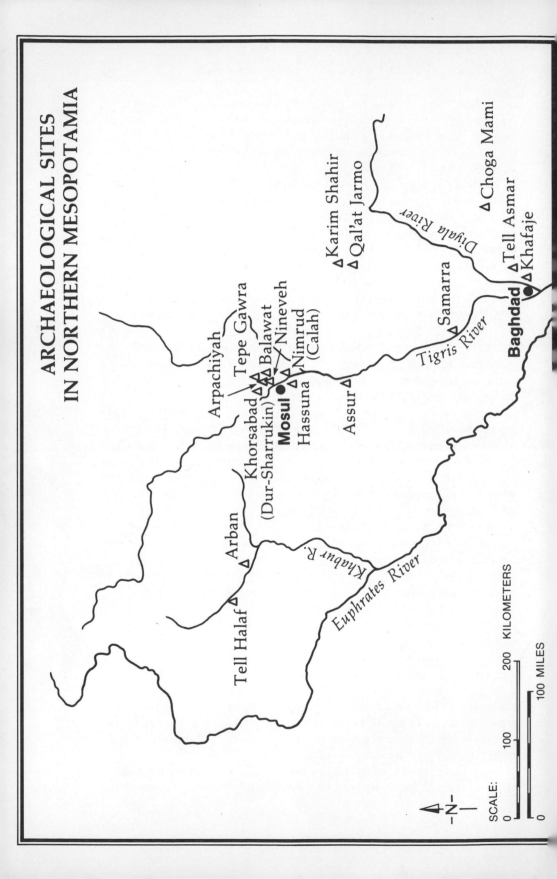

ARCHAEOLOGICAL SITES IN NORTHERN MESOPOTAMIA

Choga Mami △

Tell Asmar △
Khafaje △

Karim Shahir △
Qal'at Jarmo △

Diyala River

Samarra △

Tepe Gawra
Arpachiyah △△ Balawat
Khorsabad △ Nineveh
(Dur-Sharrukin) Nimrud
Mosul ● (Calah)
Hassuna △

Tigris River

Baghdad ●

Assur △

Arban △

Khabur R.

Tell Halaf △

Euphrates River

—N—

SCALE:

0   100   200   KILOMETERS

0   100 MILES

ties in Constantinople that Botta had built a fortress from which to dominate the countryside. Then, in October 1843, the pasha forbade any further excavations, on the orders, he said, of the Constantinople government. Botta promptly protested to the French ambassador to the Porte, and attempted to save the precious sculptures from damage by shoring them up with timber. But the villagers stole the wood at night. Botta became more and more frustrated. Antiquities were turning up everywhere and he was constrained from dealing properly with them. The workmen digging around the foundations of his house unearthed a large bull's head. The house had to be modified so that the bull could be excavated at leisure. The modifications were easy enough to make: the "fortress" was so flimsy that the early rains had washed part of it away.

Meanwhile, things were moving in Paris. The Académie des Inscriptions et Belles-Lettres, which had already obtained the first government grant for the excavations, now prevailed upon the ministers of the interior and education to "complete the excavations in a manner worthy of the French Government." The ministers were persuaded to provide not only an increased subvention but the services of a young draftsman named Eugène Napoléon Flandin to draw and record the precious alabaster sculptures before they fell apart in the hot sun. Flandin was an experienced archaeological artist who had been on an expedition to Persia and had published several books on ancient monuments. He was instructed to go out to Mosul via Constantinople, where the French ambassador would hand him a special firman (permit) for the excavations that would overrule the pasha of Mosul. Finally the ministers ordered Botta to send all the sculptures that were in fit condition to Paris, and authorized a special publication that would inform the world of Botta's discoveries.

The French ambassador worked long and hard on Botta's behalf, navigating among the complex intricacies of Turkish and Islamic law. Eventually the sultan issued a firman that authorized both excavation and the purchase of houses in the village on the mound, houses Botta could demolish to get at the buried palace underneath. The consul was also allowed to occupy his famous base house until the end of the dig. It took many months for the ambassador to secure the firman, so many that Flandin did not reach Mosul until May 4, 1844, a full year after Botta's first Khorsabad finds.

Botta could now proceed. He began by purchasing the land under the village, a process that involved him in excessive demands from dozens of villagers, and, of course, the pasha. Then he collected a labor force. The locals were unwilling to work, for their lives depended on agriculture and they could not leave their fields. Many of

Flandin's view of Khorsabad. From Monuments de Ninive
(1846–1850)

them were superstitious about working on the mound, too. But Botta was in luck. For some months the Mosul area had been flooded with Christian refugees who had fled to the plains in the face of Kurdish raids. Many of them had settled near Khorsabad and were only too glad to work for modest sums. They were, said Botta, "very robust and docile," as well as good workers. He and Flandin deployed large numbers of them on the mound, at one point more than three hundred. They dug more or less continuously until October 1844.

Flandin found the work of copying very arduous and slow-moving. It took him weeks to record the finds Botta had already made, but when that work was completed he made a plan of the elaborate palace that was emerging from the soil, while Botta copied all the inscriptions. The work was very difficult for both men. The consul had to commute from Mosul, for diplomatic business required his regular attention. Flandin was less accustomed to the heat and dirt, to the frustrations of daily life in a distant, oriental land. But the fascination of the new art styles kept both men going, even in July 1844, when the populace of Mosul demolished and looted a new Dominican convent in the town and assassinated one of the missionaries. For some hours, Flandin's life seemed to be in danger at Khorsabad, but Botta managed to get reinforcements to him in time.

By October the two men had excavated the outline of a huge, elaborate building. One uses the word "excavate" loosely, for they had no idea of controlled, scientific archaeological work. Their workmen merely followed the decorated alabaster walls of the palace wherever they led. Digging became harder when they ran out of decorated walls and had to follow mud-brick features. The techniques of excavation were simply too rudimentary for delicate tasks like tracing mud walls. All Botta really wanted to find was stone palaces and fine sculpture. After a while he and Flandin gave up, for trial trenches on other parts of the mound yielded no traces of stone palace walls. Perhaps, thought Botta, the stones had been removed for other purposes after the great palace was abandoned. But what Botta had found was the palace of the Assyrian king Sargon II. It was to be some time before Botta even learned the name of the monarch whose palace he had excavated, for no one could yet read cuneiform.

In the late eighth century B.C., Sargon II had ordered the construction of a new capital, known as Dur-Sharrukin. Sargon himself chose the site. He personally supervised the laying out of the fortified, four-sided compound of the city with its seven gates. His new palace rose at the northeast side of the quadrangle, on a vast artificial mound. A ziggurat and lesser temples were incorporated into his splendid residence, which contained dozens of chambers, storerooms, and passages.

During the memorable summer of 1844, Botta and Flandin cleared room after room, corridor after corridor. Most of them were lined with sculptured bas-reliefs of gods, humans, and animals. The Assyrian king was depicted at war, besieging cities, hunting game, engaging in elaborate religious ceremonies. The walls between the bas-reliefs were covered with cuneiform inscriptions. The major palace doorways were flanked with magnificent human-headed and winged lions and bulls. Never before had six months' excavation yielded such incredible treasures.

On November 9, Flandin left Mosul for Paris, carrying a huge portfolio of Khorsabad drawings with him. They were promptly exhibited to the Académie des Inscriptions and to the public. It is difficult for us to imagine the extraordinary sensation they caused. We are familiar with the Assyrians as Biblical figures and as a historical fact. But to the European of a century and a half ago, the Assyrians were a shadowy people who had conquered and deported the Israelites. They were a people whose actual existence many scholars doubted. Botta had brought the Old Testament to light, had found a whole new civilization, and a palace with bas-reliefs showing Assyrian monarchs engaged in warfare and conquest.

The Académie des Inscriptions set up a special scholarly commission to review Flandin's drawings and the excavations. This commission warmly praised the work of Botta and Flandin, and recommended immediate publication of the material for the benefit of artists and scholars. Their recommendation came only six months after Flandin's arrival in Paris. The sumptuous *Monuments de Ninive*, four volumes of drawings and one of text, appeared between 1846 and 1850, and became an immediate classic admired by layman and scholar alike.

While Flandin was being lionized in Paris, Botta stayed in Mosul to complete the copies of the inscriptions and to execute the last part of the French government's instructions, the removal of the best bas-reliefs for exhibition in Paris. Although the sultan of Turkey had given reluctant permission for the finds to be exported, Botta was faced with a unique and formidable task. No one in Mosul, or elsewhere in Mesopotamia for that matter, had ever moved delicate antiquities a yard, let alone fourteen miles over rough country from Khorsabad to the banks of the Tigris. Some of the stone blocks weighed two or three tons. Botta almost despaired at times during the frustrating months of packing. He was obliged to saw up the larger pieces. Wood was in short supply, so he could not make packing cases. The delicate bas-reliefs were protected with strong beams that formed a framework round the stone, a crude protection that fortunately proved effective.

But these problems were nothing compared to the difficulty of actually moving the sculptures. Botta decided to build a huge cart. He had to set up a special forge to make the axles, which took no less than six weeks to construct. His original plan had been to have water buffalo or oxen tow the cart, but not enough animals were available. So two hundred men strained and heaved at ropes attached to the cart. The huge wheels constantly bogged down in the soft, rain-soaked plain. In places the road had to be covered with boulders or planks. It took Botta eight months of exhausting labor to move the sculptures from Khorsabad to Mosul, fourteen miles that must have seemed like a thousand. One bronze-headed lion had to be abandoned when the cart collapsed. It was burned for gypsum by the locals. Fortunately the Tigris was still high enough for the precious blocks to be embarked on *kelleks* for the long journey to Basra. This task was perilous. One of the workmen died when he was crushed between a sliding block and the sculptures already on board. Even the goatskin rafts had to be strengthened with outsized timbers and extra inflated goatskins. The journey downstream was a nightmare, for the heavily laden *kelleks* were uncontrollable in rough water. A load of sculpture and Assyrian kings went to the bottom. Undeterred, Botta dispatched another consignment that reached Basra safely. In March 1846, the French vessel *Cormorant* loaded the precious antiquities. They were unloaded at Le Havre in December under Botta's personal supervision. The following May the first Assyrian room was opened in the Louvre. Botta himself spent his time working on *Monuments de Ninive* and lecturing on his finds. By all accounts he was a pleasant and easygoing man, although, Henry Layard tells us, "somewhat addicted to opium smoking. After Khorsabad, one cannot entirely blame him."

One can argue that it would have been better if Sargon's bas-reliefs had remained underground until the rigorous excavations of the twentieth century would have recovered far more than Botta ever did. But without Paul Botta's pioneer efforts, Mesopotamian archaeology might never have come of age. Botta himself never returned to Mosul. On the establishment of the Second Republic in 1847, his Mosul consulate was abruptly discontinued. He was assigned to a minor post in Lebanon and never returned to archaeology. He died in 1870. By that time, the Assyrian had become one of the best known of all ancient civilizations.

9

Layard of Nineveh

Hasten, O Bey, for they have found Nimrod himself!

Consular officials like Paul Botta were accustomed to entertaining the occasional travelers who passed through their remote outposts. European visitors were an event, a chance for news of the outside world. Botta was therefore delighted when a young Englishman named Austen Henry Layard called on him in 1842 while traveling from Baghdad to Constantinople. The two men had much in common — an interest in diplomatic gossip and local politics, and a passion for archaeology. Botta was just starting to dig into the mound of Kuyunjik. Layard was still a young adventurer, without a job or any archaeological experience. The chance to talk to a fellow archaeology enthusiast reinforced his determination to dig in Mesopotamia. When he eventually did so, Layard expanded Botta's work on a huge scale.

Austen Henry Layard was a remarkable man. During his long life he was in rapid succession a law student, a traveler and explorer, an archaeologist, a writer, a diplomat, a politician, and an art critic. If two words could be used to describe him, they would be energetic and enthusiastic. Layard's journals, correspondence, and public writings fairly wear one out, so inexhaustible his energy and so boundless his enthusiasm for solitary travel and the beauty of remote places.

Austen Henry Layard in Albanian dress. From Layard's
Autobiography (*1903*)

Layard was born in Paris on March 5, 1817, of an English family who preferred to live abroad. Much of his childhood was spent in Italy. His education was sporadic, much of it acquired by voracious reading. Henry's parents encouraged him to think independently, to indulge his curiosity, and to cultivate his powers of observation. Layard's formal education ended in 1834, when he left school in England and was articled as a clerk in an uncle's law firm in London. He hated his new life. Money was short, his lodgings small and cramped. The wintry streets of London were a far cry from the open spaces of Italy. Ambitious young Layard felt caged in and not at all content with the prospects in a steady legal career. He spent the long vacations traveling as far afield as Finland, Russia, and Italy. Real tensions developed in the family over his future.

In 1834, Henry's uncle Charles, a prosperous merchant in Ceylon, suggested he set up a legal practice there. He introduced Layard to Charles Mitford, a thirty-two-year-old businessman who had decided to start a coffee plantation in Ceylon. In traveling out there, Mitford planned to make as much of the trip as possible on horseback through the Ottoman Empire to Baghdad, and on to Kandahar and India. At first he was hesitant about shouldering the responsibility for a twenty-two-year-old who was a bad horseman and had never been to the East. Layard soon won him over by his enthusiasm and careful preparations that included lessons in trigonometry and surveying.

Layard and Mitford traveled across Europe in July 1839. In Yugoslavia, Layard bought his first saddle. "The first day we rode sixteen hours, the second fourteen, and the third twenty-six without stopping," he wrote home. He must have had a seat made of steel. A few weeks later, the travelers called on a Montenegran prince who accommodated them in a room that looked out on forty-two gory Turkish heads impaled on posts, relics of a skirmish the week before. Layard carefully recounted all the details to his nervous family in London.

After two and a half months on the road, Layard and Mitford passed through Constantinople. In January 1840 they arrived in Jerusalem after a rough journey across Syria and Turkey, where they had nightly slept in their cloaks under the stars. Layard was intoxicated with his new life and made notes on every ruin they passed — Roman, Greek, or older. Four shillings a day fed Mitford, Layard, a Greek servant, and their horses. From Jerusalem, Layard insisted on making a solo journey south to the ruined city of Petra, which lay in a remote defile occupied by hostile Bedouin tribesmen. Accompanied only by a young boy and everyone's dire predictions, he set off through the desert to Amman, the ancient Rabbath-beni-Ammon of Biblical times. The Bedouins there demanded money and nearly killed him when he

refused to pay. Another group of Arabs robbed him of all his possessions and held him hostage. For days Layard wandered with the
nomads while they argued over his fate. He enjoyed this experience
more than his hosts, for he saw many archaeological sites and gained
an understanding of the Arab character that was to serve him in good
stead later on. The Arabs had, he wrote, "a double character." The
same man would be grasping, deceitful, treacherous, and cruel on one
occasion, and on another, "generous, faithful, trustworthy, and hu-
mane." By the time he rejoined Mitford in Aleppo unharmed, Layard
was an experienced desert traveler.

Laden with only fifteen pounds of baggage each, the two travelers
arrived in Mosul in early April of 1840. Layard insisted they stay
two weeks so he could examine the mounds of Nineveh thoroughly.
The desolate earthworks made a profound and lasting impression on
him in a way no classical temples had. In the countries he had recently
visited, Greek and Roman temples and theaters rose out of the natural
landscape with dramatic effect, so that even the casual visitor could
not help but mentally reconstruct ancient buildings and cities from
the surviving ruins that lay before him. But at Nineveh, Layard wrote,
"he is at a loss to give any form to the rude heaps upon which he is
gazing. Those of whose works he is contemplating, unlike the Roman
or the Greek, have left no visible traces of their civilization or of their
arts; their influence has long since passed away. . . . The more he con-
jectures the more vague the results appear. The scene around is worthy
of the ruin he is contemplating; desolation meets desolation; a feeling of
awe succeeds to wonder; for there is nothing to relieve the mind, to
lead to hope, or to tell of what has gone by." One day, he told himself,
he would dig into the silent heaps of bricks and occupation debris.

On April 29, Layard and Mitford set off for Baghdad on a *kellek* that
would float them the three hundred miles downstream. Guided by a
single boatman who never seemed to sleep, the two men passed
Nimrud, watched birds, and looked for more ancient mounds. The
world of the *Arabian Nights* surrounded them on every side — the
fragrant oases, the creaking waterwheels, the cry of the muezzin calling
the faithful to prayer. "All my Arabian Nights dreams were almost
more than realized," wrote Layard. Even more impressive was their
reception at the British residency, where Colonel Taylor, "a small,
slight and wizened man, considerably past middle age," greeted them
hospitably. Layard and Mitford spent two months in the residency
enjoying the company of the small European community. They tried
to learn Persian as preparation for the next stage of their journey.
Layard spent many hours examining Taylor's magnificent library of
Arabic and Persian manuscripts. He learned of Henry Rawlinson's re-

cent visit and researches into the cuneiform inscriptions at Behistun. Taylor enjoyed teaching his young visitor, who absorbed knowledge about Mesopotamia like a sponge. Some young naval officers were using Chesney's *Euphrates* steamer to survey the waters near Baghdad. Henry explored the delta in their company, and visited the major archaeological sites including Ctesiphon and Babylon. The sighting of the latter moved Layard to ecstasies of delight over the desolation and the deserted mounds.

All too soon it was time to travel on to Persia. After seeing Behistun, Layard realized he wanted to spend much more time in the Near East rather than settling down in Ceylon. Mitford was all for pressing on, so the two companions parted company. Alone, Layard traveled to Esfahan, where he obtained permission to visit the Bakhtiari nomads who lived in the remote and unsettled mountain country of the region. Layard's ultimate objective was to reach the site of Susa, the Biblical Shushan. The nomads lived in the midst of fertile, highland plains that could only be reached by steep mountain tracks over high passes. "I could trace the line of route by the blood from our horses' feet," he wrote home. The local chiefs lived in fortified castles or temporary encampments near the river valleys that crisscrossed the plains. Swampy rice fields alternated with rocky hillocks and fertile grasslands where the Bakhtiari grazed their herds. The local people greeted Layard with great suspicion, convinced that he was an English officer sent to spy out the land for a possible expeditionary force against them. When he tried to travel alone across the plains the tribesmen robbed him of his compass and watch. They were so hostile and made his life so uncomfortable that he was convinced they might try to kill him. Just when he was about to leave in despair, he managed to cure a chieftain's son of fever with quinine and Dr. Dover's Powder. He was promptly adopted as a member of the chief's family and became such a trusted adviser to the rebellious tribesmen that the Persian government tried to arrest him. Layard escaped and fled to Baghdad, only to be robbed of all his possessions a few miles from the city. Meanwhile, his family were very anxious as to his whereabouts and asked the Foreign Office to make inquiries in Persia. When the British ambassador asked the vizier about him, that personage snorted with exasperation. "That man!" he cried. "Why, if I could catch him, I'd hang him. He has been joining some rebel tribes and helping them." None of this was calculated to reassure the Layard family.

Henry Layard had by now become an expert on Persian and Mesopotamian affairs, so much so that Colonel Taylor sent him to brief the British ambassador in Constantinople and to deliver dispatches. Layard rode upstream to Mosul in fifty hours through the great heat of

May 1842. There he was able to spend three days with Paul Botta. They took an instant liking to one another, inspected Nineveh and Khorsabad, and talked of digging together. Layard left Mosul determined to dig at Nineveh one day. But it was to be three years before he was able to achieve his ambition. In Constantinople the ambassador, Sir Stratford Canning, liked Layard so much that he retained him as part of his staff. Henry worked for the British embassy as an unofficial attaché engaged in sensitive intelligence work. He enjoyed his confidential role immensely, but with occasional hankerings for more freedom, especially when his family started complaining. "How I long for a black tent, a horse, a flock of sheep, and a wife in the solitary mountains," he wrote. But Layard was maturing into a quieter, more deliberate personality. By now he had an impressive command of Arabic, Turkish, and Persian. But he never forgot archaeology and followed Botta's dramatic excavations at Khorsabad with the greatest interest. Botta treated him as a close friend. "Come, I pray you, and let us have a little archaeological fun, at Khorsabad," he wrote in the spring of 1843. Unfortunately, the ambassador would not allow Layard to leave. But even Canning became interested when Flandin laid out his drawings at the British embassy. Henry Rawlinson, among others, had written from Baghdad urging that Layard be sent to dig at Nimrud, where heavy rains had exposed stonework and cuneiform-inscribed bricks. Rawlinson had started corresponding with Layard about archaeology earlier in the year. "I should be exceedingly glad indeed if the Ambassador and through him the Government could be induced to take an interest in the antiquities of this country. It pains me grievously to see the French monopoly," he wrote. His letters and Layard's pleadings finally persuaded Canning to agree to a two-month survey at Nimrud with Layard acting as his personal agent.

Layard was overjoyed. He arrived in Mosul in October 1845, giving out that he had come to hunt boar along the Tigris. By this time, Botta had left and his successor, Rovet, was eager to maintain French supremacy in archaeology. Fortunately, Christian Rassam, the British vice-consul, was a building contractor, so the excavating tools could be made secretly in his workshop. On November 8 a *kellek* bore Layard and his small party downstream to a tiny village called Naifa, near ancient Nimrud. Layard spent a restless night in the village. His mind would not relax. Palaces and sculptures danced through his brain; he imagined himself in the streets of an ancient city.

The next day he paced over the mounds while his six newly recruited Arab workmen brought him bricks and a fragment of bas-relief. He set the workmen to dig at likely spots. Almost immediately they uncovered a large chamber lined with cuneiform-inscribed slabs in the northwest corner of the mound. The same day Layard moved some men to the south side, where they found further stone-walled chambers. On the very first day of excavation, Layard had found not one Assyrian palace, but two. His first trenches had unearthed the North West Palace, built by Ashur-nasir-pal II (883–859 B.C.). This imposing structure covered six and a half acres, although Layard did not excavate all of the chambers. His southerly trenches had revealed the so-called South West Palace, built but never finished, by a later monarch, Esarhaddon (680–669 B.C.). Layard was thrilled when the earth inside the first chamber yielded some magnificent ivory figures, including a crouched sphinx and a king.

But even greater excitement lay in store. By November 28 the workmen digging the South West Palace had tunneled their way fifteen feet into the mound when they uncovered a mass of sculpted tablets. These tablets, which are now known to date from the reign of Tiglath-Pileser III (744–727 B.C.), had originally adorned his magnificent palace, of which no trace now remains. Some sixty years later King Esarhaddon, in a fit of unaccustomed economy on the part of Assyrian monarchs, dismantled his predecessor's palace and planned to reuse his sculptures. Esarhaddon's residence was never finished. Many of the sculptures were abandoned in the unfinished structure after his death in 669 B.C. They depicted, Layard wrote, "a combat with warriors in chariots, a second the siege of the city, both designed and executed with considerable spirit." He reported to Canning that "the sculptures could be removed with little care and are well worth sending to England."

At this critical moment a messenger arrived from the pasha of Mosul, the infamous Mohammed Keritli Oglu, forbidding all further excavation. Layard promptly saw red, jumped on his horse, and rode furiously into Mosul. On the way he puzzled over the sudden order. As far as he knew, the pasha had no grounds for complaint. No official objections had been raised in the first few weeks of digging. Still mystified, Layard found the pasha all smiles. Of course, Layard could go on digging at Nimrud. Still puzzled, Layard rode downstream and resumed the excavations. He had hardly begun when he was summoned to Mosul yet again. This time the pasha told him he was stopping the excavations for Layard's own protection. His life would be in danger if he continued to disturb the Moslem burials on the mound. "Your life is more valuable than old stones," the pasha assured him. In vain Layard protested that he had never seen a burial marker on the mounds. After two fruitless days of argument he rode back to Nimrud, only to find the site littered with gravestones that had literally sprung up overnight. Eventually Captain Daud of the pasha's staff sheepishly confessed that he had been ordered to move gravestones from nearby cemeteries onto the site and had done so for the past two nights. "We have destroyed more real tombs of the true Believers in making sham ones than you could have defiled," he complained to Layard. "We have killed our horses and ourselves in carrying these accursed stones!" So Layard quietly bribed the friendly captain and kept some small-scale excavations going.

The French consul was behind Layard's difficulties. Upon hearing news of the British excavations, he had sent men all over the country-side to open mounds and claim sites. Layard was forced to do likewise, at the same time urging Canning to give him more money so that he could transport some of his finds to England before Botta's sculptures, delayed in Basra, could reach Paris. He also begged for an official firman from the sultan that would overrule the mischievous pasha. But Canning was worried about the mounting expenses and waited to see what future months would bring.

In the heat and dust of November 1854, Layard now started to speculate about the identity of the buried city he was uncovering. Henry Rawlinson wrote from Baghdad congratulating him on the finds and arguing that Nimrud was "the original Nineveh." When the two men met in Baghdad at Christmas, they not only took an instant liking for each other, but argued for hours about cuneiform, archaeology, geography, and languages. The trouble was that no one could yet read Babylonian cuneiform, so the identity of Nimrud was a tantalizing mystery.

Layard's stay in Baghdad was not all archaeology and cuneiform. "At Baghdad, there are remarkably pretty women," he remarked. "Provided your dwelling is convenient, the ladies make no difficulty in walking in, not only when you want them, but uninvited." He horrified his mother by writing that he had so many "wives" he would be glad to be rid of them.

Events in Mosul were now turning in his favor. The pasha had been replaced by a new official, who encouraged the continuance of the excavations. Layard could now return to Nimrud, accompanied by Hormuzd Rassam, the seventeen-year-old brother of the British vice-consul, who was to act as his assistant. Camp was set up on the mound itself, so Layard had a panoramic view of the green floodplain dotted with black tents and huge flocks. He took care to call on the local sheikhs with gifts, thereby averting a raid on his camp. On returning from such a visit on February 20, 1846, Layard sighted two Arab horsemen riding furiously toward him. They reined their horses up on their haunches and urged Layard to follow. "Hasten, O Bey," they cried, "for they have found Nimrod himself!" Layard found an excited group of workmen clustered around a heap of baskets and cloaks. Dramatically, they withdrew the coverings. An enormous alabaster head with an imposing beard and a fine headdress rose out of the ground. Layard realized at once that they had uncovered the upper part of a winged bull, like those found by Botta at Khorsabad. The face bore a calm and majestic expression. The Arabs had been terrified when they first came across the figure. One man dropped his basket and never stopped running until he reached Mosul.

That evening the joyful Layard and his workers celebrated with several slaughtered sheep, music, and dancing. The excavations were mobbed by sightseers the next day, some from as far away as Mosul. The frightened workman who had fled from the site had announced in the bazaar that Nimrod had appeared. The town was in an uproar. The pasha asked Layard to hold off further work until the furor died down. So, while two or three men dug around the walls of the newly uncovered palace and duly discovered a second pair of winged lions, Layard spent hours contemplating "these mysterious emblems" and musing over "their intent and history."

As the weeks passed and more and more palace sculpture was unearthed, Layard became concerned about his position. He was excavating without a firman, which meant that he could export nothing. The only chance of government support was a dazzling appeal to the public. So far he had spent only eighty pounds as opposed to Botta's large sums. He become more and more frustrated as the weeks passed. Again, he urged Canning to move, but without success. Canning was waiting for the right moment to approach the government. Layard recommended publicity with a capital P. "Botta owes his success with the French Government in a great measure to the notice taken by the public of his discoveries," he wrote to Canning. In the meantime, Layard decided to honor the laws of hospitality and threw a party for the local tribesmen. He roasted fourteen sheep for his visitors, who danced all night and celebrated for three days. It was no coincidence that Layard's excavations were largely trouble-free.

It was not until mid-May, 1846, three months after the discovery of the great bulls, that Layard received the long-awaited firman granting him permission to dig and to export antiquities to England. He read this momentous document by "the light of a small camel-dung fire, the document which secured to the British nation the records of Nineveh, and a collection of the earliest monuments of Assyrian art." Unfortunately, however, he was so short of money that the excavations had to remain on a small scale for the time being. Even so, his men had now tunneled deep into the mound. A steep flight of crude steps led into the depths of the North West Palace. The deeper the tunnels penetrated, the more beautiful the sculptures. Visiting Arabs would crowd close and gasp in amazement at the figures of kings and soldiers, servants and wild beasts. The workmen were used to the sculptures by now and were as interested in the dig as Layard was. They cursed and spat at the bearded male figures, declaring they were idols, while they patted and kissed the cheeks of eunuchs, declaring they were beautiful women. When new sculptures were emerging from the ground, they would work like madmen, uttering savage war cries and letting their matted hair fly in the wind.

Layard's mode of operation, though unconscionable by today's standards, was direct enough. He simply tunneled into the huge mounds and went on digging until he hit a fine sculpture or a stone-walled palace room. His deep tunnels led along the walls of the rooms and ignored or destroyed the contents of the chambers. Although Layard was more conscientious than most of his contemporaries, he never forgot that the continuation of the excavations depended on a steady flow of fine sculptures for export. Everything was subordinated to this objective. Nimrud soon looked like a cratered battlefield.

Layard had now found so many sculptures that he had to start crating them before the locals destroyed them. So he drew on family funds. "The discovery is beginning to make a noise in Europe," he wrote to his aunt in July 1846. He struggled along in summer temperatures of 117 degrees or more, packing ten crates of sculptures wrapped in felt and matting, some of them nine feet square and a foot thick. It was a miracle that no slabs were broken as they were laboriously loaded on a *kellek* for the journey downstream to Baghdad.

After a summer in the Kurdish highlands, Layard returned to Mosul in October. He found letters from Sir Stratford Canning announcing that the British Museum had taken over financial responsibility for the excavations with a grant of two thousand pounds to cover all expenses incurred so far and for future work until June of 1847. Layard was furious at the niggardly financial provisions. Evidently the museum had no idea of conditions in Mesopotamia, nor had they allowed for Layard's proud character. The pompous instructions from the museum trustees advised Layard "to be extremely careful not to injure any sculptures" and to avoid incidents with the locals. Layard complained to his uncle that he was being treated "like a master-bricklayer." The trustees had a bargain in Layard. Where a lesser man might have returned home, he set to work to try and do as much as he could. The truth was that he was enjoying life in Mesopotamia. He had built himself a substantial mud-brick house with a thatched roof. Unfortunately, the rains came before the walls were covered and Layard had living grass for wallpaper during the entire winter. The Christian workmen lived in a house on top of the mound near the winged lions, where Layard also built a storage hut for small finds. The Arabs pitched their tents in three different areas according to their tribal affiliations. Forty tents were placed near the entrances to the trenches, another forty around Layard's dwelling, the balance by the Tigris at the spot where the sculptures were loaded onto the *kelleks*. These encampments provided Layard with an effective defense against possible raiders. Everyone was armed to the teeth, ready to fight at a moment's notice.

The dig had now acquired a considerable staff. Hormuzd Rassam paid the workmen and did the accounts. He got on well with the locals and "soon obtained an extraordinary influence among the Arabs, and his fame spread through the desert." Beyond grooms and servants, Layard employed two carpenters and a stonemason from Mosul. The workmen were divided into digging parties of eight or ten Arab basket-men, who carried away the loose earth, and two to four pickmen, who loosened the soil. Layard himself cleared the soil away from bas-reliefs or delicate small objects, as he could not trust his diggers not to damage them. The digging teams were carefully composed of Arabs from different tribes so that he would get wind of any "plots brewing" or learn if his people were appropriating antiquities for sale. He worked hard to create goodwill and to keep his men interested in their work. "I had no difficulty managing them," he wrote.

Layard had great power in the eyes of his employees. On one memorable occasion, a visiting Arab murdered the mother of a young girl he wanted to marry. Layard delivered the murderer to the authorities in Mosul, but found no one at Nimrud willing to marry the girl. "I married her, therefore, to an inhabitant of Mosul," he wrote calmly. In appreciating Layard's extraordinary archaeological achievements, one must also recognize his remarkable sensitivity and skill in managing the human side of his excavations. By his generous hospitality and firmness, he achieved miracles where his successors with better facilities were far less successful. Although he himself would rise at daybreak, spend all day supervising the digging and packing, and then work until midnight copying inscriptions and bas-reliefs, the desert Arabs found life rather dull sometimes. One evening Layard was riding home to his house when he saw his workmen driving a huge herd of sheep before them with brandished swords and loud war cries. The sheep belonged to the villagers of Nimrud. Layard asked the yelling Arabs for an explanation. "Oh, Bey," they cried, "it is not for a man to carry about dirt in baskets, and to use a spade all his life; he should be with his sword and his mare in the desert. . . . Let us then believe that these are sheep we have taken from the enemy, and that we are driving them to our tents!" And with that, they scattered the bleating sheep in all directions. The local shepherds were not amused.

The Nimrud excavations kept on producing extraordinary results. Layard now realized that he had uncovered two phases of occupation. The North West Palace was contemporary with Botta's palace at Khorsabad, but the South West Palace was somewhat later since it had been built using some of the sculptured slabs from the earlier structure. The dig had yielded no less than thirteen pairs of winged lions, and more magnificent bas-reliefs. These, wrote Layard, "represented the wars of a king, and the conquest of a foreign nation." He was especially interested in some scenes that showed men crossing a river on rafts made with inflated skins, just as they still did in his time. Although many small objects were destroyed in the tunneling, the dig did reveal pieces of armor, ornaments, helmets, fine alabaster vases, and many other artifacts depicted in the bas-reliefs. One of his most remarkable finds came from the center of the mound, where the Arabs had been set to work trenching behind the first winged bulls found at the site. Layard was about to abandon the fifty-foot-long trench when the diggers came across a magnificent black obelisk lying on its back. The obelisk was carved on four sides with twenty small bas-reliefs. Above, below, and between them were 210 lines of cuneiform inscription, looking as fresh as the day they were carved. The bas-reliefs depicted the king and his attendants receiving tribute. The cuneiform inscription was eventually deciphered as: "The tribute of Jehu, son of Omri: I received from him silver, gold . . ." The rest of the text listed Jehu's gifts. Excited Biblical historians recalled how Jehu had become king of Israel after killing Joram and destroying the ruling house of Ahab, who had been killed at the battle of Ramoth-gilead in 850 B.C. (described in I Kings 22). He had broken alliances with Judah and the Phoenicians and had paid tribute to the Assyrians. Today the black obelisk of Shalmaneser III is one of the most prized possessions of the British Museum.

The excavations at Nimrud continued until mid-May of 1847. One load of sculptures and artifacts had already gone down the river by *kellek* the previous December. So Layard began to prepare for a second load, and to move one of the great bulls to the Tigris. He was determined to take at least one of these mythical beasts to London where, he knew, it would be a spectacular exhibit. His troubles began when a load of felt, mats, and raft materials was stolen by Arab robbers only a few miles upstream of Nimrud. Layard realized that his camp could be in danger if he let matters slip. So he boldly rode out to the robber sheikh's tents and demanded his possessions back. The sheikh received him courteously and denied all knowledge of the theft. Layard made a sign to his dragoman, who handcuffed the sheikh before the bystanders could move, jumped on his horse, and dragged the chief out of the camp.

"Now, my sons," remarked Layard, calmly mounting his horse, "I have found a part of that which I wanted, you must search for the rest."

The Arabs were taken completely by surprise. Although well armed, they made no effort at resistance. Layard regaled the sheikh with horror stories of the pasha's jail and the tortures that awaited him. By the time they reached Nimrud, the sheikh was so terrified that he confessed. Tales of Layard's ruthless methods were soon passed around, as he knew they would be. The packing materials were returned the next day.

While the packing continued, Layard combed Mosul for timber to build a large wagon on which the larger sculptures could be moved. He bought Botta's iron axles from the French consulate and assembled a massive wagon of wood beams braced with iron hoops. Strong loops were fixed to both ends of the cart so that both workmen and buffalo could haul the heavy loads. Meanwhile, the workmen dug a huge trench two hundred feet long and fifteen to twenty feet deep from the excavated figures at Nimrud to the plain below. Layard then removed the earth and the mud-brick walls behind the bull (it was the first one he had found) so that it could be lowered onto its back. Next, he had the figure wrapped in felt and mats to prevent chafe, and tied with ropes so that it could be lowered to the rollers behind it. This was the trickiest part of the operation, for the ropes at Layard's disposal were too small and it was feared they might give way.

On March 18, 1847, the great day came. Greased rollers lay behind the bull, which was supported by wooden braces. The men were stationed at the lowering tackles, while some strong workers were stationed on the braces, with instructions to ease them slowly as the bull was lowered to the ground. Layard stood on the mound above the bull and ordered the wedges supporting the figure removed. The bull still stood upright, so six or seven men tilted it until the lowering ropes took the weight. The heavy figure slowly descended as the lower men propped it with the beams and the ropes strained with the load. The shrill of Kurdish pipes increased as the Arabs yelled their war cries. The women spectators screamed and gesticulated. So loud was the din that Layard was unable to make himself heard in the confusion. In desperation, he threw clods of earth at the noisiest workmen to get their attention, but in vain. All was well until the men below were forced to remove their beams as the bull neared the ground. The dry ropes creaked and strained, and then parted with a twang. The

Lowering the great bull at Nimrud. From Layard, Nineveh and Its Remains (*1849*)

The Nimrud bull on its way to the Tigris. The great mounds of the ancient city are in the background. From Layard, Nineveh and Its Remains *(1849)*

bull crashed onto the rollers in a cloud of choking dust. The workmen collapsed in confused heaps on the ground. A sudden silence fell. Layard jumped into the trench expecting a shattered figure. To his delight, the bull was intact and positioned in the correct place on the rollers. The Arabs went wild with joy, seized the womens' hands, and "commenced a most mad dance."

The bull and, shortly afterward, the winged lion, were dragged to the banks of the Tigris with superhuman effort: they bogged down in the sand and nearly capsized in potholes. A band of marauders tried to steal the felt packings one night, but Layard's guards beat off the attack with their rifles. The bull's flank bears the mark of a rifle ball to this day.

Layard had decided to float the two figures all the way to Basra by *kellek*. None of the Mosul boatmen would venture beyond Baghdad, so Layard hired a Baghdad skipper for the long journey. The raft contractor turned up with a single assistant and two donkeys laden with deflated skins. Layard argued ferociously with this villainous skipper, but eventually prevailed on him to build a higher wooden framework than usual, so the crew could squeeze under the sculptures at Baghdad and reinflate the skins without unloading them. After an abortive strike for higher wages that Layard easily frustrated, the figures were slid down a ramp onto the greased framework on the *kelleks*. About thirty cases of small objects and many bas-reliefs were loaded on the same rafts. As he watched the laden rafts disappear downstream, Layard mused on the strange destiny of their burdens. Once the adornment of royal palaces, they had been neglected for centuries. Now they were to cross the ocean and be displayed in the British Museum. "Who can venture to foretell how their strange career will end"? he wondered.

For some time Layard had been planning a dig at Kuyunjik across the Tigris from Mosul, the site where Botta had dug unsuccessfully in 1842. Although Botta had claimed that Khorsabad was ancient Nineveh and Rawlinson thought Nimrud was the place, Layard was convinced that Kuyunjik was the great city. By now Layard was sufficiently knowledgeable about Assyrian palaces to realize that Botta had not dug deep enough into the tell. The Assyrians had built their palaces on great, brick platforms. When the palace walls collapsed, the platforms were covered by sterile deposits of considerable depth, which had to be removed to expose the original structure. Once the surface of the platform was located, all one had to do was to trench along its surface to find the palace walls.

Layard decided to dig on the southwest corner of Kuyunjik. When the French consul heard of this plan, he promptly claimed the site as

French property in an effort to thwart British excavation. Fortunately, the pasha imperiously overruled him and Layard could begin. In a few days his workmen located some badly burned alabaster bas-reliefs. After a month's hectic work, Layard had uncovered nine chambers of a palace similar in design to those of Nimrud and Khorsabad, containing bas-reliefs of the king at war, besieging a city, and returning from battle in triumph. Time was so short that he was able only to make some hasty drawings and to send one fragment of sculpture — a fisherman with a wicker basket on his back — to England. "The ruins," he wrote, "were certainly those of a palace of great extent and magnificence."

For some time, details of Layard's discoveries had reached England through his letters to his family and from newspaper articles contributed by occasional visitors to Nimrud. The journalist J. A. Longworth had fascinated the readers of the *Morning Post* on March 3, 1847, with an account of his descent into the tunnels of the North West Palace. "The portly forms of kings and viziers, were so lifelike, and carved in such true relief, that they might almost be imagined to be stepping from the walls to question the rash intruder on their privacy. . . . All these figures, the idols of a religion long since dead and buried like themselves, seemed actually in the twilight to be raising their desecrated heads from the sleep of centuries; certainly the feeling of awe which they inspired me with must have been something akin to that experienced by their heathen votaries of old."

The first load of sculptures from the excavations went on display in the British Museum on June 25, the day before Layard left Mosul, and caused great excitement. Layard himself was now ill with fever and exhausted by the heat and by the long, lonely hours of copying inscriptions. He left Mosul accompanied by a large armed party that included Hormuzd Rassam, who was going to Oxford. In Paris, he found himself the celebrity of the hour. Paul Botta and other fellow scholars admired his sketches of Kuyunjik. On arrival home he found that London was agog for details of the excavations. He dined in great houses, lectured to learned audiences, and called on the trustees of the British Museum, who had good reason to be delighted with their agent's work. They immediately applied to the government for a large grant to cover the costs of publication of the Nimrud excavations, a grant application that was just as promptly turned down.

Undeterred by this rejection, Layard wrote to the trustees in January 1848, urging a major archaeological expedition to Mesopotamia. He recommended a large-scale excavation, one financed to the tune of four or five thousand pounds the first year alone. He pointed out that the French and Prussian governments had gained great prestige by their munificent support of archaeological expeditions to Egypt. Should not the British now take the lead in Mesopotamia, where even casual excavations had yielded spectacular palaces and magnificent sculpture? Besides, Layard cautioned, the Porte had now decided to start an imperial museum in Constantinople, and had issued orders for excavations to be carried out on likely mounds. Foreign expeditions might be discouraged as a result. The proposal fell on deaf ears, but Layard was given permission to write a book about Nineveh on his own initiative. He grabbed the chance with alacrity, planning "a slight sketch of the history of Nineveh." He added: "I think the book will be attractive, particularly in America where there are so many Scripture readers." Unfortunately, Layard was in very poor health. Writing was an effort, reading even more so. He spent most of 1848 staying with friends while he compiled his "slight sketch" and corresponded with Rawlinson about cuneiform.

In October 1848 fifty cases of Nimrud antiquities arrived after a long and circuitous journey from Basra to London via Bombay. The precious cargo had been transferred to another vessel in India and had sat on the quays of Bombay harbor for some time. When Layard supervised the unpacking at the British Museum, he was distressed to find that the cases had been rifled. It transpired that British residents in Bombay had opened the precious cases out of curiosity. Some pieces had even been stolen, but the British Museum did not care. They were delighted to be in the possession of so large and so fine a collection. The trustees wrote to the foreign secretary acknowledging the debt they owed Canning and Layard: "The entire collection will undoubtedly be regarded as one of the most important contributions to the materials of archaeological science which has been made in recent times." But the government offered no money for further excavations. Layard's own future remained far from secure. In December 1848 he returned to Constantinople, where the Foreign Office had given him an unpaid attachéship at the embassy. It appeared that his archaeological career was over. He left the completed manuscript of his early excavations in the hands of John Murray, the famous London publisher who had handled the works of Lord Byron and many celebrated travelers.

Early in 1849, *Nineveh and Its Remains* appeared in the bookstores and became an immediate best-seller. The reviewers waxed lyrical. On February 9, 1849, *The Times* described the book as "the most extraordinary work of the present age." Layard himself, said the reviewer, was one of the "most enterprising travelers" to be found "in the annals of our modern history." *Nineveh and Its Remains* is remarkable for its enthusiasm, liveliness, and vivid descriptions of the Nimrud finds.

Some people were surprised at the depth of Layard's knowledge, but they had never realized how many long hours he had spent in Taylor's and Rawlinson's libraries in Baghdad, or how well he spoke the local languages. Now Layard was accepted as a respected scholar as well as a competent archaeologist. Other scholars were impressed by his command of the diverse literature on the Assyrians, the general public by the incredible adventures he had undergone in Mesopotamia and by the relevance of his discoveries to the Old Testament. *Nineveh and Its Remains* highlighted a deep mystery, which, wrote Layard, "hangs over Assyria, Babylonia, and Chaldea. With these names are linked great nations and great cities dimly shadowed forth in history." The new excavations had yielded bas-reliefs of the Assyrian kings and of their subjects, of wars and conquests. Once Babylonian cuneiform was fully deciphered, people would be able to read the inscriptions on the walls of the newly discovered palaces. In the meantime, most readers were content with Layard's claim that he had revealed the "most convincing and lasting evidence of that magnificence, and power, which made Nineveh the wonder of the ancient world, and her fall the theme of the prophets, as the most signal instance of divine vengeance."

10

Nimrud and Khorsabad

*As they had been brought, so were they
taken away.*

WHILE *Nineveh and Its Remains* was the sensation of London, its
author was languishing in his unpaid post at Constantinople certain
that he would never excavate in Mesopotamia again. But he had under-
estimated the pressure of public opinion. The trustees of the British
Museum became uncomfortably aware that they had acquired a magnificent collection of about forty thousand pounds' worth of antiquities
at practically no cost, and that Layard had been treated shabbily.
Albert, prince consort, and government ministers visited the Assyrian
exhibit and were told that the new treasures had cost the country
almost nothing. Ministers and influential scholars urged the museum
to dig for more sculptures and to employ Layard to do so. The government now acted. The prime minister arranged for a ship to be sent
to Basra to pick up the bull and the lion from Nimrud that were still
awaiting transport to England. The Foreign Office appointed Layard
attaché in Constantinople at a salary of two hundred and fifty pounds
a year in belated recognition of his services. Meanwhile, the museum
trustees granted him a further three thousand pounds for renewed
excavation. Layard was to concentrate on Nineveh, to collect more
sculptures, and to record as much of the art and inscriptions as possible.

Layard was horrified at the small size of the grant. His party was to include a young and talented artist, F. C. Cooper, and an English doctor named Humphry Sandwith. Hormuzd Rassam was persuaded by Layard to leave the comforts of Oxford and join the expedition. He did so somewhat reluctantly, for he was enjoying university life. All three men were to be paid from the subvention, but after the salaries were subtracted, there was little money left for excavation and transport of finds. Again, Layard had no option but to make the most of a bad situation.

On August 28, 1849, the expedition left Constantinople for Mosul, traveling across eastern Armenia and Kurdistan through the mountains near the upper reaches of the Tigris. As they descended onto the Mesopotamian plains, the heat became oppressive. Raiding parties were everywhere. When a large party of horsemen approached, Layard sounded the alarm. The two parties approached each other warily. Then there was a shout of joy as the strange horsemen turned out to be a group of headmen from Mosul who had ridden forty miles to greet Layard. From this point on the journey became a triumphal progress. Layard stopped to visit friends. His workmen and their families lined the route and kissed his knees. As Mosul and the brooding mounds of Nineveh rose from the plain, Layard's groom arrived with his horse ready for him to ride. The travelers drew up at Layard's home as if he had never left. His old servants were already at work, the household running on oiled wheels. Layard felt as if he had been on a summer's ride. "Two years had passed away like a dream," he wrote.

During his absence, the British vice-consul had kept a few men at work on Kuyunjik to ward off the French. For a while a local English businessman, a Layard friend named Henry Ross, had watched the diggers, but he had recently left. Layard found little changed. He walked through the deep, elaborate tunnels dug by Ross's workmen. Wooden beams or earthen pillars supported the roof. Sculptures and broken clay vessels projected from the dimly lit walls. Layard gazed at sculptures lying along the southern wall of a great hall. Although much damaged by fire, the bas-relief described a military campaign, from the royal advance into battle to the triumphal return of the king. The Assyrian armies engaged the enemy in close combat among hills and by streams. Mounted archers and spearmen pursued their foe and trampled them underfoot as they begged for mercy. The returning troops threw the severed heads of the vanquished in heaps before their officers. Row after row of prisoners and great loads of booty were escorted past the king. A wide doorway at the side of this hall was guarded by two gigantic, human-headed bulls.

As he examined the Ross finds, Layard's mind was busy with preparations for digging. He recruited his old workmen, who arrived from far and wide, and set small parties of men to work clearing further chambers in the palace. By October 12, when the work began in earnest, over a hundred workmen and their families were camped at Kuyunjik. Hormuzd Rassam supervised and paid the workmen and relieved Layard of the day-to-day burdens of administering the excavation, thereby enabling him to travel to neighboring sites and to start work at his beloved Nimrud. There, Layard decided to investigate the great conical mound in the northwest corner of the site that served as a landmark for miles around. During the previous excavations, Layard had sunk a forty-foot shaft into solid mud brick from the summit but now he dug sideward into the base in the hope of better results.

He spent several days at Nimrud supervising the new excavations and renewing his contacts with the local sheikhs. One morning he rode up to the mound to find a group of strange horses picketed on the stubble. He was warmly greeted by a dragoman who silently pointed to Henry Rawlinson wrapped in his cloak and sleeping soundly in an excavated chamber. Rawlinson was exhausted after a trying ride from Baghdad, the first stage of his long journey to London. During his all-too-brief visit, Rawlinson surprised Layard by telling him that he had changed his mind about Nimrud. Originally he had thought that Nimrud was ancient Nineveh and dated to about 2500 B.C. Now, he felt that much of Assyrian history was pure myth, that Nimrud was not Nineveh at all, but the site of Biblical Calah, dating from 1300 to 1200 B.C. Since the earlier dating had appeared in *Nineveh and Its Remains,* Layard was somewhat perturbed by the new chronology. He could hardly blame Rawlinson, however, for no one had fully deciphered the royal inscriptions and sudden telescoping of chronologies was to be expected. Eventually Rawlinson was to write an outline of the history of Assyria, "in great haste, amid torrents of rain, in a little tent, upon the mound of Nineveh, without any aids beyond a tolerably retentive memory, a pocket bible, and a notebook of inscriptions."

The excavations continued throughout the fall and winter of 1849–1850. Layard commuted between Kuyunjik and Nimrud while young Cooper, the artist, lived in Mosul and rode out to Kuyunjik every day. By the end of November several new chambers had been cleared, including most of a huge hall one hundred twenty-four feet long and ninety feet wide, the walls covered with elaborate sculptures. Two enormous human-headed bulls guarded the entrance. The west wall of the hall told the story of the conquest of a hill-country people.

Some unique bas-reliefs adorned the north wall, showing how the Assyrian kings transported their huge, human-headed bulls from quarry to palace: In one, a huge block of stone lies on a round-bottomed boat on the Tigris. Wooden wedges and beams hold the precious cargo in position. Nearly three hundred men are dragging the boat with huge cables, while an overseer sitting astride the stone supervises the work gang.

Another relief shows the finished sculpture on the banks of the river. Only minor details remain to be completed. The sculpture rests on a huge sledge, carefully supported by wooden beams mounted on rollers. Four large cables, with smaller ropes fastened to them, are attached to the corners of the sledge. Gangs of laborers, each with one of the smaller ropes over his shoulder, are dragging the sledge along. As it moves forward, levers are inserted behind it to give momentum. Kneeling workmen add wedges under the levers while others sit on the levers to give additional weight. The superintending officers stand or kneel on the bull. One is beating time, another blowing a trumpet. Slaves draw carts full of spare beams and wedges behind the sledge, still others carry ropes and saws. The king in his ceremonial chariot, shaded by a parasol and attended by eunuchs, supervises this operation and the next one, a scene where his people are depicted building artificial platforms for a palace and moving a bull into place. The huge figure is being dragged and levered up the artificial mound. Hundreds of captives, many of them wearing fetters, are hard at work under the king's watchful eye. A last scene shows the bull, now held in a vertical position on the sledge, being moved to its final resting place. Beams, crossbars, and wedges keep the precious load upright. "Precisely the same framework was used for moving the great sculptures in the British Museum," remarked Layard.

For some time Layard had been corresponding with the Reverend Edward Hincks in Ireland about the cuneiform inscriptions from his excavations. With the help of Hincks and Rawlinson, it was now possible to identify some of the kings on the bas-reliefs. Hincks eventually provided a provisional decipherment of the inscription accompanying the winged bull scene: "Sennacherib, king of Assyria. The great figures of bulls, which in the land of Belad were made for his royal palace at Nineveh, he transported thither." Layard had been digging Sennacherib's "Palace Without a Rival," built in about 700 B.C. at "Nineveh, the noble fortress, the city beloved of the goddess Ishtar."

While working on Sennacherib's palace, Layard started another set of tunnels in a high mound in the northwest portion of the earthworks surrounding Kuyunjik. By the end of November the workmen had uncovered a huge gateway facing open country and guarded by two

Workmen ferrying building materials across a river in a round-bottomed boat similar to those used on the Tigris and Euphrates until very recent times. Bas-relief from the palace of Sennacherib at Nineveh, c. 700 B.C.

fire-damaged and unfinished human-headed bulls. They were fourteen feet long, bore feathered wings, and had hairy bodies. The gateway itself was over fourteen feet wide and paved with huge limestone slabs that Layard used to trace the passageway. These stone sentinels were covered with a mass of charcoal and burned brick, for the gateway had been destroyed before completion. Layard remembered Nahum 3:13: "The gates of your land are wide open to your foes; fire has devoured your bars." Visitors to the excavations came upon the bulls after progressing through dim tunnels lit by small air shafts. They were invariably impressed. "Between them Sennacherib and his hosts had gone forth in all their might and glory to the conquest of distant lands, and had returned rich with spoil and captives, amongst whom may have been the handmaidens and wealth of Israel," Layard wrote. "Through them, too, the Assyrian monarch had entered his capital

"Sennacherib, king of the universe, king of Assyria, sat upon a throne while the booty of Lachish passed before him." Part of the Lachish frieze that commemorates the king's capture of the city in 701 B.C. From the palace of Sennacherib at Nineveh

in shame, after his last and fatal defeat." The large limestone slabs still bore the ruts of Assyrian chariot wheels.

Layard now set workmen to dig on the east side of Sennacherib's palace near a human-headed bull found in 1848. Soon he found the entire southeast façade of the palace, over one hundred eighty feet long. Ten huge bulls and six gigantic human figures surrounded the entrance. Bas-reliefs showing the king's conquests occupied much of the façade. One hundred and fifty-two lines of inscriptions on the great bulls described Sennacherib's early reign and many details about the Assyrian religion and the construction of the palace.

Even more sensational discoveries came from a large chamber full of bas-reliefs that depicted the siege and capture of a large and heavily fortified city. A huge Assyrian army is camped before the walls. Battering rams and earthworks are in place. While the defenders put up a desperate resistance, part of the city has already fallen. Sennacherib himself sits in judgment over the captives. An inscription above the king's head reads: "Sennacherib, the mighty king, king of the country of Assyria, sitting on the throne of judgment, before the city of Lachish. I give orders for its slaughter."

Layard was thrilled. He had found the original depiction of the capture of a city mentioned in the Bible, seized by the Assyrians in 700 B.C. Sennacherib's army besieged Lachish when the Assyrians demanded tribute of the rebel king Hezekiah. In the Old Testament we read: "In the fourteenth year of King Hezekiah Sennacherib king of Assyria came up against all the fortified cities of Judah and took them. And Hezekiah, king of Judah, sent to the king of Assyria at Lachish, saying, 'I have done wrong; withdraw from me; whatever you impose on me I will bear'" (2 Kings 18:13). He was told to pay three hundred talents of silver and thirty of gold, so outrageous a tribute that Hezekiah had to strip gold and silver from the temple of the Lord. Sennacherib was not satisfied. His armies camped in front of Jerusalem and threatened to take it. But the Assyrian host was decimated by a sudden plague and Sennacherib never achieved his objective. He was murdered in the temple at Nineveh by his sons. Now Layard had found not only his palace but the actual record of his Judean campaign. When Rawlinson deciphered Sennacherib's inscriptions, he found reference to Hezekiah, the capture of forty-six cities, and a tribute of eight hundred talents of silver and thirty of gold, a remarkable correspondence to the Biblical account. The siege of Lachish can now be seen in the British Museum, scenes where "Sennacherib, king of the universe, king of Assyria, sat upon a throne while the booty of Lachish passed before him." Sennacherib boasted extravagantly that he had carried off "200,150 people, old and young, male and female" into captivity. With such vivid confirmation of Old Testament events emerging from ancient Nineveh, it was hardly surprising that Layard became a popular hero.

Meanwhile, the excavations under the conical mound at Nimrud were making progress. The men tunneled into the base at bedrock for eighty-four feet and came to a solid masonry wall twenty feet high. They then tunneled along the stone wall until they emerged at the edge. A huge mass of collapsed brick and mud covered this foundation, the remains, said Layard, of a square tower, not a pyramid. The structure had been cased in baked mud brick, the cone being formed of sun-dried blocks. Convinced that a royal grave lay under the structure, he proceeded to tunnel right through the stone base, "a work of some difficulty," he calmly wrote later. No tomb came to light, so he tunneled at right angles to the very center of the stone structure, then six feet into bedrock, without result. A long galley did, however, lie on top of the stone foundation, vaulted with sun-dried bricks and blocked at both ends. Layard conjectured that this was the burial chamber, robbed long ago, of the king who had built the tower. Deeply disappointed, he contented himself with estimating the height of the structure at two hundred feet.

As these tunneling operations were in progress, another gang of workmen was preparing to move the two huge human-headed lions that Layard had found in 1846. Early one morning Layard was startled by gunfire and women's screams. He dashed from his house to see a group of spear-toting horsemen driving away the locals' cattle and sheep while the bereaved owners were firing at the raiders. The women, armed with pitchforks and tent poles, were trying to rescue their animals. Layard grabbed a horse and boldly rode up to the leader of the raiding party. He demanded the cattle and sheep back, promised redress for a theft of camels that turned out to be the cause of the raid. The leader unwillingly agreed, but Layard had considerable difficulty in stopping the hostilities. His own workmen advanced on the raiders brandishing swords and spears. Others gathered up bricks from the excavations and were ready to pelt the strangers with antiquities. At this moment, Layard's greyhounds spotted a wild hare and took off in headlong pursuit. The Arabs' "love of the chase overcame even their propensity for appropriating other peoples' property." The marauders took off in wild pursuit, dropping their booty behind them.

Despite this noisy interruption, the lions reached the Tigris safely. Every available workman pulled or levered the carts as dozens of horsemen wheeled around the procession shouting war cries. "The procession closely resembled that which in days of yore transported the same great figures," wrote Layard. "As they had been brought, so were they taken away." It was months before the lions reached Basra, however. The flooding Tigris covered them with silt as they lay on the bank. Once under way, one of the lion-carrying *kelleks* went out of control and washed over a flooded embankment downstream of Baghdad. Fortunately, Captain Felix Jones, the skipper of the *Euphrates*, boldly took her alongside the stranded raft and rescued its historic treasures.

The Nimrud excavations continued to yield remarkable discoveries. Layard himself supervised the removal of the earth fill from a chamber in the North West Palace that had once overlooked the Tigris. The fill contained a series of copper vessels and jars, many of which "fell to pieces as they were uncovered," an all-too-familiar litany of nineteenth-century excavations. Bronze bells with iron tongues, cups and dishes, studs and bottoms of ivory and mother-of-pearl, many fragments of horse and chariot trappings, were extracted from these receptacles. Cauldrons sat on bronze tripods with feet in the shape of bulls' hooves or lions' paws. Circular flat vessels, and fragments of a throne came to light. A whole array of decorated bronze dishes, plates, bowls, and cups came from the same chamber, those near the floor being in an excellent state of preservation. Layard lifted as many as possible in groups and sent them to the British Museum in that state, so they could be cleaned up at leisure. The same chamber yielded weapons, fragments of military armor, glass bowls, shields and spears, also iron saws and picks. Some delicate ivory ornaments were removed with great difficulty, for the fragments tended to crumble to dust when exposed to the air. Layard spent days removing the fill of this rich chamber, and bitterly regretted he had no time to remove the contents of other rooms, tunneling as he was round the walls in search of bas-reliefs.

For all the spectacular finds from Nimrud and Nineveh, Layard was at his best when on the move. He preferred finding new sites and visiting local sheikhs to the daily routine of excavation. He sometimes found the tensions of excavation unbearable. Humphry Sandwith was totally uninterested in archaeology and preferred to idle away his time in hunting or riding. Cooper, the artist, was very ill, so much so that he could hardly draw. Layard had to check the details of his work every day. Cooper was homesick for his wife, too, and a very poor companion. Visitors were even more of a trial. Percy Badger, an ardent missionary and the brother-in-law of Christian Rassam, turned up in Mosul. He was busy writing a book on the local Christians and spent much time at Nineveh examining the excavations. Layard took a violent dislike to Badger, partly because he had a deep distrust of intolerant and quarrelsome missionaries, and the atmosphere in camp became rather strained.

A tension of a different kind was introduced by two other English visitors — Stewart and Charlotte Rowland, a young couple who were traveling to visit friends in the East. Stewart found the country very attractive because he could keep fine horses by the Tigris for almost nothing. Charlotte became entranced with archaeology when she witnessed the discovery of the rutted gateway road at Kuyunjik. Both of them liked Layard immensely. While Stewart helped supervise the workmen, Charlotte worked closely with Layard on the clearance and packing of the finds. Soon the Rowlands had moved into Layard's house at Nimrud. Even in these intimate surroundings, they all remained fast friends. Inevitably, tensions arose after a few months, perhaps because Layard may have been attracted to Charlotte Rowland. She accompanied him on many of his Bedouin visits, sitting behind him on a fast-riding camel. His letters hint at a strong attraction between them, for he refers to her "good nature and kind manner to the Arabs." At any rate, his diary refers circumspectly to painful scenes and violent quarrels, when Stewart Rowland started to beat his wife. Layard hints in other letters that Rowland had gone slightly mad and had to be restrained. Eventually, Layard was obliged to tell them to go back to England as soon as possible.

By March 1850 the Nimrud and Nineveh excavations were well advanced. Layard had managed to stretch the British Museum's three-thousand-pound subvention to cover much more excavation than he had originally anticipated. Fortunately, labor costs were very low. He paid his workmen about fourpence a day, the foremen a little more. Cooper, the artist, received two hundred pounds a year and thirty for an outfit, while Layard himself was granted two hundred pounds for his own equipment. Although the wage overhead for the Europeans was relatively high, the costs of excavation itself were much lower, so Layard could manipulate his budget. He deployed his digging teams where finds were most plentiful, occasionally throwing a feast or buying an ox for his laborers. There is no doubt that the museum got a unique bargain for its modest grant.

Most of the British Museum subvention had been expended by March, so Layard decided to take off on a long-planned trip to the Khabur Valley west of Mosul. He traveled in some style, taking along a huge hospitality tent that could entertain two hundred guests. The Khabur River flowed placidly through fields of bright spring wild flowers, a paradise after the muddy plains near Mosul. Layard was shown the mound of Arban, where floodwaters had exposed two much-damaged winged bulls of a simpler style than those at Kuyunjik.

Arab tents on the Khabur River. Painting by F. C. Cooper

A month's digging revealed a fine lion and another pair of bulls opposite the first couple. But the diggings were somewhat of a sideline. Layard spent most of his time studying and visiting with the local Arab tribes. He was later to write a long account of the Khabur peoples, an account remarkable for its vivid descriptions of Arab hospitality, of blood feuds and women who wore necklaces of "coins, coarse amber, carnelian beads and cylinders, mostly Assyrian relics picked up amongst ruins after ruins." Deserted, grass-covered village mounds could be seen on all sides.

Layard was delighted to find a new series of bas-reliefs emerging at Kuyunjik on his return: ninety-six feet of a procession of servants bearing "fruit, flowers, game, and supplies for a banquet, preceded by mace-bearers." There were attendants carrying dates and baskets of pomegranates, apples, and bunches of grapes. Some men bore partridges, hares, even strings of locusts, a highly prized Assyrian delicacy. Further chambers were guarded by huge bas-reliefs of the fish-god Dagon, small rooms that contained thousands of clay tablets and cylinders. The archives filled each room to a depth of over a foot, many of them in fragments from the collapse of the roof. The tablets and cylinders were covered with minute cuneiform signs, so small they could only be read with a magnifying glass. "The documents appear to be of various kinds," wrote Layard. "Many are historical records of wars, and distant expeditions undertaken by the Assyrians; some seem to be royal decrees, and are stamped with the name of a king, the son of Esarhaddon." There were lists of gods and registers of temple offerings, even lists of sacred days and tables of values of cuneiform letters. Within a few weeks, Layard had filled six crates with clay tablets, with many more to come. He had uncovered the royal library of Ashur-bani-pal, a find that was to place the scientific understanding of the Assyrians on an entirely new footing. "They furnish us with materials for the complete decipherment of the cuneiform character," he wrote later, "for restoring the language and history of Assyria, and for inquiring into the customs, sciences, and we may even add, literature of the people." Then he added prophetically: "But years must elapse before the innumerable fragments can be put together, and the inscriptions transcribed."

The Nimrud excavations were yielding important finds as well, especially from a buried temple near the ziggurat which yielded a sculpture of an "early Nimrud king in an arched recess, sculpted in very high relief and covered with inscriptions on all sides." The great entrances to this temple lay to the east. The main door was formed by two human-headed lions over sixteen feet high and fifteen feet long. A second temple lay a hundred feet east of the first, its entrance also flanked by two lions with bristling manes. The inscriptions from the two temples were deciphered by Hincks and Rawlinson and told of the king's military campaigns and many conquests. The minute chronicles of royal deeds surprised Layard and the cuneiform scholars, for they were more complete than those available on the ancient Egyptians. Three hundred and twenty-five lines of inscription on a huge monolith in the second temple recorded the building and rebuilding of the North West Palace, as well as military expeditions conducted with savage cruelty. Prisoners were burned alive, impaled on stakes, or otherwise tortured. Women and children were slaughtered indiscriminately.

By early summer 1850 Layard and his companions were exhausted by the increasing heat, the constant strain of dealing with their volatile workmen, and the primitive working conditions. In later years Layard was to remember his stay among the nomads and workmen at Nimrud with nostalgia, but in reality camp life was very uncomfortable indeed. Everyone lived in primitive mud-brick huts that teemed with lice and fleas and was exposed to the full force of the bitterly cold north winds that whistled over the tell in winter. At times pools of water on the mound froze over. The camp could become a muddy quagmire after a few hours of rain. The first few weeks of spring were pleasant, but then the sun would bake the plains dry and sear the camp in shimmering heat that was totally debilitating. Strong winds would bring sandstorms and dusty discomfort that was almost unbearable.

Layard himself lived in a large hut which actually boasted glass windowpanes. He had a dilapidated couch but little other furniture. The remaining members of the party fared worse and often ate their meals seated on the ground. Everyone ate much the same food as the local people — a diet of rice and vegetables with occasional feasts of sheep or goat meat. They were able to supplement the local foods with a few expensive European luxuries like jam and tea. Although Dr. Sandwith had a small chest of medicines, there was little he could do to treat the recurring dysentery and fever that laid them all low. The only treatment for more serious ailments was to retreat to the cooler air of the Kurdish highlands. Fortunately, most of the party were living an active, healthy life out-of-doors in all weathers and serious illnesses were the exception rather than the rule.

No nineteenth-century excavator could afford to ignore his local neighbors. The laws of hospitality dictated that Layard entertain anyone who visited his camp. A constant stream of visitors paused at Nimrud to look over the excavations. Layard found himself entertaining sheikhs and Turkish officials, shepherds and former workmen, even an occasional European. He was well aware that hospitality was a sacred duty in a land where there were no lodging houses and the traveler had the harsh realities of the desert to contend with. A guest could never be turned away or harmed, not even one's deadliest enemy. Shrewdly, Layard used his obligations as a host to further his archaeological objectives. By flattering his guests and giving generous hospitality he managed to forestall any plans for an armed raid on the camp. He also made sure that all Europeans carried arms and did not stray far from camp alone. He set a twenty-four-hour guard on the excavations.

When it was clear that everyone was feeling the strain, Layard shut down the Nimrud excavations and set off for the Kurdish highlands. He left a gang of workmen tunneling into Sennacherib's palace at Kuyunjik, where they soon found bas-reliefs of campaigns in the lower Mesopotamian marshes, of military victories, prisoners of war, and day-to-day life in his domains. In the fall, Layard returned to pack nearly a hundred crates of bas-reliefs and other finds, which he floated safely downstream to Basra. He himself left Mosul on October 16 for an uneventful ride by *kellek* to Baghdad. He was lucky. The countryside was in open rebellion against the Turks and no one was safe. One of his rafts was attacked but the crew beat off the raiders and killed several of them.

Layard had come to Baghdad with plans to shift his operations to Babylonia and specifically to dig at Babylon itself. He found Baghdad an island in a sea of rebellion, its only safe means of contact with the outside world the British East India Company's steamer under the com-

mand of Felix Jones. When unsettled conditions delayed him in Baghdad, he set some of his experienced laborers from Mosul to work on
mounds near the city, but with little result. On December 5 he set out
for Al-Hillah and Babylon, where he befriended the local pasha. This
kindly gentleman presented him with two lions. The younger one
soon died of mange, but the second, a full-grown specimen, was well
known in Al-Hillah. He was a friendly beast whom everyone liked
except the butchers. The lion would occupy their stalls and not allow
them back until he had eaten all their stock. When not eating meat, the
lion would chase fishermen from their wicker boats and eat the suc-
culent catfish they had just landed. "The pasha," wrote Layard cynically, "rather encouraged a mode of obtaining daily rations, which, although of questionable honesty, relieved him from butchers' bills."
The lion would lie in the sun and allow little boys to pet him when he
was not hungry.

The Babylon excavations were a great disappointment. The ruins
were a far cry from the relatively compact tells and earthworks at
Nimrud or Nineveh. Babylon was a veritable sea of mounds, very difficult to survey and excavate. It was impossible for Layard, as for Rich
before him, to correlate the historical descriptions of the great city with
the ruins they saw. There were no signs of city walls, nor of the
famous palace of Nebuchadnezzar with its Hanging Gardens. Nevertheless, Layard put his diggers to work on the two principal mounds —
Mujelibe and the Kasr. The workmen tunneled deep into the mounds
at different levels but found little more than masses of mud bricks or
"numerous relics of a doubtful period." Layard investigated the underground chambers originally dug into by Rich forty years before. Rich
had found modern skeletons in wooden coffins. Layard found more of
them and a "foul and unbearable stench" that permeated his tunnels, a
scent of decaying wood and wild animals. "Even the Arabs," he recalled, "were compelled to leave their work for a few days." He was
puzzled by the lack of bas-reliefs. All he found were huge quantities of
glazed bricks in brilliant colors. He bought a few cylinders and small
gems from the local dealers in Al-Hillah, but found almost nothing
himself.

The Babylon discoveries were "far less numerous and important
than I could have anticipated," Layard wrote. He doubted whether the
site would be worth investigating on a large scale. After all, he rationalized, if Alexander the Great had employed ten thousand men to uncover the rubbish from the temple of Belus and had failed to find it,
it was hardly surprising that his small group of Arab workmen would
be unsuccessful. The truth was that his crude excavation methods were
not up to the complex task of tracing buildings or individual levels in

the mounds. Without the familiar bas-reliefs to go by, he was at a complete loss on how to proceed.

Layard had wanted to dig at Birs Nimrod as well, but the country was too unsettled. A heavily armed escort accompanied him there, an escort that promptly fell onto a party of Arabs, stripped them of their cows and sheep, and severely wounded their owners, who would have been killed if Layard had not objected. Peace restored, he climbed to the summit of the Birs and gazed over a vast, marshy landscape. The analogies between Birs Nimrod and the collapsed Assyrian temples at Kuyunjik and Nimrud were obvious, he thought. "The ruin is a specimen of the perfection of the Babylonian masonry," he wrote. He refused to speculate as to its association with the Tower of Babel in the Scriptures, preferring to associate it with the ancient city of Borsippa, an interpretation favored by both Rawlinson and modern scholars.

In January 1851, Layard rode further south into Babylonia with the intention of digging into the tells at Nippur and Uruk.* The desolate plains of the region were little known to Europeans, although William Kennet Loftus had carried out some abortive excavations at both sites in 1849. Political conditions were now exceedingly dangerous. But Layard sought the protection of the sheikh of the Marsh Arabs, in whose swampy country of reed-hut villages Nippur lay. He was greeted by the sheikh's sons, who arrived in black boats built of rushes and bitumen that skimmed over the water with remarkable speed. The sheikh's village was all mats and reeds, the houses divided by canals. Layard was forced to live in the mosquito-ridden village, where, at least, he was safe from robbers and wild animals. He rented two large boats to act as commuter ferries for his men. The workmen dug into the mounds of Nippur for several weeks and found large numbers of glazed-earthenware coffins of the Parthian period (250 B.C.–A.D. 226). These contained human remains that almost invariably crumbled to dust as they were uncovered. Deep trenches revealed massive brick foundations and cuneiform-inscribed bricks, but none of the spectacular finds associated with Nimrud or Kuyunjik. Again, Layard was discouraged. "I am much inclined to question whether extensive excavations carried on at Nippur would produce any very important or interesting results," he reported.

Political conditions were now deteriorating rapidly in the delta, so much so that Layard was unable to reach Uruk. He surely would have been murdered if he had tried. Then he contracted pleurisy and fever from the marshy environment, becoming so weak that he resorted to desperate measures and administered himself a dose of blistering fluid used on sick horses. This drastic remedy gave immediate, if temporary,

* Uruk (the Biblical Erech) is now called Warka by the Arabs.

relief. He rode the whole way to Baghdad almost collapsing from fever, but arrived unscathed. His workmen were less fortunate. They were stripped of all their possessions by desert robbers.

After a few weeks of rest in Baghdad, Layard had recovered sufficiently to return to Mosul. There he found Thomas Septimus Bell, a young arist sent out by the British Museum as a successor to Cooper, who had been invalided home. Bell turned out to be competent and hard-working, although very young and inexperienced. Layard set him to work at once copying newly discovered bas-reliefs from Kuyunjik. Sennacherib's palace was still yielding new artistic treasures: four new chambers with scenes of Assyrian armies returning from successful campaigns with prisoners and loads of booty. Another series depicted royal soldiers fighting marsh peoples in reed boats just like those Layard had recently used at Nippur.

By April 1851, Layard had had enough. Although the British Museum was pressing him to continue, he was fed up with their inadequate financial support and complained constantly about the amounts of his own money he had been obliged to spend. He was justifiably proud of his accomplishments at Kuyunjik and Nimrud. No less than "seventy-one halls, chambers, and passages" in the palace of Sennacherib had been opened, covered with, "by a rough calculation, about 9,880 feet, or nearly two miles, of bas-reliefs, with twenty-seven portals, formed by colossal winged bulls and lion-sphinxes." Yet only a small proportion of the palace had been fully examined. But Layard, the perfectionist, was obsessed with his failure to uncover anything of value at Babylon and Nippur, and his inability to reach the great mound at Uruk. Above all, he was depressed about the state of the country. Political conditions had deteriorated sharply in recent months and travel was exceedingly dangerous, even for Europeans. He was tired of insolence from townspeople and the complexities of Arab hospitality, even if his memories of desert tents were to remain his most lingering and nostalgic experiences of Mesopotamia. He left Mosul on April 28, 1851, never to return to Nineveh or Nimrud again. The excavations were left in the charge of Christian Rassam and young Bell, who was drowned at Bavian soon afterward. Their instructions were to keep a British presence at the site to prevent the French from moving in on the excavated palace. No large-scale operations were contemplated. They were to await new instructions from the British Museum.

Layard arrived in London in July 1851 and was swept into a social whirl. He was lionized by the duke of Wellington, Lord Cowley, and other prominent men. When the crates of bas-reliefs from Kuyunjik and Nimrud arrived at the British Museum, Layard spent long hours

The reception of the Nineveh sculptures at the British Museum.
From the Illustrated London News, *February 28, 1852*

supervising the unpacking. At the same time he felt increasingly bitter about the offhand attitude of the museum trustees to his discoveries. For instance, they had no idea of local conditions, and were content to send out another young and inexperienced artist who knew nothing of the country or the people. Layard was well aware of the furious competition for Assyrian antiquities that was about to break out and complained to the secretary of the museum that the trustees were allowing the French to overtake them. Relations between the museum and Layard became rather strained as a result. But while Layard retreated into seclusion to write a sequel to *Nineveh and Its Remains,* which was still selling well, thousands of Londoners flocked to the British Museum to see his latest discoveries. Eventually the sheer weight of public opinion goaded the trustees into casting around for a successor to Layard, who had refused to go out again. It was a year before the museum renewed its work at Nineveh.

In January 1852, Layard's fortunes improved dramatically. A change of foreign secretary brought Lord Granville to the Foreign Office. He promptly appointed Layard his under secretary. The appointment caused some surprise, but was widely acclaimed as a just reward for the discovery of Nineveh. As it turned out, the job only lasted eleven days, for the government resigned in crisis and Layard with it. He now stood for Parliament and in July was elected Liberal member for the constituency of Aylesbury in Berkshire. Since a political career was less demanding in those days, Layard was able to spend much time in society and working on his new book.

A fascinating stay with the Reverend Edward Hincks in his remote country parsonage at Killyleagh in Ireland gave Layard new insights into the thousands of lines of inscriptions from Kuyunjik and Nimrud. Hincks had the rare combination of talents that make up a successful decipherer — an ingenious mind, great linguistic abilities, and an inexhaustible fund of patience. For years, he had pored over the history of the Assyrian kings and had deciphered the names of Sargon, Sennacherib, and Esarhaddon. Now he was working on the main bodies of the inscriptions, the texts that followed the standard formulas of kingly titles. Layard was able to use his preliminary results, and those produced by Hincks's rival Henry Rawlinson, to attempt a general account of the Assyrian kings in his new book. *Discoveries in the Ruins of Nineveh and Babylon with Travels in Armenia, Kurdistan, and the Desert* was published by John Murray in March 1853. The public devoured its seven hundred pages eagerly.

Layard's second book is more authoritative, the work of a man who knew he had discovered a unique civilization. The decipherment of cuneiform had enabled him to develop a provisional chronology of the

Assyrian kings, one which, he readily admitted, would be altered radically when his new clay tablets from Kuyunjik were deciphered.

He attempted a description of the Assyrian state, "at all times a kind of confederation formed by many tributary states." He stressed the independence of each ruler and their perpetual internecine warfare. This, he claimed, was the truth behind the Biblical references to the Assyrians and the Israelites. The nonpayment of tribute led to an Assyrian military expedition, to the reduction of a few towns and the enslavement or resettlement of their populations — interest, as it were, on the unpaid tribute. Throughout *Nineveh and Babylon*, Layard returns again and again to the connections between the Old Testament and his archaeological finds. This, he knew, was the crux of the profound interest in all things Assyrian on the part of the general public. For all his scholarly pretensions, he was a journalist and popular writer by inclination.

Austen Henry Layard's archaeological achievements are, quite simply, staggering, especially for a man with no formal training. He had no idea how to keep records of finds or of different archaeological levels. He simply worked out his own solutions as he went along. Anyone visiting Nineveh, Nimrud, or the British Museum is amazed at the results he obtained with inadequate financial resources, no special equipment, certainly no cameras, and, on his first expedition, no skilled assistance except that of Hormuzd Rassam. The British Museum owns sheet after sheet of drawings of bas-reliefs made by Layard's own hand that are the only record of finds he was unable to ship home. Unfortunately, it was too much for one man. Hundreds of bas-reliefs and inscriptions were found but never recorded and are now lost. Layard had the great archaeologist's instinct for the vital rather than the trivial, and a nose for discovery that led him unerringly to royal palaces and spectacular finds. The prodigious energy of the man made up for many of his scientific shortcomings.

Layard gave up archaeology after the publication of *Nineveh and Babylon*. He was only thirty-six years old. Next he embarked on a successful career as a politician and a diplomat, eventually becoming British ambassador in Constantinople and Madrid. No carefully trained students stepped into his shoes to take over where he left off. His successors were little more than treasure hunters, out to acquire as much loot for the major museums or their private gain as they could. It was to be almost half a century before the self-taught amateurs and treasure hunters were to be replaced by the systematic, careful, scientifically trained excavator.

IV

TABLETS, TELLS, AND TACTICAL EXCAVATIONS

11

Early Archaeologists in Sumer

The depths of its mounds are as yet untouched.

In REPLACING LAYARD, the British Museum faced a problem: almost nobody was qualified to direct archaeological excavation in Mesopotamia. Not only had few people ever dug there, but hardly anyone in England had even visited the area. Clearly, any excavation would have to be under the general supervision of Henry Rawlinson in Baghdad, even if he had no time to direct it in person. The trustees asked Rawlinson to suggest someone, and after extensive consultation and correspondence, Rawlinson recommended one of the few people with archaeological experience in Mesopotamia, a geologist named William Kennet Loftus. Rawlinson was particularly impressed with Loftus because he was a man of initiative and resource who was not afraid to work in dangerous territory. Determined and aggressive, Loftus was very much a man of action, happiest in the field. His excavation experience had been acquired on the desolate mounds of southern Mesopotamia, which Rawlinson believed held the clues to early Mesopotamian civilization. Conceivably, he felt, the British Museum could be persuaded to expand their operations into the south at the close of the Nineveh dig.

Loftus had gained his first archaeological experience while serving

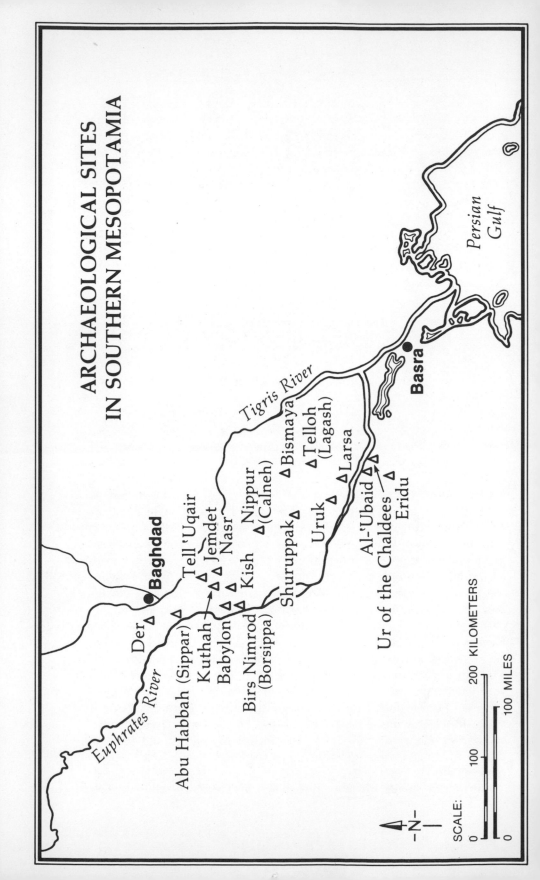

ARCHAEOLOGICAL SITES
IN SOUTHERN MESOPOTAMIA

Baghdad

Persian Gulf

Basra

Tigris River

Der

Abu Habbah (Sippar)
Kuthah
Babylon
Birs Nimrod (Borsippa)

Tell 'Uqair
Jemdet Nasr
Kish
Nippur (Calneh)

Shuruppak
Bismaya
Telloh (Lagash)
Uruk
Larsa

Al-'Ubaid
Ur of the Chaldees
Eridu

Euphrates River

SCALE:

0   100   200 KILOMETERS

0   100 MILES

as the geologist to a boundary commission charged with mediating a complex frontier dispute between Persia and Turkey. The commission's work brought Loftus to the Near East in 1849, the year Layard's first sculptures from Nimrud were on exhibition in London. In December, the members of the commission were to travel by steamer from Babylon to Ahvaz on their way to the disputed areas. Always eager for adventure and a change of routine, Loftus obtained permission to take an alternative route overland from the Euphrates to the Tigris to examine the geology of the marshes on the way. Accompanied by his friend W. A. Churchill, Loftus traveled light with a small armed guard. Even so, their lives were in danger, for the tribes of the desert and marshes owed allegiance to no one. As they rode toward the Tigris, Loftus was amazed by the abundant traces of ancient civilization littering the desolate plains — canals, earthworks, and earthen mounds, the remains of ancient cities that had once been flourishing settlements. He made a special point of visiting the mounds of Uruk.

As the two men approached, they saw the mounds of the ancient city towering above the grass-covered plain. Herds of gazelle were grazing on the new grass and bounded away to safety when the guards pursued them with loud cries. "Three massive piles rose prominent before our view. The whole was surrounded by a lofty and strong line of earthen ramparts, concealing . . . all but the principal mounds." Loftus and Churchill spent two hasty days at the site, trying to draw at least a rudimentary plan of the mounds and fortifications. "Each step that we took, after crossing the walls, convinced me that [Uruk] was a much more important place than had been hitherto supposed, and that its vast mounds, abounding in objects of the highest interest, deserved a thorough exploration," Loftus wrote. The two travelers reached the boundary commission's camp full of enthusiasm for their new site. Their sketches and reports, and their few small finds, so interested the commission leader, Colonel Williams, that he allowed Loftus to return for a few weeks of digging, telling him to "procure specimens of the remarkable coffins of the locality, and such objects as might be easily packed for transmission to the British Museum."

Loftus was on the road within a few days, accompanied by four servants, two guides, and fifteen horses and mules. The protection of a local sheikh enabled him to work in relative safety. For three harassing weeks he rose at dawn and labored all day in the fine dust. It was exhausting work, made even harder by extremely cold nights.

On his first visit Loftus had noticed dozens of clay coffins outcropping from the Uruk mounds. "Even the tombs of ancient Thebes do not contain such an aggregate amount of mortality," he wrote. The coffins lay in literally every corner of the site. Loftus tunneled as deep

The slipper coffin makes its way from Uruk to the Euphrates.
From William Kennet Loftus's Travels and Researches *(1857)*

into the artificial platform as he dared — some thirty feet — and still came across a solid mass of burials. Urns and large dishes contained skeletons, but most common of all were glazed, slipper-shaped coffins of clay. The lids were cemented in place with lime mortar and were ornamented with elevated ridges and figures of warriors. The rich, green enamel on the exterior contrasted with the blue on the inside. All these "slipper" burials dated to the Parthian period and were obviously of recent date.

The coffins sometimes contained skeletons that crumbled to dust when exposed to the air. Rings, amulets, bangles, and gold ornaments often accompanied the bodies. Over the years the local Arabs had broken open hundreds of coffins annually in search of gold ornaments. Loftus observed them at work. The grave robber would drive a spear into the soft soil until he struck an obstruction. Then, burrowing like a mole, he would grub and pick his way to his quarry, break open the lid, and root around among the bones with his dagger in search of gold. The coffin was then broken into pieces to get at others below. Most of the mounds were honeycombed with burrows and broken potsherds that testified to centuries of treasure hunting. On several occasions coffins unearthed during the excavations were rifled while Loftus's back was turned.

Every time he tried to separate a coffin from its tightly packed neighbors, it fell apart. After breaking at least a hundred, he devised a method using a mixture of paper, flour, water, and gum that enabled him to lift three to send home to the British Museum. Even so, the operation caused Loftus much anxiety, for his exuberant workmen had to carry the extracted coffins nine miles across rough ground to the Euphrates. The porters almost danced the coffins to the river, their companions feigning mock attacks that caused the workmen to lift their spears in defiance and almost drop their precious burden. When the coffins reached the river, the local villagers staged a mock funeral with wailing and dancing. Loftus could do nothing but watch as his precious finds were tossed to and fro by the crowd.

Loftus resumed his work with the commission at the time that Rawlinson and others were poring over the tablets and inscriptions from Kuyunjik in the north. The more Rawlinson examined the Layard finds, the more convinced he became that the ancient texts would provide useful pointers for the future excavator of the southern Mesopotamian mounds. He theorized that Uruk and Ur of the Chaldees had been settled first. "The names of the eight primeval cities, preserved in the tenth chapter of Genesis, are not intended to denote capitals then actually built and named," he wrote. The names designated localities where the descendants of Noah established the first colonies, names that became famous in later times and were associated with city-states. Rawlinson's hypotheses caused widespread interest. He became more and more eager to start new excavations at Uruk and other tells, and was convinced that the mounds would yield finds as spectacular as those from Khorsabad, Nimrud, and Nineveh.

Just as Loftus was about to set out for Kuyunjik to take up his appointment as Layard's successor, the British Museum decided to send him to Susa instead. As it turned out, the Susa excavations were unsuccessful, and Loftus returned home in 1852. At this juncture, the Assyrian Exploration Fund appointed him to dig in southern Mesopotamia. Forthwith he made elaborate preparations to return to Uruk. A well-known artist, William Boutcher, and a friend named Ker Lynch, accompanied him.

Uruk presented an even greater scene of desolation than in 1849. The river had not flooded in recent years and the drought had driven the local people elsewhere. Loftus had the greatest difficulty recruiting laborers. His supplies had to come from a small town miles away. Camels had to bring water to camp from the river, and also to Uruk, which was nine miles from Loftus's base. Blinding sandstorms developed on all but the calmest days, enveloping the excavations in dense clouds of choking dust. Sometimes the workmen got lost on their way back to camp. But Loftus was undeterred. He was determined to uncover the city that had once flourished on this desolate spot.

Uruk is the largest archaeological site in the south, consisting of a series of long mounds that extend over an area more than six miles in circumference. A canal once flowed through the site. On either side of its now-dry bed lie mounds of occupation debris up to fifty feet high. The most imposing structures were in the southwest portion, crumbled masses of brickwork and rubbish, the remains of three ziggurats and a huge Parthian temple. Loftus concentrated his first efforts on the highest mound, a pyramidlike heap of sun-dried brick named Buwariyya ("reed matting") over two hundred feet square. He tunneled into the mound and found some brick buttresses, also layers of unbaked brick and reed mats. He quarried further in search of inscribed cylinders, but found none and assumed they had been destroyed in the collapse of the structure.

His primary objective was to find bas-reliefs and art objects. So he moved his workmen over to a "walled quadrangle" eight hundred and forty feet from the Buwariyya. This structure, known as the Waswats in Loftus's time, consisted of a series of courts, gateways, and enclosures that seemed like a possible site for a palace. The structure stood on a huge artificial platform over fifty feet high and was covered with deep deposits of collapsed brick and occupation debris. The masses of decaying brickwork made the excavations very hazardous, especially since materials for shoring trenches were unobtainable.

Loftus concentrated on finding walls, the insides of which might be adorned with sculptures. He uncovered a long façade, which he estimated to be over one hundred and seventy-five feet in length. The plain wall was adorned with stepped recesses and had once been decorated with terra-cotta cone bricks. It had evidently been plastered in antiquity. While the exterior was relatively easy to excavate, the interior was a different matter. An entrance lay at the northeast side, leading to a large court flanked by rooms on either side. The walls were so thick that Loftus was convinced for a while that he was digging into a solid structure. Eventually he managed to clear seven chambers, but no sculptures came to light, only plastered walls and the remains of date-wood beams. The only traces of decoration were some fragmentary glazed bricks. "Rubbish completely filled every chamber; so that, having ascertained the non-existence of sculpture in two apartments, I did not deem it advisable to explore further," Loftus commented. The bricks used in the construction of this edifice were all marked with a deeply-impressed triangular stamp or with "an oblong die bearing thirteen lines of minute cuneiform characters." The Uruk architecture was quite different from that of the northern palaces. There was, after all, no suitable stone for sculptures in southern Mesopotamia, Loftus surmised, so it was hardly surprising that the ancients had used the local building materials. Since he had just uncovered the first Sumerian building known to modern times, his puzzlement was hardly surprising.

Loftus now sank some trenches into a smaller structure nearby on a level with the desert. He uncovered a thirty-foot length of a wall built of terra-cotta cones three and a half inches long. The cones were arranged in semicircles, with their rounded bases facing outward. "Some had been dipped in red and black color," he wrote, "and were arranged in various ornamental patterns." The site was littered with thousands of these cones, which "were undoubtedly much used as an architectural decoration."

The three months that Loftus spent at Uruk did little more than scratch the surface of what was obviously a highly complex and long-occupied settlement. Loftus himself was somewhat disappointed by the results of his diggings. He blamed his lack of success on the absence of building stone, on the inaccessibility of the place, and on the huge deposits of Parthian burials that mantled most of the site. His portable finds were especially disappointing: a scatter of inscribed cones and bricks and a few tablets. But enough had been done to show that Uruk was worth future exploration. "[It] may still be considered as unexplored," Loftus wrote. "The depths of its mounds are yet untouched."

Rawlinson followed the progress of Loftus's excavations with great interest. As his long term of office in Baghdad drew to a close he managed to free time for some southern excavations on his own. Soon after Loftus's departure for England in 1853, he dug briefly at Birs Nimrod (Borsippa), near Babylon. By then Rawlinson was wise in the ways of Mesopotamian architects and searched for commemorative cylinders in the corners of the great mass of brickwork, which had long been identified as a ruined ziggurat. His excavations were rewarded with dramatic success. The clay commemorative cylinders of Nebuchadnezzar came to light, recording how "Nebuchadnezzar, king of Babylon," had rebuilt and repaired the "building named the Stages of the Seven Spheres which is the wonder of Borsippa." Rawlinson published the cylinders in the *Journal of the Royal Asiatic Society*, the first positive identification of Birs Nimrod as an actual Babylonian location, rather than the hypothetical Tower of Babel.

Not content with this triumph, Rawlinson now sent J. E. Taylor, the vice-consul at Basra, on exploratory journeys into Babylonia in search of early Biblical cities. Taylor spent some time at a series of low mounds near the town of An Nasiriyah that were some three thousand yards in total circumference and associated with a two-storied structure about seventy feet high. These ruins, known as Muqayyar ("bitumen" or "cemented with bitumen"), are a high spot on the low-lying plain and are often isolated by the floodwaters of the Euphrates. Pietro della Valle had collected some cylinder seals here in 1625, and Baillie-Fraser had visited the site in 1835. In the manner of the day, Taylor tunneled into the heart of the two-storied structure, one of the best-preserved Babylonian temples because it was free of the debris of later millennia. He soon convinced himself that the "whole building was built of sun-dried bricks in the center, with a thick coating of massive, partially burnt bricks of a light red color, with layers of reeds between them." Pausing to admire the buttresses and drainage holes, Taylor now turned his attention to the southwest corner of the temple, where he found a perfectly preserved inscribed cylinder in a niche in the bricks six feet below the surface. Three other cylinders came from similar niches in the remaining corners, together with another, even more important cylinder in the north wall.

Excavations elsewhere at Muqayyar yielded inscribed bricks, dozens of burials, and abundant traces of lengthy urban occupation. The cylinders and bricks found in the temple structure proved to be highly informative. Rawlinson was forced to reevaluate his earlier theories. He now correctly identified Muqayyar with the Biblical Ur of the Chaldees, associated in Genesis with the patriarch Abraham. The temple turned out to be that of the moon god Sin. It had been built by a king named Ur-Gur about 2700 B.C. and restored two thousand years later by the Babylonian monarch Nabonidus, whose commemorative clay cylinder Taylor recovered. But Rawlinson was electrified to find that each of Nabonidus's commemorative inscriptions ended with a prayer for his eldest son Bel-shar-usur, none other than the Biblical Belshazzar, whose feast was spoiled when "the fingers of a man's hand appeared and wrote on the plaster of the wall of the king's palace." Bel-shar-usur served as coregent with his father and was the last Babylonian king. He was murdered soon after the Persians conquered Babylon. Taylor's excavations at Muqayyar were the only source of information on Ur of the Chaldees until well into the twentieth century.

Taylor also dug into Abu Shahrain, a smaller complex of mounds south of Ur, where he found traces of a large ziggurat and inscribed bricks that later identified the site as the Sumerian city of Eridu. Rawlinson now had solid historical data from cuneiform records to modify the provisional identifications of Biblical cities he had published in 1852. His new identifications of the locations of Ur and Eridu have stood the test of time. Perhaps fortunately for archaeology, the country round Ur and Eridu was so robber-infested that few European travelers visited these two sites until the twentieth century. The Turkish authorities insisted that anyone visiting Ur sign a letter releasing the Ottoman government of any responsibility for their safety.

The English were not the only Europeans interested in digging in Babylonia. The news of Loftus's first work at Uruk reached Europe just as the French were considering a new official expedition. No less a personage than the French minister of the interior, Léon Faucher, was in London in the summer of 1851, both to visit the Great Exhibition and to view the Assyrian finds in the British Museum. He examined them meticulously, then sent a request through diplomatic channels for permission to make plaster casts of some of the originals for the Louvre. He returned to Paris convinced that the French government should become involved in Mesopotamian excavations a second time; otherwise, all the prizes would fall into alien hands and French prestige would suffer. The political situation in France had settled down again. Armed with a special report from a commission of the Académie des Inscriptions, Faucher requested, and obtained, a grant of 78,000 francs from the Commission of the Budget for a "Scientific and Artistic Expedition" to Mesopotamia and Persia. The expedition was to be led by Fulgence Fresnel, a experienced Arab scholar, and former consul at Jiddah. Jules Oppert was the linguist and cuneiform expert of the party, while Félix Thomas served as artist and architect. They arrived in Mosul in March 1852.

The expedition set off for Baghdad after three weeks of preparatory work at Khorsabad, Nineveh, and Mosul. Fresnel, Oppert, and Thomas spent over three months in Baghdad debating what to do next. Rawlinson had strongly advised them to work in Persia rather than Babylonia on account of the disturbed political conditions outside the towns. But in July 1852, a rumor in the bazaars announcing the discovery of a golden statue of Nebuchadnezzar at Babylon spurred Fresnel into action. Accompanied by two regiments of Turkish troops who were on their way to Al-Hillah, the three men began excavations in the mound of Kasr at Babylon. The results were discouraging at best. They found the usual inscribed bricks, stamped, so Oppert showed, with nearly forty different signs, and glazed tiles with fragments of mosaics on them. Trenches sunk into other mounds nearby and into the summit and base of the so-called Babil tell were just as disappointing. The French worked in the Babylon area for nearly two years, gathering a scatter of antiquities and inscribed bricks from dozens of mounds and ruined buildings. Fresnel and Oppert were unable to explore the vast site fully. Nor did they throw any new light on the topography of the ancient city. Perhaps their most significant discovery came from a mound adjoining Birs Nimrod. A small, dated tablet identified the great mass of brickwork as the remains of ancient Borsippa. Unfortunately for Oppert, his translation did not appear until Henry Rawlinson had already identified the site from his own excavations there.

The French expedition broke up in February of 1854. Oppert returned to France via Mosul, where he spent six weeks with Victor Place, the new French consul, helping him decipher many of the inscriptions from his excavations at Khorsabad. Félix Thomas also went to Mosul, and assisted Place in the marathon task of recording the details of Sargon's palace. Fresnel remained in Baghdad and died of fever there the following year. The expedition's finds were tragically lost in the Al-Qurneh disaster of May 1855, when Arab raiders overturned the rafts bearing a huge load of Mesopotamian antiquities from both Assyria and the south. In spite of this, Oppert shouldered the burden of publishing his colleagues' work. His two-volume monograph appeared in 1859 and was noted for its brilliant analysis of the inscriptions from Khorsabad, Nineveh, and Babylon, and for Thomas's fine drawings. Despite Oppert's work, the finds from the southern sites were unspectacular compared with those from Khorsabad. It was to be a quarter of a century before anyone dug scientifically into the ancient cities of the south.

12

Place, Rassam, and the Royal Lion Hunt

*Thus, in my position as agent of the British
Museum, I had secured it for England.*

Wʜɪʟᴇ ᴛʜᴇ ғʀᴇɴᴄʜ busied themselves in Babylonia, Rawlinson was
still trying to find a permanent successor to Layard in Assyria. With
Loftus excavating at Susa and then at Uruk, the problem became
urgent, for there was a danger that the British government would withdraw the grant of fifteen hundred pounds for renewed Assyrian excavations. Not only that, but the French had reactivated their consulate
at Mosul. In August 1851, Léon Faucher had obtained funds not only
for the scientific expedition, but also for a renewal of the Khorsabad
excavations. Eight thousand francs was specially allocated for Khorsabad. The French foreign ministry scrutinized their personnel files for
an energetic young diplomat to direct their new Assyrian excavations,
and appointed Thomas Victor Place the new French consul at Mosul.

Place was born at Corbeil, France, on July 18, 1818, the son of a
wealthy merchant who lost all his money in speculative investments
when Place was sixteen years old. Place made his way in the world on
his own and became a career diplomat at the age of twenty-one. He
was regarded as a bright young man and served as secretary to a special
mission to Haiti and as a junior consul in Cádiz, Naples, and the
Republic of Santo Domingo. He was to serve as consul in Mosul for

three eventful years, from May 19, 1851, to November 20, 1854. Place had no archaeological qualifications whatsoever. "I recognize that one of the principal interests of the Mosul Consulate is the discovery of Nineveh," he wrote. "The administrators of the Museum have so advised me." But he had to beg a copy of Botta and Flandin's *Monuments de Ninive* from the Louvre. No one seemed interested in training him to excavate. He traveled out to Mosul with Jules Oppert and Félix Thomas, two of the three members of the scientific expedition, which was to operate in the south at the same time as Place dug at Khorsabad. The leader of the expedition, Fulgence Fresnel, was already in Mesopotamia. Place arrived in Mosul with a firman from the sultan that authorized him to dig more or less where he wished. The Académie des Inscriptions had told him to occupy as many sites as possible just as fast as he could.

Diplomatic secrets seldom lasted long in Mesopotamia. Rawlinson got wind of the Académie's instructions even before Place arrived in Mosul, and promptly increased the tempo of excavation at Kuyunjik at his own expense. At the same time he arranged to meet with Place at Samsun on the Black Sea to negotiate a division of sites for excavation. They reached a harmonious agreement whereby Place was given a clear field at Khorsabad, while the British retained Sennacherib's palace at Kuyunjik. Rawlinson raised no objection to Place's working at the northern edge of Nineveh, nor was exclusion from Nimrud mentioned. Minor sites were apparently considered fair game for everyone. Rawlinson hastened back to Mosul and directed the Kuyunjik laborers to concentrate on a chamber called the Hall of Bulls, which was yielding large numbers of inscribed tablets. At the same time he importuned the museum for both a director and an artist, preferably someone of mature years.

The museum ignored Rawlinson's pleas and sent out Charles Hodder, another young and inexperienced artist who knew nothing of the East and even less of archaeology. He reached Mosul on April 10, 1852, where he found an impatient Rawlinson trying to manage the excavations in Sennacherib's palace until his arrival. No major sculptures had been found for months, merely a steady stream of clay tablets that, said Rawlinson, "filled eight large boxes and would last students for fifty years." Rawlinson was taken aback at Hodder's youth and inexperience, but set him to work on the bas-reliefs from Sennacherib's palace. He himself watched the French and again tried to recruit Loftus, whose Susa excavations had proved abortive. As previously told, Loftus decided to return home and soon left for Uruk, even though political conditions were in one of their unsettled phases.

For some weeks, Rawlinson enjoyed the company of Captain Felix

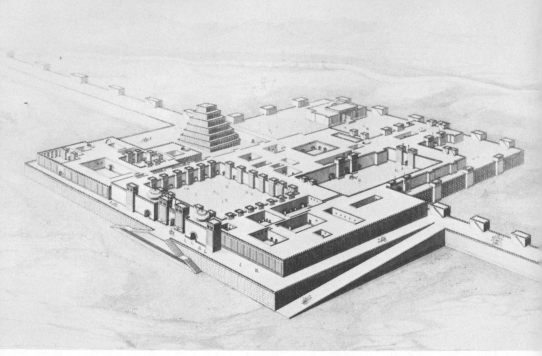

Reconstruction of Sargon II's palace at Khorsabad after the
French excavations

Jones, who was an expert surveyor in command of the river steamer
Nitoris. Jones had accompanied him to Behistun on the second visit and
had rescued Layard's Nimrud lion from the floodwaters of the Tigris
two years before. The British Museum had now commissioned him to
make a detailed survey of the area between the Tigris and the Great
Zab rivers, "yielding," they said, "to a general desire of seeing a complete picture of Assyria in her present desolation." The survey took
several months, but Jones was delighted to find that Rich's map of
Nineveh was accurate. His own survey, he said, stamped Rich's "narrative with the broad seal of truth." Jones's map was the primary source
on Nineveh for nearly a century.

Meanwhile, Victor Place had arrived in Mosul to find that only eight
thousand francs of the government subvention could be used for Assyrian excavation. He told his government that they had not given him
enough. But with the aid of Botta's foreman and many of his workmen,
Place reopened the Khorsabad excavations. For some weeks his laborers found almost nothing, so he talked of abandoning the site. Rawlinson again offered him the northern part of Kuyunjik, an offer Place
declined, for he felt it would be difficult to avoid encroaching on Layard's long-held preserves. Just as Place was about to give up, his workmen came on some bricks inscribed with King Sargon II's name. From

then on, the excavations never looked back. For two years Place excavated the remaining chambers of Sargon's palace on the summit of Khorsabad, an area three times larger than that explored by Botta. Like Layard, he dug the site by tunneling around the walls of each room. He set himself the objective of reconstructing the ancient appearance of the palace as well as finding bas-reliefs and inscriptions. He succeeded brilliantly. Fortunately he had the services of the scientific expedition's artist, Félix Thomas, who returned from Babylonia just in time to work on the intricate details of the sculptures and bas-reliefs before the finds were shipped downstream. Place recovered not only the floor plan of the palace, but four outlying gates flanked by bulls and other fine sculptures. Although his excavations did not yield as many bas-reliefs as Botta's had, they produced dozens of small objects in clay, glass, and metal. Even the bakery and Sargon's wine cellar full of painted storage jars came to light.

Place was able to publish a reconstruction of Sargon's palace in his sumptuous monograph *Ninive et l'Assyrie*, which appeared in Paris in 1866–1869. Even if his complex tunnels made an accurate survey difficult and at times he attributed to the Assyrian architects a concern for symmetry that they may not, in fact, have had, Place's excavations showed that Sargon's city had covered at least 741 acres. His palace was erected on a huge brick platform that supported the royal residence, several temples, a ziggurat, and a large open plaza. The northwest wing consisted of large halls decorated with winged bulls and bas-reliefs that glorified Sargon's deeds in peace and war. Each room had walls between nine and sixteen feet thick to provide insulation against the heat of summer and the cold of winter.

Place's systematic excavations were a scientific contribution of lasting value, for his reconstruction was based not just on observations in the field but on deciphered inscriptions as well. His monograph remained the standard source on Khorsabad until 1927, when the site was reopened. Tragically, nearly all his finds perished in the wreck of a raft near Basra in 1855, the same mishap that wiped out the scientific expedition's work and many British finds, too.

Henry Rawlinson returned to his post in Baghdad soon after Place started work at Khorsabad and was informed that the trustees of the British Museum had decided to appoint Layard's former assistant, Hormuzd Rassam, as director of excavations under Rawlinson's general supervision. Rassam was gratified to receive such an important appointment, one that allowed him two years of excavation in Assyria. He arrived in Mosul in October of 1852 and took up residence in the home of his brother Christian Rassam, the British vice-consul. Mosul was full of gossip about the French excavations at Khorsabad. Place had

put teams of sixteen workmen digging into sites all over the countryside in the hope of claiming their contents for France. In doing so, he
was merely obeying the instructions he had received from the Académie
des Inscriptions. By all accounts, he was a quiet, conscientious diplomat
of impeccable integrity. His British rival was a very different type of
person, one who at best can be described as ambitious, devious, and
ruthless in his methods. Rassam's very personality exacerbated the ri-
valry that surrounded most of his operations in Mesopotamia.

It is difficult to judge Hormuzd Rassam's character and motives. His
introduction to archaeology came when he served as Layard's loyal and
hard-working assistant, a superb mediator between a respected foreigner and his workmen. Now, he was to stand on his own feet, a local
man fully accepted by the people of Mosul as a long-standing member
of their community, but employed by a foreign organization. Unques-
tionably, Rassam had been strongly influenced by Layard and the long
periods of time he had spent in England. He espoused English customs
and mannerisms, but was acutely aware of his inferior "native" status
in the eyes of many Englishmen. He desperately wanted to be recognized as a great archaeologist. From the very beginning, he believed
that the way to recognition was through spectacular finds and ship-
loads of antiquities. He assumed, wrongly, that people would not care
exactly how he came by them.

Rassam's mettle was tested soon after his arrival. He learned that an
inhabitant of Nebi Yunus had unearthed a huge, human-headed bull
while digging a cellar for his house. Nebi Yunus was the one Nineveh
mound where no one was allowed to dig because of the holy mosque
on its summit. When news of the find reached the vice-consulate,
Rassam send Hodder to make a drawing of it. But the young artist returned home empty-handed. Place had already hurried to the scene and
had tried (unsuccessfully) to remove the bull. The pasha of Mosul now
intervened, convinced that buried treasure lay under the house. He informed all parties that the Turkish government needed antiquities as
much as anyone and sent a large gang of convicts to dig away at the
site. He did, though, allow Rassam to copy the inscriptions. He even
asked him for some experienced workmen to assist his convicts. The
excavations lasted for nine months but were hampered by the high
prices the landowners asked even of the pasha for digging on their
property and by the heavy chains the convicts always wore. There was
little to show for the work except two human-headed bulls, a bronzed
lion, and an inscribed marble tablet which indicated that Sennacherib
had built his stables and military warehouses there.

In intervals between watching the French, Rassam sent workmen to
dig as close to the limits of French territory at Kuyunjik as he dared.

He was expecting Place to start work on his Nineveh concession shortly. Meanwhile, he packed up the already-famous bas-reliefs of the siege of Lachish found by Layard, and scattered workmen on literally dozens of obscure mounds around Mosul, most of which yielded absolutely nothing. Since Place's men were operating near Nimrud, Rassam reopened that site and dug in an area east of the Central Palace. The dig soon revealed shattered fragments of a huge obelisk. It had stood near a great doorway guarded by a stone bull and a lion, both bearing inscriptions of Ashur-nasir-pal II. The North West Palace was still yielding a seemingly inexhaustible supply of bas-reliefs, this time of the king hunting lions. Unfortunately, the sculptures were badly damaged.

Both Place and Rassam had their eyes on the large mounds of ancient Assur, another Assyrian capital, investigated very superficially by Layard some years before. Before Rassam had arrived, Place had worked there, attracted to the locality by its legendary fame as the first city built by the god Assur when he came to the land of the rivers. But the dig had proved unproductive and the French had moved on elsewhere. When rumors of Rassam's plans reached the French consulate, Place (according to Rassam) determined to reestablish his excavations first. One of Rassam's brothers was getting married so Hormuzd delayed his departure for the celebrations. The day before the wedding he heard that Place's guides had set out. Immediately, he and Hodder leaped on board a large *kellek* with his equipment and some workmen and floated down to Nimrud. From there he organized a party of ninety men and reached Assur in three days. While he was en route, a galloping messenger from Mosul brought him letters from Place protesting that the French had prior claim. "I could not understand the logic of M. Place's argument," he wrote. After all, Layard had found as much as anyone there! So he ignored the complaints and pressed on, spurred by reports that the French were also on their way. Delayed by a storm, Rassam arrived later than he planned, but he immediately sent a small gang of workmen across the Tigris with Hodder to claim possession of the choice spots. There were loud cheers when a flag was hoisted on the summit of the highest mound. But, as Rassam himself approached, he heard sounds of conflict and war cries. He arrived in time to prevent bloodshed between his men and the French, who had just arrived. The unfortunate French overseer was being kept at bay, the rival Arab guide was stretched out full length on the ground, the two work gangs almost at blows. With considerable difficulty, Rassam managed to establish peace. The French, who had come overland with few tools or supplies, were permitted to dig on the eastern side of the mound while Rassam commandeered the best locations. When an indignant Place turned up three days later, he had no option but to agree to an apportionment of the mound between the two nations — to his disadvantage.

Although the French soon abandoned their trenches in disgust, Rassam persisted for three weeks. The results were disappointing, for the mud-brick buildings on the mound had crumbled. Layard had earlier found an inscribed terra-cotta cylinder bearing the name of Tiglath-Pileser I on the site. Rassam found two others, during later visits, at the corners of a square masonry platform. Tiglath-Pileser's inscription was used as the basis for the Royal Asiatic Society's cuneiform decipherment exercise in 1857.

The Assur excavations were typical of the intense competition that surfaced when Rassam started operations. Rival gangs of workmen chased each other over the countryside. A site was abandoned after superficial examination if it produced nothing. Both parties were looking for palaces and sculptures, as well as for gold and other treasure.

During the hot summer of 1853, Rassam spent much of his time packing sculpture for shipment overseas, fulfilling promises made by Henry Rawlinson. The British Museum received many prize pieces; others went to the Louvre, for Rawlinson had given Place permission to ship duplicates from Nimrud. A fine collection, including some magnificent and unique examples of Assyrian artistry, went to the Crystal Palace Company, the commercial organization operating the great Exhibition Hall. This collection eventually ended up in the Berlin Museum when the company disposed of its assets. Rawlinson has been criticized for his actions in dispersing this material to a commercial company, but in fairness to him it should be said that he was preoccupied with saving as much sculpture as possible from certain destruction.

Even the Americans started to collect some finds. An American missionary, the Reverend W. F. Williams, applied for permission to ship some duplicates to the Smithsonian Institution in the summer of 1852. With the approval of the American ambassador in London, the trustees of the British Museum, and Henry Rawlinson, a number of Ashur-nasir-pal's bas-reliefs were sent to various destinations in the United States.

When cooler weather returned, Rassam again scattered his workmen all over the countryside, "for nearly two hundred miles around," he boasted. His main efforts, however, were concentrated on the northern sector of Kuyunjik, where, he felt, the only chance of spectacular results lay. By this time Rassam seems to have been getting desperate for success. His funds were nearly exhausted and Hodder was sick. The only way to achieve results was by digging forbidden ground, that ceded to the French by Rawlinson. Place had never tried to dig on his concession in the year or more since he had been ceded it, and the landowner had been paid off by the British for years. Rassam assumed he would prefer that the English, rather than the French, excavate there. In his desperation he resolved on a secret dig at night.

On December 20, 1853, Rassam took a small team of trusted workmen to dig by moonlight at three spots in French territory, in an area where Layard had sunk some shallow trenches. Rassam ordered his men to dig much deeper, stopping work each day at dawn. The first night yielded accumulations of painted bricks and inscribed marble fragments; the second, a marble wall, which petered out after a few feet. Rassam was deeply disappointed, for, impetuously, he had reported the discovery of a new palace to Rawlinson and the British Museum the day before. So the third night he oversaw the men himself, digging around the short marble wall. The men worked in shifts without respite in a frantic search for the alleged palace. After three hours of work they uncovered a magnificent bas-relief of an Assyrian king standing in his chariot as he was about to set out on a lion hunt. The sculpture formed part of a wall of a long hall into which the men were tunneling blindly. Suddenly the earth fell away from the side of the wall, revealing the king in his chariot. The workmen paused in astonishment. "Images," gasped one of them and everyone pressed forward to wonder at Ashur-bani-pal in his chariot. The workmen sang and danced for joy. "For a moment I did not know which was the most pleasant feeling that possessed me, the joy of my faithful men or the finding of the new palace," remarked Rassam.

The early part of the night's work had been a nightmare for Rassam because word of his nocturnal diggings had filtered out in Mosul. He was not afraid of the French but of the Ottoman authorities, who were, he knew, fascinated with buried treasure. The discovery of the palace relieved his anxiety, for it was an unwritten law that whoever excavated a palace had rights to it. "Thus," wrote Rassam proudly, "in my position as agent of the British Museum, I had secured it for England." He now boldly kept a new shift of workmen digging in the daytime. Victor Place was at Khorsabad when news of Rassam's coup arrived. He hastened to Kuyunjik to find his rival and the new discovery surrounded by hundreds of fascinated spectators. He protested the trespass but to no avail. Rassam calmly told him that Rawlinson had no authority to give away the concession anyhow, for the British had indemnified the landowner since Layard's time. And with that, Place had to be satisfied. After acidly congratulating Rassam on his good fortune, he left, uttering threats of protests to higher authority.

By the end of that remarkable day, Rassam's workmen had cleared all the upper part of the hall. A sequence of bas-reliefs, about five feet high, depicted the story of the entire lion hunt. First, Ashur-bani-pal is seen entering his chariot while attendants prepare the horses and hand him weapons. Next, the king is standing in his chariot about to set off (the first relief to come to light). Then, in succession, he is shown in vigorous pursuit of a lion, bow drawn; spearing his prey; and engaging yet another lion in combat. Additional reliefs picture him in other heroic postures of the chase. The haunting depiction of a lioness, dying in agony, is part of the sequence. So are scenes of caged beasts waiting release for the hunt, and pictures of all the bustle of a royal hunt and the ceremonies associated with it. Above the reliefs extended courses of crumbled, sun-dried bricks painted with other hunting scenes and war scenes, most of which had perished in the intervening centuries.

When Rassam started to clear the floor of this remarkable chamber he came across a great concentration of clay tablets thickly strewn about in apparent chaos. One has the impression that Rassam regarded tablets as somewhat of a nuisance in the midst of his palace. He simply instructed his men to gather them up and stack them in packing cases. Had he realized that this cache was to turn out to be one of the most important treasures of information on the Assyrians ever recovered, he might have been more careful. Just over three years before, Layard had recovered a part of Ashur-bani-pal's library in two small chambers in the South West Palace. Now Rassam, working in the North Palace, had stumbled across the main body of his archives, stored in the great hall of the royal residence, on the face of it a most unlikely place for a library. Rassam never bothered to record the exact provenience of the priceless archive. He casually wondered whether the tablets had been stored in the hall after the king's death while Kuyunjik was under siege. In retrospect it seems probable that the library was kept on a floor above the great hall and tumbled down when the hall ceiling collapsed. A team of British Museum experts was still unpacking, cataloguing, and deciphering Ashur-bani-pal's library twenty years later.

Every workman at Rassam's disposal was now deployed at the North Palace in teams of seven: a digger, a basket filler, and five carriers. These massive efforts began to show results when another long chamber came to light southwest of the lion-hunt hall. It contained bas-reliefs that depicted an orchard with tame lions and dogs exercising among the trees. Nearby was a twenty-foot-square room adorned with scenes of Ashur-bani-pal's campaigns in Persia. The chamber was guarded by two pairs of colossal mythical figures, one with a lion's head and an eagle's talons. These hideous personages were the equivalent of the winged bulls or lions found at the entrances to other Assyrian palaces. Much of the palace had been destroyed and later quarried for building materials. Alas, Rassam had no option but

"In my lordly sport, they let a fierce lion of the plain out of his
cage, and on foot I shot him with arrows, but did not kill him."
Detail from one of Ashur-bani-pal's lion-hunt bas-reliefs at Nineveh
(*c. 645* B.C.)

to make a superficial examination of his new palace, for the discovery
came, as these finds often do, just as he was running out of funds and
preparing to return to England. As it was, he postponed his departure
for three months to clear the rooms southeast of the lion-hunt hall. The
situation was tricky. Hodder had come down with an intestinal complaint so serious that he had to be sent to Baghdad for medical attention
and then home. Rassam had no one to help him record the elaborate
bas-reliefs before their removal. His excavations were hurried and
careless. And Rawlinson was so preoccupied with official business in
Baghdad that he could pay only a flying visit to Mosul to see the
finds. He selected the best pieces for shipment and offered the duplicates to the French for the Louvre.

Six months before Rassam had discovered the North Palace, a group
of influential people in London, including the prince consort, had

formed a private endowment known as the Assyrian Exploration Fund, with the intention of carrying on work in Mesopotamia once official funds ran out. This new digging sponsor came as somewhat of an embarrassment to Rawlinson, Rassam, and Place, for it introduced another competitive element in an already-crowded field. An irritated Rawlinson suggested that the fund work in the south.

Nothing loath, the directors of the fund hired William Kennet Loftus to work at Uruk for the second time (as described in the previous chapter). When the excavations proved unproductive, Rawlinson prevailed on Loftus to release the artist Boutcher to work at Kuyunjik. Boutcher reached the North Palace in time to receive a briefing from Rassam and to carry on where Hodder had left off. His drawings are the only surviving record of Ashur-bani-pal's palace.

In early April of 1854, Rassam all but closed down the excavations at Kuyunjik and Nimrud, leaving Boutcher with a single team of excavators. Reaching England after a bitterly cold journey, he discovered that the trustees had obtained another fifteen hundred pounds from the treasury specifically for the removal of the North Palace sculptures. They promptly asked him to return to Nineveh, which he agreed to do. But on the eve of his departure he was offered an appointment as a political administrator at Aden under the East India Company, a post that offered permanent employment. The trustees allowed him to take up this opportunity and informed Rawlinson that the grant was still available and should be used. This put Rawlinson in a difficult position. By now he had reluctantly authorized Loftus to dig at Kuyunjik after Rassam, but had made it clear that only the museum had a concession to remove sculptures from there. Rawlinson may have distrusted Loftus's motives, for he had learned that Loftus's employers had been offered five hundred pounds by Kaiser Wilhelm IV of Prussia to assemble some sculptures for his collections. Wilhelm IV had already supported the famous Lepsius Expedition to Egypt, which had yielded fine scholarly results. Apparently he did not want to miss an opportunity to make a mark in Assyria as well.

Loftus dug for weeks on the west side of the North Palace without result. He was planning to give up when his workmen found a wall of sculptured slabs at a level twenty feet below Rassam's cuttings. The new trench was rapidly approaching the North Palace, indeed threatened to undermine it. In considerable agitation Christian Rassam, who was watching over the situation for Rawlinson, put six gangs of workmen on the old dig in an attempt to forestall any raiding of sculptures. Just when the situation was becoming delicate, news arrived that the Assyrian Exploration Fund had decided to merge its efforts with those of the British Museum. To Rawlinson's relief, Loftus and Boutcher

A kellek *carrying a Nimrud bull. Painting probably attributable to F. C. Cooper*

promptly became the museum's employees. They unearthed magnificent garden scenes and more pictures of the chase. The rooms in which the new reliefs were found were marked on a master plan compiled by Boutcher. Many years later Rassam published the plan without any acknowledgment of the source. Boutcher's drawings were widely admired, and those that have survived justify this admiration.

Boutcher was eager to try a new device as well, "to apply the Photograph." He ordered a "new instrument from Paris, adapted to the wax-paper process," which he felt would be most suitable for the climate. Unfortunately, his new instrument never reached him. But Victor Place did use a camera with some success at Khorsabad. Unlike Egypt, where photographers like Francis Frith were working as early as 1857, Mesopotamia's ancient mounds did not receive real photographic attention until the 1880s, by which time irreparable damage had been done to the ziggurats and royal palaces.

By the end of 1854 the first excavations in Assyria were drawing to a close. Henry Rawlinson felt that his work was done. He left Loftus to select forty cases of Kuyunjik finds that were to follow eighty cases of Rassam's lion hunt and tablets to London. The remainder of the Kuyunjik materials were either given over to the French or abandoned. Place had packed 235 crates onto heavily loaded *kelleks*, including material from both Kuyunjik and Nineveh for the Louvre and the British Museum, as well as his Khorsabad finds. Kaiser Wilhelm had twenty-four cases in the same shipment. The *kelleks* reached Baghdad safely but were delayed there because of a shipping shortage caused by the Crimean War. In spite of warnings from Rawlinson that political conditions were highly unsettled downstream and that the flood embankments could burst suddenly, the convoy left Baghdad on May 13, 1855. Five days later the *kelleks* were attacked and plundered near Al-Qurneh. The marauding tribesmen tipped the crates into the Tigris and killed several of the crewmen. When news of the disaster reached Basra, frantic attempts were made to salvage the precious cargoes. Seventy-eight crates of the original shipment were recovered, twenty-six of them destined for the Louvre. Kaiser Wilhelm never received his sculptures. Only two crates of Place's Khorsabad finds ever reached Paris. The loss to science was incalculable. Fortunately, the fifty crates containing Ashur-bani-pal's lion hunt were not shipped until the next year and reached England safely.

A few months before the Al-Qurneh disaster, the Assyrian Exploration Fund wound up its affairs. All the British Museum's funds were exhausted, so Loftus's Kuyunjik excavations were never published, partly on account of "the present disturbed state of the East." When the fifty crates of his finds arrived in London, the museum had to store them in the basement. There was no space to put their contents on display. The trustees had already decided not to apply for further government support for Mesopotamian excavations. All the palaces of Assyria had apparently been discovered and most of their treasures removed. So much sculpture had been found, indeed, that there was a positive embarrassment of Assyrian kings in London and Paris. The public had lost interest in the subject as the sensations of the Crimean War crowded the front pages of the newspapers. Only the scholars continued their passionate interest in the hundreds of cuneiform tablets shipped home by Layard, Rassam, and Loftus.

Henry Rawlinson left Baghdad for the last time in 1855. His forceful visits to the British Museum ensured that decipherment, classification, and study were continued. Loftus died of heatstroke aboard ship on his way home in 1858. Victor Place returned to Paris to write his study of Khorsabad. What he felt about the Al-Qurneh disaster is not recorded. He never returned to archaeology but continued his diplomatic career in Turkey and New York until his death in 1875. The French were as uninterested in further excavations as their rivals. When the French consul in Mosul, Victor Place's successor, applied for official funds to dig, the minister in Paris replied firmly, "No, the excavations are completed, we have spent enough." It was to be nearly twenty years before foreign archaeologists were to dig in Mesopotamia anew.

13

The Deluge Tablets

I saw at once that I had here discovered a portion at least of the Chaldean account of the Deluge.

AFTER THE CRIMEAN WAR, the focus of Assyrian scholarship shifted from the field to the quiet of libraries and museums. A small band of cuneiform scholars continued to sift through the huge archives of clay tablets from Ashur-bani-pal's library at Kuyunjik. Since the tablets were the property of the British Museum, the experts tended to congregate in London, where scholars from all over Europe would gather in the cramped study room of the Department of Oriental Antiquities. The work of translation took years to complete, for many of Ashur-bani-pal's tablets were in a poor state and had never been sorted out, pieced together, or even cleaned properly. In the 1860s and 1870s, there were no textbooks on cuneiform or Assyrian grammar. Everything had to be learned at first hand, by copying, translating, and annotating tablets, and by relying on the experience of older scholars. Rawlinson and his friend Jules Oppert were instrumental in training the Assyriologists who were to make even closer correlations between the Scriptures and ancient Mesopotamia than the pioneers had succeeded in doing. In 1862 Rawlinson himself published a provisional chronology of Assyrian history that provided a basis for comparing Assyrian events with the Old Testament. A year later he translated a tablet that gave a history of Assyria and Babylonia. The philologist Edwin Norris, who had published the authoritative Elamite version of the Behistun inscriptions in 1855, spent years working on an Assyrian dictionary. Though it remained unfinished at his death in 1872, the three volumes that were published were invaluable as a basic source on Assyrian vocabularies, to be set alongside a steady stream of grammatical studies from French scholars like Joachim Menant, who worked on King Hammurabi's Babylonia inscriptions. By 1876, it was a widely studied script, but one still based almost entirely on the Kuyunjik tablets.

The Department of Oriental Antiquities was in the genial charge of Samuel Birch, one of the most influential orientalists of the late nineteenth century. Birch reported to the secretary of the museum but relied heavily on colleagues like Rawlinson for advice and overseas contacts. Incredible though it may seem, Birch never visited Egypt or Mesopotamia. Yet his tiny, cramped office over the museum heating plant was a major center of Egyptology and Assyriology in Europe for half a century. Birch was a vigorous, hard-working man "of generous build." He sported a short, white beard in later life and a mustache trimmed, it was alleged, to make him look ferocious. Whatever the weather, he wore a black broadcloth coat and light trousers. His black, chimney-pot silk hat was, his friend Wallis Budge wrote, "quite the worst in the museum, which is saying a good deal." One American visitor described him as looking like a "cross between a jockey and a bishop."

It was Birch who bore the full load of the mass of Near Eastern correspondence that descended on the museum. He advised scholars all over the world about cuneiform, hieroglyphs, and excavations. Visitors arrived in droves, too, not only serious scholars, dealers, and publishers, but casual inquirers and the inevitable cranks. Conspicuous among the latter were "experts" on Biblical chronology who were trying to reconcile newly translated tablets from Nineveh with the Scriptures. They would invariably begin by challenging the accuracy of the translation, then produce large charts that purported to give the exact day and month, even the hour, when events in the Bible occurred. Birch always remembered the gentleman who, when asked when Adam and Eve were expelled from the Garden of Eden, consulted his chart and replied, "They were turned out at sunset on Friday the twentieth day of the month Tebheth, four thousand, seven hundred and thirteen years before Christ." It transpired that they had lived in the garden for eighty-nine days, seven and a half hours. Argument with such visitors was useless, so Birch used to sit back and let them run on until they ran out of patience, breath, and ideas.

Birch was also busily engaged in acquiring Egyptian and Mesopotamian antiquities from dealers in the Near East and all over Europe. Although official excavations had ceased after Rassam's expedition in 1855, unofficial diggings, especially near Baghdad, supplied a steady stream of cylinders, tablets, and other antiquities for museums and collectors on both sides of the Atlantic. A flourishing illegal trade started in Baghdad and ended in dealers' stores near the British Museum and the Louvre. Nearly all these finds, many of them priceless tablets, had no known provenience and forgeries were commonplace.

Birch had another invaluable quality. He encouraged enthusiastic young scholars to become involved in the work of his department. He allowed them free access to his records and the departmental collections on condition that they work seriously at translation or tablet preparation. As a result, his hospitable office and study room became a mecca for gifted students, among them one George Smith.

Smith was the classic, ivory-tower scholar, a quiet and shy man with a nervous manner whose only interest in life appeared to be Assyrian texts. He was an engraver's apprentice by trade, but became interested in cuneiform while very young, having read Rawlinson's work and corresponded with him. "He had a broad, high forehead, and keen eyes set rather close together," wrote a colleague, who commented on his "curiously pointed fingertips."

Smith succeeded in deciphering a new account of Shalmaneser's war against Jehu, the king of Judah, which caused considerable interest when it was published in 1866. Soon he was hired by the British Museum to assist Rawlinson in the preparation of additional volumes of *Cuneiform Inscriptions of Western Asia*. Between 1867 and 1871, Smith closeted himself in a small room in the museum and produced a whole series of important translations of Assyrian and Babylonian history. The staff of the department saw little of him — he kept to himself. He was absorbed in translation and neglected cataloguing for the more exciting and arduous work of interpretation. His main preoccupation was Ashur-bani-pal's library. He divided hundreds of tiny fragments into seven broad categories of subject matter, one of which was mythology. In 1872, when he came to sort through this pile more carefully, he came across "half of a curious tablet which had evidently contained originally six columns." He scanned the columns and noticed in the third one a reference to a ship resting on the "mountains of Nizir, followed by the account of the sending forth of the dove, and its finding no resting place and returning. I saw at once that I had here discovered a portion at least of the Chaldean account of the Deluge." The earnest students in the study room were electrified when Smith laid down the tablet on the table and jumped up and rushed around

One of the fragments of the eleventh tablet of the Epic of
Gilgamesh, which gave George Smith a version of the Babylonian
story of the Flood. The tablet came from Ashur-bani-pal's library
at Nineveh.

the room "in a great state of excitement, and, to the astonishment of those present, began to undress himself." When he calmed down Smith reexamined the first fragment and found it covered about half the story. A more thorough search of the pile revealed eleven other fragments of the same epic. Oppert and Rawlinson had lit upon traces of this legend before, but it was not until Smith pieced it together that its true significance was appreciated.

It was a thoroughly dignified and fully dressed George Smith who lectured to an overflow audience of the Biblical Archaeological Society on December 3, 1872. Rawlinson presided over the meeting, which was attended by Prime Minister Gladstone and a distinguished gathering of archaeologists, philologists, and theologians. Smith's lecture was a masterpiece of modesty that generated prolonged discussion afterward. "The meeting," said *The Times* in a glowing review next day, "concluded at a late hour."

What Smith revealed was a version of a deluge myth that showed marked resemblances to the story of the Flood in Genesis. He translated the eleventh tablet for his lecture audience, the one that dealt with the "Chaldean Deluge." The hero Izdubar learns from a seer named Hasisadra how he survived a great flood sent by the gods to punish humankind. The tablet told how Hasisadra made a large ship which was planked and caulked with bitumen. Into it he loaded all his family, "the beast of the field, the animal of the field, the sons of the people, all of them, I caused to go up." Then the flood came and "destroyed all life from the face of the earth." It rained for six days and nights but cleared on the seventh. The ship went aground on the "mountain of Nizir." Hasisadra "sent forth a dove and it left. The dove went and turned, and a resting place it did not find, and it returned." Eventually a raven was dispatched and did not come back. So Hasisadra released the animals, became a god, and lived happily ever after.

George Smith was well aware that the texts he had discovered would be by no means the only account of the Babylonian flood. He suspected, rightly, that they could be traced to even earlier myths. We know now that that they were part of a masterpiece of Sumerian and Akkadian literature called the *Epic of Gilgamesh*. The flood story comes from the eleventh tablet of the epic. Gilgamesh hears the tale of the flood from the mouth of its hero, Atram-hasis ("exceedingly wise"). The original Babylonian flood legend came from another poem, the *Epic of Atram-hasis*, which was a history of humankind. A large part of this epic is lost, but enough is known about its content for scholars to reconstruct the original story of the flood in reasonable detail. The Sumerian prototype of the Babylonian *Epic of Atram-hasis* was found in the archives at Nippur, a hundred lines of an original three-hundred-line epic.

All versions of the flood story are a highly dramatic narrative of gods and people. The *Epic of Atram-hasis* tells how the world was created and how the gods felt that someone should be in charge of it. The mother-goddess Mami created the first man, made of the flesh and blood of a minor god mixed with clay. Humankind is born, the first cities built, and kingship established. But the world's population becomes so numerous and troublesome that the chief god, Enlil, decides to destroy humanity with a great flood. The devout king of Suruppak, Atram-hasis, is warned of the impending flood by the god Enki. He builds a large boat, takes aboard his family, some craftsmen, and the "beasts of the field." Gilgamesh then hears the sequel, which is lost in the original *Epic of Atram-hasis*. The deluge destroys everyone else, but Atram-hasis' ship floats on the waters and grounds on Mount Nisir (Pir-Omar Gudoun) east of the Tigris. He sends out first a dove, then a swallow, to reconnoiter the earth. When they return, he dispatches a raven, who never comes back. Atram-hasis and his crew then recolonize the world. As a reward for his faith, Atram-hasis and his wife are granted immortality by Enlil. Gilgamesh fails in his quest for the same eternal life, for death is the lot of mortals.

Smith's revelations caused an ecclesiastical and scientific sensation. Public interest in Mesopotamian archaeology enjoyed a dramatic revival after twenty years of indifference. The Deluge Tablets were displayed at the British Museum and drew large crowds. But the account was incomplete. In his lecture Smith had told how he had managed to piece together most of the epic from duplicate tablets. But there remained tantalizing gaps, especially one of seventeen lines from the very first column of the first tablet. The *Daily Telegraph* saw a unique opportunity for a news story and promptly offered the British Museum a thousand guineas for a new excavation at Nineveh to find the missing lines, provided Smith led the expedition and sent regular accounts to the paper. The trustees accepted their offer. Smith took a six-month leave of absence and left for Mosul on January 20, 1873.

Smith was hardly an ideal choice as director of a major excavation. He had never traveled outside Europe, nor had he any experience with handling Arab workmen, let alone of excavation. In those days the latter was no disqualification, for no one had thought deeply about archaeological technique. One must admire Smith's single-minded courage and devotion to his beloved tablets, for his health was far from robust. He first traveled to Paris to visit the Louvre, where he inspected the Khorsabad finds, then continued on to Marseilles, Palermo, and Antakya in Syria. After only a day in Antakya, he was on the road for Mosul. The trip took a month, Smith's first taste of the vagaries of Eastern travel and of flea-ridden lodging houses.

The pasha of Mosul received Smith courteously enough, but declared that instructions he had been sent from Baghdad prohibited foreigners from inspecting or excavating any archaeological sites in his district. When the pasha forbade Smith even to look at the sites, Smith called on the French consul for help, there being no British representative in Mosul at the time. When that failed, he decided to float down to Baghdad while awaiting the firman from Constantinople that the British Museum had applied for months before. He stopped briefly at Nimrud and Assur and spent a valuable month at the British residency while he examined Babylon, Birs Nimrod, and other sites. Like so many travelers, Smith lamented the lack of excavation at Babylon, and longed for a chance to dig in the mounds there. He realized they were a potential gold mine of information, one that would no doubt confirm the records on the tablets he had already worked on.

It was April 3 before Smith could start excavating. By then the firman had come through and he had ridden back to Mosul. There he found Layard's old foreman, Toma Shishman, who was, commented Smith, "very fat and short-winded." He claimed to know everything about the mounds, and that his services were indispensable. Smith was not impressed, and in any case planned a small-scale excavation at Nimrud first. He hoped to obtain there additional inscriptions that would throw light on the reign of the relatively unknown monarch Tiglath-Pileser II, as well as to verify information known from previously excavated and deciphered tablets. His excavations were conducted with a priceless advantage: his fluent knowledge of cuneiform, which could be used on the spot to establish the identity of buildings, sculptures, or the content of inscriptions. Smith focused his attention on the Temple of Nebo, where he duly found a tablet describing Tiglath-Pileser II's reign. The excavations continued for a month, while he checked inscriptions unearthed by Layard in the South West Palace, attemped to find foundation cylinders in the huge ziggurat tunneled into twenty years before, and uncovered new chambers in the South East Palace. The finds, by Layard's standards, were far from spectacular, but Smith did obtain some valuable inscriptions. It was a sign of the economic impact of the Layard excavations that the village of Nimrud had fallen on bad times since his departure.

On May 7, 1873, Smith turned his attention to Kuyunjik, starting excavations at three locations in the library areas of Sennacherib's South West Palace, and the southeast corner of Ashur-bani-pal's palace. Unlike his predecessors, Smith had no interest in bas-reliefs, just in terra-cotta cylinders and clay tablets. Any form of excavation was difficult, for the palace sites were honeycombed with abandoned tunnels and deep trenches. Some inscriptions came to light in Sennacherib's palace, but the North Palace of Ashur-bani-pal was a mess. The local people had quarried for building purposes the stones exposed by Rassam. Heavy boulders had to be shifted with crowbars to get at the archaeological deposits. The work proceeded slowly until the evening of May 14, when Smith sat down to examine the cuneiform tablets found during the day's work. To his amazement, one of them "contained the greater part of the seventeen lines of inscription belonging to the first column of the Chaldean account of the Deluge, and fitting into the only place where there was a serious blank in the story." As soon as the tablet was copied, Smith telegraphed the *Daily Telegraph*, which published the sensational discovery on May 21, 1873. The missing fragment had come to light only a week after the Kuyunjik digging began.

To Smith's astonishment, the *Daily Telegraph* now instructed him to close down the excavations. They had achieved their editorial objective and were no longer interested. Smith had enough time to sift through the debris of previous excavations and to find some more interesting cylinders and tablets, including some dealing with creation legends, but dutifully left Mosul on June 8 after only a month of digging. It was some months before the finds reached London. The Turkish authorities in Izkenderun seized them as illegal exports. Only the direct intervention of the British ambassador in Constantinople secured their release. The tablets still reside in the British Museum, labeled DT (Daily Telegraph).

The complete Deluge Tablets continued to cause a sensation in London, so the British Museum decided to send Smith out on a second trip to Nineveh, in order to benefit from the rest of the sultan's firman. Only four months after returning to London, Smith was on his way to Mosul again. He found the Turkish authorities far from sympathetic to his return. The sultan had decreed that half of all the finds must go to the Imperial Ottoman Museum in Constantinople. When Smith pointed out that his objective was to find fragments of inscriptions, the authorities laughed in disbelief. From this point on he excavated in an atmosphere of distrust, forbidden to work anywhere other than at Kuyunjik.

For years, Smith had been convinced that Layard's library chamber in Sennacherib's palace contained but a portion of the royal archives. Layard had literally shoveled an irregular mass of tablets into baskets and shipped them in crates to England in bulk. Smith believed that the tablets found by his predecessor had fallen into the chamber from rooms on the second story when the palace was destroyed. To test this hypothesis, he excavated an oval area some seven hundred feet around, ordering his men not to tunnel into the mounds, but to remove the huge piles of excavated soil from the surface of the deposits first. He recovered many tablet fragments from these heaps in the process, then dug through the hard-packed upper levels of the mound. At first only modern objects came to light. Then cuneiform tablets became more and more plentiful as the trenches penetrated to greater depths. Smith was clearing the fill from halls and chambers that Layard had tunneled through by following the walls. Numerous tablets were found on the floors: invaluable bilingual lists, historical and mythological data, and histories of Sargon II, Ashur-bani-pal, and other monarchs. Eventually over three thousand priceless tablets came from three months of excavation. Smith's hunch had proved to be absolutely correct.

At the beginning, Smith had employed only forty men, but the pressure of time imposed by the firman (it would expire in March 1874) was such that he engaged more and more diggers until an incredible army of nearly six hundred men were laboring away. "When they were at work, the mound presented an interesting appearance of bustle and activity," remarked Smith in one of the classic understatements of archaeology. It was a miracle that he found anything at all in the chaos. To add to his anxieties, the Turkish authorities were a constant nuisance, interfering with the dig and charging him with desecrating Moslem graves, of not paying adequate rent for the ground. At times the weather was so cold that pools of water on the mound were frozen all day. Then the Tigris overflowed and the vast labor force had to be ferried across the river by boat from Mosul.

On March 12, 1874, Smith closed down the dig and prepared to leave for England. But the pasha of Mosul claimed half his finds and only let him depart when the sultan of Turkey gave orders that he be allowed to leave provided he left half his duplicates behind. Smith lacked the authority and experience that Botta and Layard had enjoyed in dealing with the Arabs and the Turks. His bookish personality must have seemed incongruous to the authorities. But the scale of his operations show that he was no weakling and was determined to achieve his declared objectives. In the 1870s, it was far harder to work in Mesopotamia than in Layard's day, for the Turkish government was now well aware of the significance and value of Assyrian antiquities. Fortunately, the objectives of the British Museum's operations had shifted from sculpture to small objects, and especially to clay tablets, so Smith was able to take most of his finds with him.

The furor over the Assyrian tablets continued unabated upon Smith's return to London. He succeeded in matching many of the tablets from his new excavations with those from his earlier diggings and Layard's collections. In 1875, the museum sent him out for a third dig, but this time he went to Constantinople first, so he could help the British ambassador obtain a new firman. He ended up waiting there for five months, arriving eventually at Mosul in March of 1876, too near summer to start work. He decided to return to London at once, and against everyone's advice, he insisted on crossing the desert to the Mediterranean in the heat. Already weary from months of negotiation and arduous travel, Smith contracted dysentery about four days' ride from Aleppo and died on August 19, 1876. Right up to his final journey, he worked on his cuneiform tablets, including a remarkable specimen that gave an account of the construction of the temple of Belus at Babylon. The ziggurat had been built with seven great steps, then capped with a temple that was visible from a great distance.

Smith's possessions and his precious tablets were shipped on to London by the British consul in Aleppo. His travel notes showed that he had worried about the safety of his precious tablets right up to the end. As he lay dying, he scribbled in his small notebook that the thirty-five tablets "are in my long boots . . . in my trunk." His last entry added: "my work has been entirely for the science."

Smith's unexpected death left a sudden vacuum in the British Museum. The tremendous surge in public interest over the Deluge Tablets had not passed by the dealers in Baghdad, who promptly shipped large new shipments of cylinders and tablets to London, Berlin, and Paris. Birch and Rawlinson were worried by the increased illegal traffic. Clearly the new tablets came from unexcavated sites in the south, tells like Nippur and Telloh. A group of scholars now urged the museum trustees to apply for a firman to dig not only in Assyria but in Babylonia as well. The epic poems from the Kuyunjik libraries made repeated reference to Uruk, Eridu, and other southern sites, which promised rich rewards for those patient enough to excavate them over a long period of time.

While the trustees agreed that further excavation was desirable, the problem was to find a suitable archaeologist to direct the work, someone familiar both with tell excavation and with local conditions. It so happened that Hormuzd Rassam had just resigned his political appointment in Aden after a fascinating and checkered career that took him as far afield as Zanzibar and Abyssinia. He had been asked to work with George Smith and had refused, but now he accepted the unsalaried post of director of excavations. His appointment heralded the beginning of a new scramble for Mesopotamian antiquities, one that focused not on sculptures but on archives and on cuneiform tablets and cylinders. It was to be an appointment the trustees were more than once to regret.

14

Gates and Palaces

All the Assyrian and Babylonian mounds,
where ancient cities and temples were found,
require a regular digging up.

THE OCCASIONAL SOCIAL reforms of the nineteenth-century Turkish sultans placed considerable emphasis on public education and included the
founding of the Imperial Ottoman Museum of Antiquities. The beginnings of the museum go back to the mid-nineteenth century, but at
that time the collections consisted of little more than some scattered
archaeological finds dumped in an ancient church courtyard. In 1877,
the sultan decided to reorganize the museum along the lines of the
Bulak Museum in Cairo. His purpose was not only to house some local
antiquities in the East, but also to stem the rapidly increasing traffic in
illegal antiquities that had centered in Baghdad from the 1850s onward.

The sultan designated a quaint early Turkish palace, the Tshinili
Kiosk, as the museum building. The first Turkish director general of
the museum was Hamdi Bey, a quiet yet effective man who had received art training in Paris. After an early career as a government administrator in Baghdad and elsewhere, Hamdi Bey found his niche in
the director-generalship. Hampered by inadequate funds and government apathy, he nevertheless succeeded in making the museum a viable
repository for antiquities and managed to obtain the funds for a larger,
permanent building. Hamdi Bey collected antiquities from all over the

Ottoman Empire and directed excavations in Lebanon and Mesopotamia for the Turkish government. Anyone applying for a firman had to negotiate with him on the details. Hamdi Bey was highly sensitive to the interests of his government. He revised the antiquities laws in 1881, making them even more stringent. The new permits specified precise physical and time limits for the excavations and gave instructions for the disposal of the finds. Every excavation was required to pay the wages of a Turkish government commissioner, who joined the dig and supervised the work on Constantinople's behalf. For a quarter of a century the dedicated and hard-working Hamdi Bey, "slightly built" and with "a pair of dark, extraordinary eyes that looked through one and beyond," controlled the destiny of excavations in Iraq.

The Imperial Ottoman Museum had only just been founded when Hormuzd Rassam arrived in Constantinople to negotiate a new firman for Assyrian excavations. Forewarned by George Smith's difficulties in 1876, Rassam was prepared to be patient. After three and a half months, he left empty-handed. Anglo-Turkish relations were at a low ebb, the British ambassador, Sir Henry Elliot, unsympathetic, and the Porte downright hostile. Just as the British Museum was giving up hope, the Foreign Office appointed Austen Henry Layard the new British ambassador to Constantinople in April 1877. Although Russia and Turkey were at war and the sultan was preoccupied with military affairs, Layard approached him personally. Such was the weight of his authority and prestige that a firman on very generous terms was forthcoming at once.

Rassam reached Mosul and Baghdad in December and started work at Kuyunjik on January 7, 1878. He had not been near an archaeological site for nearly twenty years. A great deal of archaeology had been carried out in Europe and Egypt since then, and excavation techniques were slowly changing for the better. But Mesopotamian archaeology had remained a backwater, unaffected by the new, more rigorous excavation methods that had been pioneered by German scholars at Olympia in Greece since 1874. The Germans never dug at Olympia without artists, an architect, and photographers in attendance. Their results were promptly published in sumptuous monographs. Hormuzd Rassam was totally unaware of these developments. His instructions from the trustees were simple and specific: "Find as many fragments as possible from the libraries of Assur-bani-pal and Sennacherib, for the completion of the records which were already amongst the national collection in London." Rassam, however, had set his sights higher. He remembered the fame and fortune that had come Layard's way a quarter century before. Unwilling to concentrate all his energies on such a tame undertaking as mere clay tablets, he decided to look for new, unexplored sites that would yield spectacular finds like Layard's lions and sculptures. These, he felt, would gratify the British public, "especially those who valued such discoveries either for their Biblical or literary studies."

As soon as Rassam's arrival became known, dozens of Layard's former workmen descended on Mosul, not only the veteran diggers, but their sons and relatives as well. He wanted four or five hundred men, an expense that was bound to strain his limited purse. For some reason the Arabs liked working for Rassam, probably because he was a respected local man and there was no other employment. So he took advantage of them and paid only about three fourths of the regular laborer's wage for the Mosul area. As a result he was able to engage a larger number of men than would otherwise have been possible. His long experience of manpower problems under Layard enabled him to get away with this economy, sweetened as it was with the occasional gift of an ox for a feast. Within a few weeks, digs at Kuyunjik and Nimrud were in full swing.

The Kuyunjik and Nimrud excavations were conducted by Rassam at a distance, but with Christian overseers who knew something of inscriptions and clay tablets. Instead of following the walls of Ashur-bani-pal's palace, they continued Smith's work, clearing chambers and breaking down brick walls that were in the way. The overseers found numerous tablets, the most important find a cylinder with thirteen hundred lines of cuneiform inscription describing the conquests and empire of Ashur-bani-pal. Nimrud yielded a temple built by Ashur-nasir-pal II, located near the North West Palace. The walls were gone and the beautiful glazed ceiling tiles were in thousands of fragments.

These excavations were a sideline with the indefatigable Rassam. Fortunately for him, he was operating with a temporary, telegraphed firman that spelled out no restrictions. When the official one came — it imposed the usual strict conditions, including a provision for sharing finds with the Ottoman government — Rassam kept it to himself. Without Layard and his own friends in Mosul, he would have been in trouble. The sultan had written that an official commissioner, on salary from the British Museum, was to be present at all excavations. This clause was removed on the insistence of Layard, who also pulled strings to allow Rassam to export everything. The new breed of firman was restrictive even for a highly responsible excavator. For a licensed plunderer like Rassam, a tailor-made permit was impossible. He had to use all his diplomatic and bargaining skills to achieve his objective at a time when excavation in the Layard style was becoming an anachronism.

Nowhere did Rassam need his skills more than in his excavation of the mound at Balawat, fifteen miles east of Mosul. Some time before, an Arab digging a grave into Balawat had come across a large bronze plate embossed with human figures. He had broken it up and sold it to the French consul and some of Rassam's friends. The latter in turn sent some fragments to Rassam, who hastened to investigate. He was relieved to find that the discovery had been made in a part of the mound that was devoid of gravestones. But the local villagers would be certain to object if he dug there, on the grounds that he might disturb recent graves nearby. So Rassam came to terms with the landowners and started work with his own men, knowing that trouble would come as the first spadeful was turned. He was right. Yelling villagers forced a stop to the dig, as Rassam knew they would. After prolonged negotiations, he promised to employ some local people to watch for graves and to stop the digging when necessary. To Rassam's relief, his stratagem worked and there were no further problems.

The very next day the workmen came across huge bronze panels lying at an angle in the ground. The tops lay four feet from the surface, the bases fifteen feet below it. The plates had to be removed in large pieces, for they started to crack on exposure to the air. They proved to be the coverings of a huge gate with double doors, originally hung from a wooden frame. Each door had seven eight-foot bronze panels, set in cedarwood. The bronze hinges had rotated in stone sockets. "The plates which are embossed with a variety of subjects such as battle scenes, triumphal processions and religious performances, are divided into two panels surrounded by a border of rosettes," wrote Rassam. He had found the bronze gates of Shalmaneser III, now one of the great treasures of the British Museum. Balawat has since been shown to be the site of a temple to Mamu, the god of dreams, and of a palace called Imgur-Enlil, which was entered through the bronze and cedar gates Rassam had found.

The Balawat excavations were a constant source of anxiety to Rassam. The local workmen quarreled with his regular crew, many of them still concerned with possible grave desecrations. Bitterly cold winds blew over the site and nearly froze the nightwatchmen who guarded the gates. So he set his men to recover the bronze work as fast as possible and to tunnel into other parts of the mound. A second pair of bronze gates, these belonging to Ashur-nasir-pal II, came to light near the first examples. These were set on brick platforms. A temple housing a "marble coffer, containing two beautifully inscribed tablets hewn of the same material," was discovered at the north side of the site. The burned-down temple contained not only inscriptions but a large quantity of human bones. Although these burials were obviously ancient, the workmen raised such a hullabaloo that the bones had to be reburied. Rassam also found an Assyrian well which he cleared to the bottom in search of treasure thrown into it in time of danger. He found nothing. So troublesome did the local workmen then become that Rassam removed the bronze gates and shut down the excavations.

Naturally, the trustees were delighted with Shalmaneser's bronze gates. They decided to take advantage of Layard's presence in Constantinople by applying for another firman, this time a permit that would enable Rassam to dig in Assyria, Turkey, and if that were not enough, Babylonia as well. While awaiting word from Layard, Rassam returned to Mosul in November of 1878, to be greeted by a huge crowd of well-wishers. He opened up Kuyunjik again and went about looking for new sites to excavate. For two months he visited large numbers of mounds, dug feverishly at Nimrud, and again at Assur, with little success. A severe attack of fever so reduced his energy that any work was an effort. He also felt frustrated. Everywhere huge sites awaited excavation, many of them, presumably, full of spectacular finds. Yet he found little. "All the Assyrian and Babylonian mounds, where ancient cities and temples were found, require a regular digging up," he wrote many years later. The trouble was that the days of "digging up" were now numbered. Spectacular finds would only come from carefully planned, systematic excavations conducted under close supervision for months, even years, at a time.

In January 1879 he found himself in possession of a two-year firman that enabled him to excavate in three different provinces of the Ottoman Empire at the same time! It was the firman of Rassam's dreams. He immediately hastened to Baghdad, where the British agent, Colonel Nixon, immediately agreed to keep an eye on the excavations south of the city when Rassam was elsewhere.

Rassam's first target was Babylon, so he took some trusted overseers and set up his headquarters at Al-Hillah. His arrival created great concern among the Arab brick diggers, who had quarried Babylon for generations. Recently, some Baghdad merchants had bribed them to collect cylinder seals and other small antiquities for export to Europe and the United States at a hundred times their Babylon price. Their clandestine diggings were easily combined with brick quarrying, so much so that the workmen would contract with two or three dealers, then break up cylinder seals and sell parts of the same specimen to different people. Rassam himself bought a Babylonian cylinder that had been sawed in half with such a crude saw that nearly half an inch of the inscriptions had been destroyed.

With characteristic cunning, Rassam moved in on Babylon by hiring a brick contractor from Al-Hillah to negotiate with the diggers. The contractor agreed to pass on all the inscribed bricks he received, while Rassam made a similar arrangement with the other diggers. In this way he obtained a temporary monopoly on all finds from the site. When a few dealers tried to bribe his workmen, Rassam quietly turned a blind eye, for his monopoly arrangement worked well. He got most of the antiquities and the diggers received both a wage and the profits from the plain bricks as well.

In addition to ensuring a monopoly on casual finds, Rassam started large-scale operations at the site. After a few abortive days on the Kasr, he moved his men to more promising mounds nearby, where he opened huge trenches in search of palaces on the scale of those in Assyria. While no large stone structures or sculptures were likely to come to light, Rassam felt sure he would recover at least the rooms of a brick-built palace. "By following a certain method," he wrote, "we came upon signs of standing walls, which surprised my diggers not a little." But the major finds were few and far between, although he did unearth some cylinder seals. The truth was that his excavation methods were simply too unsophisticated to trace mud-brick structures. Nor did Rassam have the patience to dig on any one site for any length of time. While he was working Babylon, he moved in on Birs Nimrod, where he found brick diggers feverishly looking for antiquities. He used the same tactics as at Babylon and "placed a few gangs of work-men to excavate in four different spots." He found a large building erected by Nebuchadnezzar, numerous glazed bricks, and little else.

Leaving his overseers in charge, Rassam casually took a boat down-stream to visit the large mounds of Telloh, the site of the Sumerian city-state of Lagash, which he described as "very curiously shaped." Telloh was a mile in circumference and consisted of a series of mounds in one of which the French vice-consul in Basra, Ernest de Sarzec, had found a series of diorite statues and many inscriptions in 1877–1878. Rassam's firman did not extend as far south as Telloh. Nevertheless, he gathered together a gang of Arabs and set to work on Sarzec's site. He dug into the highest mound, recovered a mass of clay cone bricks, two inscribed gate sockets, and a series of red stone maceheads, which, he said, were "a kind of weights." Sarzec had left the largest of his diorite statues in the mound and had reburied it. Rassam calmly dug it up "to take a squeeze of the inscription on it for the British Museum" and left it exposed. The local Arabs broke it up after his departure. After three days fighting broke out among Rassam's workmen, so he aban-doned the excavations. He was furious when he learned that Sarzec was already negotiating for a permit for Telloh. To head off Rassam the cunning Frenchman had kept quiet about his application. Taken completely by surprise, Rassam remarked pettishly that he would have found as fine statues as the French if he had been able to dig a few days longer.

Rassam continued his frenetic travels as he made his way upstream, again digging into likely sites. He traveled on horseback, by boat, on foot, in dust storms, torrid heat, and blinding rain. All manner of travelers hung on his coattails: Swiss tourists, military missions, and officers' wives, one of whom had to spend the night shivering under a tarpaulin in a rainstorm. "I could not invite her to share my tent, for fear of causing scandal," Rassam pompously remarked. Back in Mosul, he now closed down Assur and Nimrud, where his excavations were unproductive, and advanced on his ultimate target — the mound of Nebi Yunus at Nineveh, hitherto unexcavated because of the violent objections of the guardians of the mosque on its summit. Rassam was confident he could outwit them where others had failed.

During his months of work at Kuyunjik, Rassam took care to employ plenty of Nebi Yunus villagers. He visited their homes and cultivated the acquaintance of the leading inhabitants, as well as the priests. After a while a number of prominent families suggested that he dig in their backyards. Rassam went one step further. He quietly purchased two or three tumbledown houses with the consent of the shrine's guardians (who were paid a fee), with the intention of digging under their foundations and then giving the land back to the original owners together with the necessary building materials to rebuild. Quite naturally, the owners were delighted. The mosque guardians were equally delighted when Rassam not only negotiated with them about off-limits areas around the mosque but agreed to erect some baths within the sacred precincts. Of course, he could keep any antiquities found in the deep foundation trenches he would need to dig in order to build the charitable baths! Rassam was ready to start work at once, but the local authorities in Mosul demurred and referred the matter to Constantinople. After prolonged negotiations and inquiry after inquiry, the minister of public instruction flatly refused permission for the Nebi Yunus excavations. Although Rassam assailed the officials responsible for being anti-British, he was now persona non grata in Constantinople. Even Layard's influence could help him no more. Nebi Yunus remains unexcavated to this day. We can be thankful that Rassam's workmen were prevented from ruining a series of Assyrian public buildings that may, one day, fill in many of the gaps caused by the haphazard excavations of the nineteenth century.

Hormuzd Rassam's archaeological career was now nearing its close. He returned for a last season under the Layard firman in 1880, this time at the beginning of the summer. He crossed to the Euphrates from Aleppo with a mule train to save time, reaching the river at Hit, where he engaged a bitumen boat in which to float down to Babylon. The heat was intense, reaching 107 degrees even on the river. At

Babylon Rassam nearly collapsed from heat prostration, but found that his "native overseers" had unearthed plenty of clay tablets. But the excavations were unproductive by Rassam's standards. He retired for the summer months to dig near Lake Van in Turkey, and returned to Mosul in the fall for a further season in Babylonia. All this time his nephew Nimrud was overseeing small-scale excavations at Kuyunjik, looking for clay tablets. There was always a chance that the authorities might relent and allow him to dig at Nebi Yunus.

Rassam came south with the objective of widening his excavations beyond Babylon and Birs Nimrod. This time he had his eye on the ancient Babylonian site of Kuthah, a huge tell over two hundred and eighty feet high that lay fifteen miles northeast of Al-Hillah. He also planned a search for the Biblical city of Sepharvaim (the Babylonian Sippar). Kuthah, locally known as Tell Ibrahim, was relatively inaccessible, so Rassam concentrated on Sippar, which he finally located at Abu Habbah, a tell twenty miles southwest of Baghdad. The ruins of the walled city contained a small ziggurat. The surface of the mound was littered with pot fragments and bricks. Rassam came on Abu Habbah almost by accident. He hastened to dig there, camping close to a nearby shrine and supervising the excavation in person. This time success rewarded his efforts. The workmen uncovered a chamber paved with bitumen. Some impulse caused him to break through the floor. To his astonishment, a terra-cotta box containing a magnificent, inscribed marble tablet came to light. The tablet bore a relief of the sun god seated in a shrine and commemorated the restoration of the god's temple at Sippar by King Nabu-apal-idinna. An inscription in front of the shrine identified the city and the name of the temple from which it came.

Rassam continued to dig at Abu Habbah at intervals until 1882. He estimated that a complex of buildings consisting of at least four hundred rooms surrounded the ziggurat. He excavated about one hundred and seventy of them, from which he removed large numbers of inscribed cylinders and tablets. The Sippar archives were preserved on unbaked clay. Eventually he recovered between sixty and seventy thousand tablets, "a large number of which fell to pieces before we could have them baked." It took years to decipher the piles of tablets. Most of them turned out to be business records concerning sacrifices, the manufacture of jewelry and other objects, and a complicated bureaucracy of priests, scribes, and temple officers. The revenues of the great temple of Shamash were recorded for generations, like the accounts of a large commercial concern, which it fundamentally was. One cylinder recorded how Nabonidus, the last king of Babylon, had a passion for antiquarian pursuits. The cylinder described how he decided to check his historical records by digging into the cities of his predecessors. Eighteen cubits below the surface Nabonidus came across a foundation stone laid by Naram-sin, the son of Sargon of Akkad, "which for 3,200 years no previous king had seen." *

Except for the clay tablets, Rassam was disappointed by his Abu Habbah diggings. Nor was a hasty month at Kuthah any more revealing. "I had no less than twenty tunnels and trenches opened in it," he wrote. "There were no indications whatever in them to give me any hope of discovering Babylonian remains." He found some bricks inscribed with Nebuchadnezzar's name and surmised that they had been brought there from elsewhere. His tunnelings missed the Babylonian city of Kuthah completely, buried as it is twenty feet below the surface.

Rassam kept his overseers scattered all over Mesopotamia perennially searching for a spectacular palace or finds that would enrich the British Museum galleries in his name. Although the trustees were delighted with the Abu Habbah tablets, Rassam continued to search for buried treasure with methods that horrified even the Turkish authorities. In July 1882, when the firman expired, he waited in Baghdad in the vain hope that the Porte would renew it. Once it became clear that the sultan had no intention of letting him loose on Mesopotamia again, Rassam went back to London. But he left Arab workmen posted at each of his major sites to protect them against unauthorized excavations. Rassam fully expected to return.

---

* Sargon I of Agade was the founder of the Akkadian Dynasty and conquered the Sumerian king Lugalzaggesi in about 2370 B.C. Sometimes called "the Great," Sargon I ruled over a confederacy of city-states that extended from Sumer to the Mediterranean. His capital has never been found. Sargon II, the Assyrian king who ruled from 721–705 B.C., built the great palace at Khorsabad near Nineveh, the palace discovered by Paul Botta in 1843.

15

A Scramble for Tablets

With all your gettings, get tablets.

T HE BRITISH MUSEUM continued to pay Rassam's watchmen in Mesopotamia for four years while the cuneiform experts in London sifted
through the Abu Habbah archives. Rassam himself visited the museum
regularly to meet with Birch, Layard, and Rawlinson, in the hope that
he would be employed to dig more sites. In 1886, Samuel Birch began
to receive disturbing reports from Baghdad about the sanctity of sites
under British Museum guard. His correspondents reported that the
museum's watchmen were apparently conniving in illicit excavations at
the sites under their charge, indeed were engaged in illegal digging
themselves. Then a German orientalist wrote that a party of his
scholarly friends had bought a fine collection of antiquities at Nineveh
from Rassam's watchmen. Even more distressing, they had purchased
no less than three hundred Babylonian tablets from the guardians at
Abu Habbah. The closely knit network of Assyriologists buzzed with
gossip and rumors when one of Birch's former assistants, W. St. Chad
Boscawan, reported that the Berlin Museum had recently acquired
magnificent collections of Babylonian commercial and legal tablets
from a Baghdad dealer. These specimens could only have come from
one of Rassam's guarded sites. Since Boscawan was retained as a cunei-

form consultant by most of the European dealers, his report was taken seriously by the museum. Henry Rawlinson was consulted and suggested that the trustees apply for a new firman to dig at Kuyunjik. At the same time, the person appointed to oversee the excavations could try and locate the source of the tablets and other specimens that were reaching Europe illegally. This time the trustees rejected Rassam in favor of a young man named Wallis Budge, a trained Assyriologist who was to achieve world fame as a collector and a popularizer of Mesopotamian and ancient Egyptian archaeology.

Wallis Budge was a precocious youth, whose family had served in the East for generations. His schooling was harsh but proved useful in later life, for his teachers encouraged him to study Hebrew and the historical background of the Scriptures. At an early age he met Charles Seager, a prominent Semitic philologist of the time. Seager introduced Budge to Samuel Birch and to cuneiform at about the time George Smith was working on the Deluge Tablets. When Birch gave Budge the run of his office, George Smith told him the only way to learn cuneiform was to "copy a piece of text every day, and, by trying, to translate the signs in it." The industrious Budge found himself taking informal classes in Egyptian hieroglyphs and cuneiform. There were no textbooks, so everyone copied down the script from the blackboard and handed in his translation at the next session. Budge was soon in close touch with all the early Assyriologists: Rawlinson, Oppert, and even Layard, who urged him to go out and dig rather than study inscriptions. Budge made other influential friends, too, among them William Gladstone, who was one of those who helped him gain admittance to Cambridge University to study Semitic languages in 1878.

By this time Budge was producing a steady stream of translations of Assyrian tablets. During the next five years he added Arabic, Ethiopic, and Talmudic literature to his repertoire. In 1883 Gladstone and others nominated him for an appointment as assistant in the Department of Oriental Antiquities under his friend Samuel Birch. Budge was to spend his entire productive and controversial career in the service of the British Museum. He now found himself faced with the prospect of becoming an Egyptologist as well, for the department was so understaffed that one had to acquire competence in a whole range of archaeological and historical fields.

Budge's newly acquired Egyptological skills led to his first collecting expedition to Egypt in 1886–1887, a mission that taught him the wily tricks of tomb robbers and antiquities dealers, and enabled him to smuggle twenty-four cases of antiquities out of the country under the furious nose of the British consul general, Sir Evelyn Baring. The trustees of the British Museum were delighted: Budge's acquisitions were of fine quality and had been obtained at very moderate cost. A born collector, Budge was a sociable person with a penchant for bargaining and an eye for new acquisitions. He had the gift of ignoring official regulations and getting away with activities that would have landed most men in jail. The British Museum recognized him for what he was—a superb acquisitor.

This was the young Assyriologist whom the trustees appointed to take over where Rassam had left off. Just as he was about to leave for Baghdad, Budge received information that a unique collection of clay tablets had been found at Tell el-Amarna in Egypt, tablets that bore, his correspondent said, a remarkable resemblance to cuneiform tablets that had been brought to Cairo from Baghdad some years before. Budge realized that this discovery was potentially of the greatest importance: the tablets might throw light on the relationships between Assyria and Egypt in Old Testament times. So he traveled to Baghdad via Egypt and acquired the Tell el-Amarna tablets on the way. They turned out to be a unique archive of diplomatic correspondence of great historical value, which Budge spirited out of Egypt in the face of determined opposition from officials of the Egyptian Museum. Unrepentant, Budge sailed for Basra and then traveled by river steamer to Baghdad, a city which did not impress him. There was, he complained, "appalling noise and confusion" that he thought "indescribable." Although the residency had rented a house for him, Budge hesitated to live in it because "it was in the native quarter and so far from the river." Fortunately, the captain of the *Comet*, an Indian Merchant Service steamer, invited him to stay on board. The berth gave him far more freedom of action, something Budge needed if he was to be an effective collector. He found himself pursued by irate customs officials who were convinced he was carrying contraband whiskey. In fact, the box contained the precious el-Amarna tablets. After much yelling and commotion, the captain of the steamer managed to persuade officialdom that Budge was no drug or alcohol smuggler.

For all his devious ways, Wallis Budge was meticulous in making official contacts. He called on Colonel William Tweedie, the British consul general, who was at the end of a long and distinguished career in government service. Budge was ushered into the presence of a "tall, spare man, of military bearing, and he possessed the calm demeanour and quiet dignity which I have noticed to be characteristic of the official who has had much experience in dealing with orientals of high rank." Tweedie wore "a sort of turban cap" and was wrapped in a cloth cloak to ward off the chill of the winter morning. Budge was mildly disconcerted when his host started talking not about antiquities but about the Arab horse and its pedigree. Then he realized that Tweedie was sizing him up and weighing his letters of introduction from Rawlinson and others.

After some minutes of rambling conversation, Tweedie spoke very frankly. He could do little to help Budge. British prestige in Baghdad was a pale reflection of what it had been in Rawlinson's day, and in any case, the British Museum had no power to appoint watchmen over Mesopotamian sites anyway. Furthermore, natives would always steal antiquities and Budge could not stop it. Tweedie pointed out that Rassam was very unpopular with the authorities, for he never finished a dig and hopped from one site to another. Besides, the Turkish inspector of antiquities in Baghdad was well aware of the purpose of Budge's visit and had called on Tweedie to point out that no foreigner was allowed to deal in antiquities. In other words, Budge could visit sites and eat at the residency, but he had better behave himself. "I can promise to give you a new kind of curry every night for a month at a stretch," ended Tweedie, "so good a cook has God given me." And with these encouraging words, he gave Budge lunch and a tour of the residency with its fine portrait of Rawlinson and magnificent stained-glass windows.

After this strange interview, Budge spent hours wandering around the bazaars and made a point of visiting as many dealers as possible. The wealthiest dealers lived in the meanest hovels. As Budge became trusted, he found that the dealers would produce fine antiquities and exquisite jewelry from holes-in-the-wall and cellars. He quietly added choice pieces to his British Museum collection, using techniques that had paid dividends in Egypt: show an appreciation for fine things, pay fair prices, and take time to buy.

Budge now called on the Turkish inspector of antiquities, who complained loudly about Rassam and promptly introduced him to more dealers. For the next few days, he busied himself buying up hundreds of Babylonian tablets from Abu Habbah and other sites already sampled by the British Museum. Many of the dealers were, alleged Budge, none other than the very watchmen appointed by Rassam to guard the museum's interests. He was now certain that the London rumors were true. He carefully packed away the tablets in twenty-five wooden boxes, and to avoid the customs officials, he smuggled his purchases on board the *Comet* at night, loading them on the side that faced away from the customhouse. The prices he paid were fully three hundred percent lower than those in London, so low in fact that he became suspicious. It turned out that the dealers and the authorities had made a deal, whereby he would be arrested upon departure, the tablets confiscated and then returned to the dealers — for a consideration. But they had met their match in Wallis Budge. He calmly announced that he was off to Al-Hillah to buy more tablets. The watchers relaxed their supervision of the steamer after Budge vanished. Meanwhile, the skipper of the *Comet* quietly departed for Basra with a visiting Persian nobleman on a state visit to India aboard. Budge learned a few days later that his precious tablets were safely on their way to England locked in the strong room of a British–India mail steamer.

This piece of blatant smuggling was soon common knowledge. Budge found himself much criticized for actions he considered entirely ethical. After all, he argued, he was only recovering property stolen from British Museum sites. "I felt," he wrote many years later, "that I had done what anyone would have done who had the welfare of Babylonian and Assyrian archaeology and his employers' interests at heart." His only regret was that he had to spend more public money to recover property that had come from excavations financed by the museum in the first place. Budge had no worries. He had powerful backers, among them Henry Rawlinson, who had urged him: "With all your gettings, get tablets."

Budge next traveled to the major sites in Babylonia excavated by Hormuzd Rassam. He found illegal digging in full swing. Babylon's mounds had now been stripped of most of their bricks. The diggers quarried in old excavation trenches, extracting bricks by day and antiquities by night in fear that Turkish officials would confiscate them. Abu Habbah had been destroyed by illegal digging. Rassam's former workmen were smuggling tablets into Baghdad every month. One of the so-called workmen willingly admitted his thefts. After all, he said cheerfully, no one pays my wages! Budge bought over seven hundred and fifty tablets from local dealers and workmen and made contacts for future sales. At the same time he acquired a knowledge of how the illegal antiquities trade worked right under the often-compliant noses of the Turkish authorities. Being a collector himself, he could sympathize with the tricks played by the workmen to smuggle tablets into Baghdad. One man at Abu Habbah would walk into town wearing a long cloak with hidden pockets full of tablets. Others would smuggle their finds in loads of bricks or charcoal. The dealers bought everything that came in and promptly sold their stocks in Berlin, London, or Paris. The demand for tablets was inexhaustible as the major museums tried to acquire as many as they could. Budge bought all the specimens he could afford. Again he smuggled his finds past the authorities, who then telegraphed the sultan for permission to detain him. A friendly postal official arranged an accident to the telegraph wires near Baghdad and Budge got away safely.

He returned to London full of self-righteous indignation about the chicanery of the watchmen and dealers. He urged the British Museum to fire all their retainers in Babylonia. Significantly, no Kuyunjik tablets were coming on the London market, for it seemed that Hormuzd Rassam's nephew Nimrud was watching closely over the excavations. Most of the Babylonian antiquities reaching London came from Abu Habbah. There was nothing anyone in Europe could do to stop the illicit digging there.

The British Museum now decided to reopen their excavations at Kuyunjik, specifically to recover as many tablets as they could. The trustees had started to compile a catalogue of the Kuyunjik tablets. Obviously it should be as complete as possible. Wallis Budge was dispatched to Constantinople to apply for a new firman in person, working both through the British ambassador, Sir William White, and the director of the Imperial Ottoman Museum. He stayed in Constantinople for seven weeks, exercising his considerable charm both on Hamdi Bey and on the minister of public instruction. Unlike many other scholars, who did their best to insult the Turks, Budge had the gift of getting on with them and understood their sensitivities — a great asset. But only the personal intervention of the British ambassador with the sultan finally produced the firman. The conditions were specific and stringent. The British Museum might retain any clay tablets found, but all other finds were to go to Constantinople. A Turkish commissioner would be present at the excavation at all times, his salary paid by Budge. Since the proposed excavations had a highly specific purpose, Budge agreed to the conditions. Although it was now December, he set off for Mosul at once, accompanied by the British ambassador's son. They traveled by a steamer full of mutinous Turkish soldiers as far as Antakya, then overland to Mosul via Aleppo and the village of Jerablus on the Euphrates, where Budge examined the ancient mounds of the city of Carchemish. The journey was arduous and cold. Their caravan was looted by Shummar Arabs just short of Mosul.

The caravan finally arrived to a warm welcome, for wild rumors of a bloody resistance to the Arabs had reached the town. Budge stayed with Nimrud Rassam, then rented the front part of an old house, where he hoped to get some privacy. It was a vain hope. Neighboring families dumped their garbage in his courtyard, their chickens flew into his stable. All the cats and dogs of Mosul fought at the front door.

The sultan's firman made the preliminary arrangements for the excavations an easy matter, especially since Budge "facilitated" the process with some timely gifts. He walked over Kuyunjik with Nimrud Rassam and decided to start on a modest scale by sifting through the heaps of dirt left by Hormuzd Rassam's excavations of 1852–1854. Fifty workmen sorted through the contents of the chambers at the southwest corner of the mound, where Rassam had found Ashur-bani-pal's library. Eventually two hundred men joined the excavations, which lasted until the end of June 1889 and for an additional three weeks in November 1890. Nearly six hundred tablets were carefully recovered from old spoil heaps and unexcavated chambers. Budge spent much time soothing the Turkish commissioner, who turned out to be ineffectual and timid, so much so that he spent most of his stay in Mosul. In his spare moments he purchased manuscripts from dealers. In February 1889 he left Mosul for Baghdad by raft, glad to escape the sordid little town. "The smells in the town were numerous and powerful at the best of times," he commented, "but with the coming of warm weather, the reek from the tanneries down by the bridge became more penetrating, and when to this the fumes from the hot sulphur springs to the north of the town were added, the result is easier imagined than described."

Budge received a cool reception from the dealers in Baghdad. They had not forgotten his strategies of a year before. But the official atmosphere in Baghdad was transformed. A new British consul general had been appointed, Colonel Adelbert Cecil Talbot, whose diplomatic skills were more polished than those of the eccentric Tweedie. Budge received a personal call from the pasha, many formalities were waived, the customs hardly inspected his baggage. "It seemed to me that most Turkish rules and regulations were especially made to be broken on payment by the breaker," remarked Budge cynically. He succeeded in buying all the Abu Habbah tablets he could afford without any difficulty — and with official help.

Budge made one more visit to Mesopotamia, this time in 1890. He returned to Mosul to collect the Kuyunjik tablets found in his absence, crossing the desert to Mesopotamia overland from Damascus, a trip that took twenty-three days. Everyone had warned Budge not to try this itinerary, but he refused to listen. He was lucky. His muleteer guides were both honest and clever men, who managed to avoid the Arab raiders that beset the route. He spent three weeks in Mosul closing down the Kuyunjik excavations and packing the finds, then waiting for a firman to dig at Der in southern Mesopotamia, a site known to contain numerous tablets. Budge had purchased some finds from there the previous year. As usual, the permit application was delayed interminably. This time the chicanery was on a large scale.

As Budge's *kellek* neared Baghdad, he was hailed by an Arab who told him that the Baghdad authorities had been digging at Der for months. The actual excavations had been entrusted to local dealers. Budge's Arab informant revealed that the dealers and their overseers had recovered hundreds of cylinder seals, three rooms of clay tablets, and dozens of coins. They had smuggled their finds into Baghdad, where they awaited his pleasure.

Budge was speechless with rage and frustration, but there was nothing he could do. Any excavations would be a mockery, despite their respectable legality. His Arab friend could not understand his anger. "Be not sad of heart," he cried. "We have all the tablets in Baghdad, we are your friends, and we have kept all the tablets for you. You will buy them and they shall get out of the country quickly, and you will be able to live with your English friends in Baghdad and not be obliged to sit in the desert with the jackals and the vultures and burn by day and freeze by night. You will have plenty of rice to eat and clean water to drink, and there are now many oranges in Baghdad." Budge's reply is not recorded!

Upon arrival in Baghdad, Budge found that the pasha blandly denied all knowledge of any excavations. So he turned to the dealers and bought no less than twenty-five hundred tablets in three evenings, all of them from Der, and many of unique historical value. He then packed these into boxes and sent them to Basra at once before purchasing another seven thousand less-important tablets to be sent off later. His only consolation was that the market was depressed and prices were low. Not content with purchase alone, Budge talked discreetly to some of the illegal diggers and established that there were probably some isolated pockets of tablets awaiting recovery in the site. A week after his arrival in Baghdad, the long delayed firman arrived. In late January 1891, Budge set out for Der, only twenty miles away. The excavations started in pouring rain, but two hundred men were soon swarming over the mounds opening up the extensive trenches started by the illicit diggers.

As usual, the conditions of the firman required a Turkish commissioner to be present at all times. An elderly gentleman, immaculate in "bright red wool tarbush, fez, a black frock coat, light trousers, and patent shoes," sat on a sofa outside his special tent. This unassuming, very religious gentleman never visited the excavations but his servant watched everything with a lynx's eye. It was he who told Budge that the workmen were selling a lot of his tablets on the side to Baghdad dealers, despite careful security precautions. The inspector advised him to buy the illicit finds back from the dealers. Once the men tumbled to his strategy, they brought the tablets to Budge direct, in exchange for regular bonus payments. Thus, it paid them to be honest. "Of course," wrote Budge, "this was to compound a felony, but it was the only practical way of obtaining the tablets."

Leaving Nimrud Rassam to supervise the excavations, Budge traveled downstream in search of yet more tablets, purchasing fine collections from Abu Habbah and other mounds. The weather was so wet that the Der excavations had to be curtailed in late February. By this time Budge was satisfied that he had not missed anything significant and that most of his proposed excavation area had been gutted before his arrival. The excavation camp was dismantled on February 19 and Budge rode back to Baghdad. To his frustration, he met a funeral procession on the narrow path that led to the city. Ten men and four women were trudging along with a loaded bier. They chanted and wailed as they monopolized the track. Fuming at the delay, Budge rode up to the Bridge of Boats behind the mournful procession. He was disconcerted to learn that the mourners had told the bridge guards he would pay their toll charges. There was nothing to do but to pay up, for the mourners had even told the guards the deceased was Budge's personal friend! It turned out the funeral procession was a complete fake. The vehicle had been used by Budge's dealer friends to smuggle a large consignment of tablets into the city.

Budge had many friends interested in his finds. They gave him much sage advice on how to circumvent rules and regulations, and he was never at a loss for a stratagem or an ingenious solution to an export problem. Wallis Budge believed that all Baghdad officials were bribable (he was probably right) and that the safest place for clay tablets was out of Mesopotamia, where they could be deciphered and studied after cleaning and restoration. This time Budge returned to London not only with twenty-five hundred cuneiform tablets, but with over two hundred priceless Arabic, Syriac, and other manuscripts exported by the simple expedient of donating a comfortable sum of money to the pasha's "favorite Baghdad charity." More important, he left Baghdad with long-term connections that gave him a regular conduit for purchases of tablets and cylinder seals from local dealers. The British Museum was enriched for years.

The following year, Budge was appointed acting keeper of the Department of Egyptian and Assyrian Antiquities in the British Museum, a sign that the trustees approved of his collecting activities. Not everyone was fond of Wallis Budge. His smuggling was looked upon with disfavor in some academic circles. The Arab overseers who had lost their jobs as a result of his investigations were only too eager to badmouth him to foreigners in Baghdad. Hormuzd Rassam was particularly unhappy. Sensitive as he was about his reputation as an archaeologist, he considered the dismissals a personal affront. Disturbing rumors about Budge's reports on his activities in Baghdad reached his ears almost weekly. Soon the two men were barely speaking to each other. In the second week of July 1891, Budge was talking to Rassam, Layard, and others in the Assyrian student room at the museum when he suddenly accused Rassam of being a party to the theft of Assyrian antiquities from British Museum sites. He went on to say that the Abu Habbah tablets sold to the department and to the Berlin Museum had been exported by overseers who were in fact Rassam's relations. Furthermore, the British Museum's consignments from its own excavations at the site had consisted of "rubbish." The prize tablets, he alleged, had gone elsewhere. Layard expostulated. He was already upset with the museum because he felt they had downplayed Rassam in their displays. Rassam demanded an apology from the principal librarian of the museum, who wrote back that Budge denied he had ever made the alleged statements. When Layard pursued the matter, Budge prevaricated in what Sir Austen called a "mean, shuffling, and untruthful manner." He wrote to a friend: "I may say they [Budge's charges] were pressed upon me."

Budge had sent a report on the Baghdad situation to his supervisors. In his confidential document he made several charges. Not only did he allege that the overseers were Rassam's relatives, but that Rassam himself had sold antiquities from official excavations to dealers in Baghdad and London. Rassam, he alleged, never visited his excavations but lived comfortably in Baghdad smuggling spirits into the city. This confidential report caused the principal librarian to advise Budge to lie low.

While the British Museum attempted to placate Layard, Rassam seethed with anger. Against all advice, he sued Budge for slander and claimed a thousand pounds in punitive damages. The columns of *The Times* and other newspapers hummed with comments as the case awaited trial. Questions were asked in the House of Commons. How many missions had Budge undertaken with public funds? How much had he spent, where had the funds come from? The first lord of the treasury replied that a special grant had provided funds and urged members not to ask for more specific details as it would be "to the detriment of public learning if his conduct were discussed in the House." In other words, the British had acquired remarkable antiquities at a modest cost. Even if questions were being asked by Budge's colleagues, the museum was very happy with his work.

Rassam and Budge came to court for five days in late June of 1893. After hearing from both plaintiff and defendant, and from Austen Henry Layard on Rassam's behalf, the jury decided in Rassam's favor to the tune of fifty pounds. The damages were promptly paid by Budge's museum colleagues, the legal fees by the trustees. Rassam's reputation suffered more than Budge's, for the papers made it clear they felt it was a frivolous case. "While we admit the general justice of the verdict," wrote *The Times* on July 4, 1893, "it is impossible on the whole not to regret that the plaintiff did not take the advice of his friends . . . and refrain from bringing the action." The *Daily News* went even further and described the trial as "a sort of antiquarian festival. These distinguished persons have not been in the intimacy of Assur-bani-pal for nothing. Their measures of time are not as our measures: otherwise the better part of a week would hardly have been devoted to the settlement of such a case."

Hormuzd Rassam continued to seethe impotently until his death in 1910. He appealed to the archbishop of Canterbury, a museum trustee, for a renewed investigation of the affair. When that got him nowhere, he withdrew from any involvement in Assyriology and retired to Hove on the south coast to write a book on his excavations. The completed manuscript, *Asshur and the Land of Nimrod*, was rejected by several London publishing houses before it eventually found a home in the United States. Rassam's *magnum opus* is dedicated to his late friend and supporter Austen Henry Layard, who had died three years before. It comes as a disappointment after his mentor's brilliant narratives, and at best is a self-serving document, a defensive and smug account of an archaeological career full of chicanery and intrigue. Rassam's inferiority complex peeps through on many pages, as he tries to defend his methods and ethics. But the book did him no good, for archaeological colleagues were now openly attacking his methods. The French archaeologist Charles Fossey described Rassam's work as "diggings that more closely resemble rape and pillage than scientific excavations."

The tragedy of Hormuzd Rassam was that he and, to a certain extent, Wallis Budge, were anachronisms. Just at the moment when Rassam was trying to justify his actions, the first long-term excavations into the very southern mounds he had tried to pillage had begun. These excavations were not only to reveal the hitherto-unknown Sumerian civilization but to conjure up the palaces and temples of ancient Babylon from their desolate isolation of centuries.

16

Sumer Discovered

Since the discovery of Nineveh . . . no discovery has been made which compares in importance with the recent excavations in Chaldea.

As EARLY AS 1872, George Smith had predicted that his "Chaldean account of the Deluge" was a late version of a folk legend that had been in existence for untold centuries. Once the cuneiform experts in Europe began to decipher the mass of new tablets from the Budge and Rassam investigations in Babylonia, they realized that Smith had been on the right track. The Assyrians had copied a literary tradition that had come from the Babylonians, who had in turn copied it from yet another people. Had there been an early urban civilization in southern Mesopotamia that had served as a prototype for both the Babylonian and Assyrian?

It had been the French consul in Mosul, Paul Emile Botta, who had first revealed the Assyrians to an astonished world in 1842. Now another French diplomat was to make a startling discovery in southern Mesopotamia. In January 1877, Ernest de Sarzec, a consular official with considerable experience in Ethiopia and Egypt, was transferred to Basra as vice-consul. Sarzec was about forty years old, an active, tall man. He had, we are told, "expressive features" and was familiar with desert life. He combined his consular duties with a profound interest in oriental art. At the time, Basra was a torrid outpost of the Ottoman Empire.

It had a sleepy trade with India and a very small European colony that suffered greatly from fever and lethargy. Sarzec was too active a person for an obscure life of soporific trade and occasional desert hunting excursions. He decided to spend his leisure time exploring the ancient civilizations of Babylonia. While on a visit to Babylon and Birs Nimrod, he got in touch with dealers and illicit diggers, contacts that were strengthened in Basra through a prominent local Christian and steamship operator, J. Asfar. Asfar, who dealt with antiquities on the side, introduced him to local merchants who regularly bought artifacts from Arabs upstream. The diggers kept on talking about a site called Telloh, where inscribed bricks, cones, and an inscribed torso of a man had come to light. Asfar urged the new consul to investigate Telloh more closely, perhaps even to dig it. Sarzec made secret preparations for an excavation. Well aware that Hormuzd Rassam was charging around Mesopotamia with bands of laborers, he said nothing publicly and took the risky step of digging without an official firman. This, he felt, was the best way to claim the site, which in any case was under only nominal Turkish jurisdiction. The real political power lay in the hands of the local pasha, Nasir, who had founded the town of An Nasiriyah and named it after himself. Sarzec cultivated Nasir sedulously, and as a result he could travel and excavate anywhere he liked in the pasha's domains.

Only two months after arriving in Basra, Sarzec was hard at work at Telloh on the first of a long series of brief excavation campaigns. Telloh consisted of four miles of sites extending along the bank of a dried-up canal that formed a branch of the Shatt-el-Hai. Sarzec spent two preliminary seasons, in 1877 and 1878, digging massive trial trenches in the principal mounds. The very first time he rode over the largest of them, he picked up part of the shoulder of a magnificent diorite statue. He started his excavations on the fifty-foot mound from which this fragment had been eroded. The mound turned out to consist of a platform of unbaked bricks upon which a substantial building had once stood. In a recess in the outer northeast wall of the building, Sarzec's workmen recovered the torso of the very figure from which the inscribed shoulder had come. Sarzec was unable to remove such a large piece, so he took an impression of the inscriptions on it and buried the statue under soft earth. (This was the statue that Rassam uncovered in his hasty, illegal dig of 1879. It will be recalled that he left the statue exposed and the locals destroyed it.)

Once Sarzec had established the general character of the building on the platform, he set his men to work across the entire site in long rows. Telloh had not been reoccupied in later times and this technique produced a rich haul of tablets, jars, inscriptions, and two large terra-

General view of Sarzec's excavations at Telloh, showing the
level underneath a Sumerian royal palace. This photograph was
taken by Sarzec himself. From Sarzec and Heuzey, Découvertes
en Chaldée (*1884*)

cotta cylinders of a ruler named Gudea. The preliminary excavations
yielded quantities of cuneiform inscriptions that were the most comprehensive ever found from the earliest periods of Mesopotamian history.

The enterprising Sarzec realized he had made a major discovery. Telloh was the site of a very early city indeed, one where the temples and
other buildings were not mantled in feet of debris from later occupation or in deposits of Parthian slipper coffins. He suspected he had
found a complete early settlement of a hitherto-unknown Mesopotamian
civilization far earlier than that of Babylon. So convinced was he of the
importance of his finds that he obtained a leave of absence from his
consular duties, sailed to Paris, and tried to put his work on a more
permanent basis. He was referred by the Ministry of Foreign Affairs
to Léon Heuzey, the curator of the Department of Oriental Antiquities
at the Louvre. Heuzey at once recognized the significance of the
Telloh finds, which he identified as a magnificent collection of early
Mesopotamian art and artifacts of hitherto largely unknown type, except for a couple of isolated statues acquired for the Louvre some years

before. Sarzec was soon fast friends with Heuzey, who at once committed the Louvre to acquire the Telloh material for 130,000 francs. At the same time, Sarzec was encouraged to return to Basra and carry on the excavations at his own expense until the French ambassador could obtain a firman for Telloh before anyone else got wind of the finds. His application beat Rassam's to the punch and the French secured official permission for a long-term campaign of excavations on the mysterious city.

In 1880–1881, Sarzec returned to Telloh, accompanied by his new wife. This time the excavations were subsidized by the French government. He was to return to Telloh almost every year until 1900. The first official season was devoted to a thorough and unhurried examination of the great building he had found in 1877–1878. Sarzec was soon able to announce the finding of nine other large diorite statues, as well as fragmentary bas-reliefs and numerous inscriptions. The workmen probed deeply into foundation walls of structures buried below the major ziggurat, recovering pre-Babylonian artifacts and art objects far older than anything ever dug up before.

Sarzec returned to Paris in triumph in the summer of 1881, bringing a huge collection of Sumerian art with him. These finds caused a great sensation at the Fifth International Congress of Orientalists in Berlin and before the French Academy in Paris. Jules Oppert, that pioneer of cuneiform, delivered a famous address on Telloh to the congress, an address that began: "Since the discovery of Nineveh . . . no discovery has been made which compares in importance with the recent excavations in Chaldea." Heuzey published the first part of his magnificent *Découvertes en Chaldée par Ernest de Sarzec* in 1884, the first compendium of information on the Sumerians. What Sarzec had uncovered was the world's earliest literate society.

For years Hincks, Rawlinson, and others had suspected that a more primitive script and civilization had preceded the Semitic Babylonian cities. In a lecture in January 1869, Jules Oppert had argued that the early rulers of the south were often called "king of Sumer and Akkad." Thus, he argued, the non-Semitic peoples who had preceded the Semitic Akkadians should be called "Sumerians."

At the time, most cuneiform experts disagreed with Oppert, arguing that there was simply not enough material from the clay tablets in the Kuyunjik archives to document the Sumerians. In any case, the Ashur-bani-pal archives were assembled at least a thousand years after the demise of Oppert's new civilization. Only a few inscriptions from delta sites were known, and those were of very limited value.

Now Sarzec's new excavations had changed all that. The inscriptions and tablets documented the history of Lagash, a Sumerian city-state of the third millennium B.C. Lagash had been ruled by a series of powerful governors. No less than six of Sarzec's diorite statues depicted Gudea, the seventh and most famous of them. These Sumerian statues brought the Assyrian bas-reliefs found by Botta, Layard, and Rassam into a new focus. Fully fifteen hundred years earlier than the Assyrians, the Sumerians were producing works of art that exhibited both a naturalism and a freshness not found in the later bas-reliefs. One of the first examples was a bas-relief called the Stela of Vultures, which dates to about 2400 B.C. It depicts a group of armed men and their leader marching in formation. The stela attracted the attention of H. G. Wells, who once described natural man as "a spasmodic and untrustworthy fighter." When he wrote about the Sumerians, he said: "There you see him in a sort of phalanx, advancing with his shield locked with that of the next man and their spears at a level making an invincible line. All down the changing historical record, that body of disciplined infantrymen appears and reappears." The stela itself was erected by the Sumerian king Eannatun to mark the boundary between the state of Lagash and its archrival Umma. Their respective rulers quarreled incessantly about irrigation water through the centuries.

Sarzec's excavations could hardly be described as scientific, for his men were simply instructed to follow mud-brick walls and recover as many small finds as possible. Few plans of the excavations or the structures they revealed survive. At least, Sarzec had the sense to realize that systematic, long-term excavation would provide much greater dividends than hasty diggings in search of caches of tablets. His efforts at systematic exploration saved much of the site from destruction by tablet hunters.

Unfortunately, dealers from around every corner descended on Telloh each time Sarzec wound up his excavations there. His attempts at security were so lax that the illicit diggers could work openly in the daytime. Many of the tablet hunters were former Rassam laborers who were continuing their lucrative arrangement with Baghdad dealers. They smuggled their tablets into the city hidden in the usual flowing cloaks or in baskets of fruit. For months the tablet diggers searched feverishly for the royal archives and official tablet repository of Lagash. They eventually found it in a small, compact mound whose small chambers were packed with baked clay tablets by the thousand. Just as the tablets came to light, Sarzec returned to Basra to hear the rumors of a spectacular illegal discovery. The diggers hastily covered up their find and started work elsewhere on the site until he was out of the way. They denied all knowledge of the find and managed to prevent Sarzec from digging in the small mound. Some time later the diggers opened up the chambers at leisure and sold thirty-five thousand to forty thousand tablets to the Baghdad dealers. The Lagash archives were exported to museums all over Europe and to the United States, to be followed in later years by larger antiquities, including more Gudea statues. Telloh was so large that adequate policing of its precincts was almost impossible. But the plundering of the excavations should in no way detract from Sarzec's remarkable achievement, sandwiched as it was between consular duties in Baghdad and Basra.

His phenomenal finds rekindled interest in the excavation of southern Mesopotamian cities throughout the scholarly world. The Germans began a systematic excavation at Babylon in 1899 after a lengthy series of preliminary investigations. They were preceded by excavations under the sponsorship of the University of Pennsylvania in 1888.

American interest in Mesopotamia stemmed from a profound concern with the historical veracity of the Old Testament. After the publication of Layard's books, no orientalist could overlook the connections between the Bible and archaeological sites in Mesopotamia. The result was the formation of the American Oriental Society. "England and France have done a noble work in Assyria and Babylonia. Now is the time for America to do her part. Let us send out an American expedition," cried a speaker at the society's annual meeting in New Haven in 1884, where the finds from Telloh were discussed. The society formed a committee to raise funds and elected a prominent journalist the chairman. The Archaeological Institute of America soon found itself with $5,500, given for the purpose of sending out a party of American scholars to spy out the land and look for promising excavation sites. Dr. William Ward led this "Wolfe Expedition to Babylonia," which was named after Catherine Lorillard Wolfe of New York, who had given most of the money for the trip. The expedition followed in Loftus's footsteps and visited many of the major sites, cameras and surveying instruments in hand.

Ward's report was submitted to the institute in June 1885. He recommended large-scale excavations, but the report met with little enthusiasm, for popular interest in Mesopotamian archaeology had faded. Nothing might have happened had it not been for the Reverend John P. Peters, newly appointed professor of Hebrew at the University of Pennsylvania. Peters was an energetic and hard-driving man who started courses on Semitic and archaeological topics at the university in 1886–1887, courses designed to titillate the interest of the educated, affluent public. He received strong support from the provost of the university and from E. W. Clark, a prominent local banker who headed a fund-raising drive. Between 1888 and 1900, the community raised over $100,000 to support American excavations in Babylonia and especially at the site of Nippur, the Biblical Calneh.

The fund-raising drive and overall direction of the "Babylonian Exploration Fund" were in the hands of a fifteen-person committee. Peters was named director of the first expedition; Hermann Hilprecht, the newly appointed professor of Assyriology at the university, was secretary. Plans for the expedition matured rapidly, with several members, among them Hilprecht, agreeing to serve without salary. The comfortable committee rooms at the university buzzed with activity: firman applications were written and plans for the purchase of tablets devised. Unfortunately, no one had a clear idea what conditions would be like in the field.

Peters spent three frustrating months in Constantinople obtaining a firman. He combated malicious gossip, indifference, and open hostility, much of it caused by his own grandiose demands that he be allowed to dig several sites at once. After a shaky start Hamdi Bey and Peters became good friends, which helped accelerate the permit. Eventually, the six members of the expedition converged on Aleppo and Baghdad in late 1888. Peters met his Turkish commissioner, whom he found to be living at the house of a notorious dealer, a former headman on Rassam excavations. The dealer was a general merchant who, wrote Peters tactfully, had "conducted a considerable business in antiquities ever since Rassam left Babylonia." The Turkish commissioner had a notorious reputation for taking bribes. "Those were days of intrigue, treachery, and suspicion," recalled Peters in his book on Nippur. The Germans digging at Babylon told Peters to keep the commissioner drunk and well fed, and happy by systematic bribery. Peters also kept him in line by threatening to expose his thefts of tablets to the authorities and had little trouble. The commissioner did help the expedition find some experienced diggers at Babylon who were expert at locating tablets and mud-brick structures. Small wonder, for they made their living by illegally digging for antiquities.

The firman allowed the Americans to dig either at Birs Nimrod or Nippur. After a brief visit to the former, everyone agreed they should concentrate on Nippur. While Peters and the expedition's Turkish commissioner rode to the miserable town of Ad Diwaniyah to pay their respects to the local authorities, the rest of the party, accompanied by twenty-two trained workmen from Babylon, their families, and a caravan of animals loaded with equipment, struck out direct for Nippur. The three-day journey only confirmed the rumors they had heard about Arab blood feuds and highly unstable political conditions. At one point a group of raiding horsemen descended upon the column, which somehow managed to evade them. On the third morning the ziggurat and mounds of Nippur appeared, towering above the plain. Hilprecht's heart sank. Even at a distance he could see that at least fifty years would be needed to dig Nippur adequately: "What would our committee at home have said at the sight of this enormous ruin, resembling more a picturesque mountain range than the last impressive remains of human constructions."

Nippur lay in the center of a morass of swamps and dried-up canals. Bands of hostile Arabs watched from a distance as the Americans approached. "Greeted by the wild dance and rhythmical yells of some fifty Cafej warriors who had followed our movements from a peak of the weather-torn ruins, we took possession of the inheritance of Bel," recalled Hilprecht. They pitched their tents on the summit of the southwestern portion of the ruins, a windy vantage point that provided an all-round view and some warning from surprise attacks. The Arab workmen erected reed and palm-leaf huts in a square around the tents. The huts served as stables, kitchens, storerooms, and workshops, and as protection from "sand storms and the thievish inclinations of the children of the desert."

While Peters received Arab visitors, Hilprecht and the other Assyriologists combed the surface of the site to choose the places to excavate. Hilprecht was anxious to dig in a large, open area northwest of the conspicuous temple precincts, where he expected to find storerooms and tablets. The impetuous Peters disregarded his expert colleague's advice and set workmen to dig a small mound in an area where Parthian slipper coffins had come to light and the early, pre-Babylonian levels were far below the surface. Once additional workmen were available, Peters consulted with the expedition architect and dug into the corners of the ziggurat in search of foundation cylinders. The first ten days of digging yielded only a few inscribed bricks and an isolated cuneiform tablet bearing the name of King Sargon I of Agade. Peters began to get worried. He saw his funds evaporating without tangible results to show for them. At this point, Hilprecht again urged a dig in the northeast section of the ruins and asked for a few workmen to dig some trial trenches. After considerable hesitation, the worried Peters agreed and gave him two gangs of workmen for a week to prove or disprove his hunch. Within a few hours, tablets began to emerge from the trenches, and by the end of the first six-week season, Hilprecht had recovered more than two thousand tablets, most of them dating to around 2000 B.C. The better-preserved tablets, found in a baking kiln, were for the most part records of business transactions; the rest were literary, mathematical, and medical texts. The literary tablets, most of them fragments, made Hilprecht suspect that he was close to the temple library. Peters allowed him five extra gangs of diggers in March, but the excavation ended, when time ran out, a few feet from a series of tablet-filled chambers that Hilprecht was not to discover for eleven years.

Peters himself continued to concentrate on the ziggurat, at one point directing two hundred and fifty men as they trenched through rock-hard mud brick and rubble. For nine weeks the Americans dug on uneventfully, "the topography of ancient Nippur becoming more lucid every day."

Funds were running out fast when serious trouble erupted between the Hamza and Behahtha tribes of the Afej Arabs, both of whom claimed the mound and insisted on furnishing laborers for the dig. The workmen would shout war cries and insults at the foreigners and quarreled with the Turkish escort, who took delight in picking fights with them. No one had any privacy. Arabs wandered unmolested through tents and storerooms. The camp could be seen from miles away, and was under no sheikh's protection. It would only be a matter of time before someone raided it. The Americans were surprisingly naive, for they omitted to build a guesthouse for visitors and to provide hospitality for those who called on them. They were horrified by the local people and their morality. "Even in a city like Hillah, respectable Arabs will give their daughters for a beshlik," recorded the shocked Peters. The locals held the Americans in open contempt and threatened again and again to burn down the camp. In April, a bread oven was destroyed, four sheep stolen. It was rumored that the Americans' horses would be the next to go. On April 15, the Turkish guards frustrated an attempt to steal the horses and fired on the intruders. Unfortunately, one of the thieves was killed by a rifle bullet through the heart. The next four days were full of anxiety. Compensation was offered and refused and the emissaries beaten. Arab horsemen pressed on the camp. The excavations were closed down and preparations made for immediate departure. "The days and nights which followed were full of exciting scenes," remembered Hilprecht. On April 18, the Arabs set fire to the reed huts of the camp before dawn. In minutes the camp was a pile of smoldering ashes. The Americans battled to save their effects while the Arabs gleefully plundered. Half the horses perished, together with valuable guns and saddle bags and $1,000 in gold. But the antiquities were saved. The expedition retreated in confusion on horseback and by boat through the swamps to Al-Hillah. Most of the Americans promptly resigned and Peters was recalled to the United States. Twenty thousand dollars had provided but the sketchiest impression of Nippur and the whole season had been a debacle.

Somewhat to everyone's surprise, the backers of the first season

Arab workmen dancing in the temporary camp at Nippur.
Photograph from Hilprecht's Exploration in Biblical Lands (*1903*)

readily agreed to a second in 1889–1890. Hamdi Bey interceded personally with the grand vizier and the Nippur permit was renewed over the objections of the local authorities. Peters was again placed in charge of the expedition, but this time he took no Assyriologists or specialists with him. This extraordinary decision on Peters's part immediately reduced the excavations from a scientific investigation of a complex site to a form of treasure hunting à la Rassam. Peters was anxious to obtain as many antiquities as possible for the minimum cost, without the interference of scientists. Objects, he felt, would please the public and bring in more money for excavations. He resumed the excavations on January 14, 1890, with a team of two hundred workmen.

This time the atmosphere at Nippur was quite different. Drought conditions and a devastating cholera epidemic had so decimated the local Arabs that they were delighted to see the Americans back and to work for them. Nothing much was said about the incident of the previous year. This time an improved camp was pitched just south of the mounds and built under the protection of a local sheikh. Unfortunately, however, Peters refused to pay a blood indemnity of $44 for the death of the robber, feeling that to do so would be a sign of weakness. This gaffe caused serious problems and constant security worries for the Americans. Rumors of the fabled wealth of the visitors had spread far and wide and caused local tribesmen to flock to the mounds to stare. They were particularly interested in the gold fillings in Peters's teeth, which, wrote Hilprecht, "excited their lust."

The Americans were constantly on their guard for raids or conspiracies. Fortunately for them, they were believed to possess great magical powers, which had brought on the cholera in revenge for the raid of the year before. Peters cured some minor ailments to reinforce this belief and lost no opportunity to demonstrate his prowess. Perhaps he overdid it when he laid on a spectacular firework display one evening. During the day he had wandered over a mound near the camp, looking mysterious with a compass and muttering strange incantations. After dark he stole out of camp and ignited several rockets from the bottom of a trench. The workmen and their families were at dinner and screamed in fear. Terrified that the stars were falling from heaven, the more timid fled to hide in the huts. "At last we came to our *pièce de resistance*, the tomato-can firework. At first this fizzled and bade fair to ruin our whole performance. Then, just as we despaired of success, it exploded with a great noise, knocking us over backward in the trench, behind a wall in which we were hidden, and filling the air with fiery serpents hissing and sputtering in every direction. The effect was indescribably diabolical." The workmen fled for cover in sheer terror. But even this impressive pyrotechnical display did not prevent quarrels, thefts, droughts, and floods. By increasingly shrewd human relations and years of experience, the Americans mastered what Hilprecht rather charmingly calls the "peculiar dangers of the Babylonian climate."

The first season's excavations had shown that Nippur had been occupied for several thousand years, from prehistoric times right up to the ninth century A.D. Now Peters had to fill in the details of the story. The dig concentrated on the ziggurat. The surroundings of the temple had been protected by two huge walls with watch towers. Storerooms and kitchens, as well as houses, formed an integral part of the walls. Peters broke into the outer shell of the ziggurat and discovered a smaller stepped tower inside it. His "tunnels and wells" showed that "many kings of many ages had honored the temple of Bel at Nippur." He found structures built by "Ashur-bani-pal and Ur-Gur, who reigned in about 2700 B.C.," and even claimed he had found Sargon of Babylon's ziggurat. The excavations were so haphazard, however, that nothing but a general impression of the temple came to light. Peters's knowledge and archaeological experience were totally inadequate for the complex task that faced him. Wallis Budge, always a tart observer of his colleagues, remarked that "more travelers than one who have seen the site of the American excavations at Nippur have failed to see there any exhibition of scientific digging."

The frenetic pace of Peters's excavations recalled that of Layard and Rassam. He tunneled into Hilprecht's mound and unearthed two thousand tablets without any notion of the strata they came from. When a mound on the southeastern side of the site suddenly started to yield tablets, he moved gangs of tablet diggers to the new locality. Soon they shoveled out a chamber thirty-two feet long and sixteen feet wide crammed with unbaked tablets that had once been stored on wooden shelves round the walls before the building was burned down. Most were tax lists and business documents of great value for establishing the chronology of the Babylonian kings. Peters kept few notes. The only plans of the site were those compiled by a visiting Hungarian engineer, who made plans of some of the major structures. Wisely, Peters shipped a large consignment of antiquities downstream before the dig finished. The angry tribesmen, who were still after blood revenge, had planned a raid for the final night. Another dramatic firework display enabled the Americans to slip away unharmed.

A third campaign at Nippur lasted three years, from 1893 to 1896. It bore the firm imprint of Peters's excavation strategy, but was under the field direction of J. H. Haynes, the photographer and business manager of the first two excavations. A firman was readily granted, partly because Hamdi Bey had great sympathy for the persistence of the Americans, and also because Hilprecht, now recovered from a lengthy illness, had spent many months in Constantinople reorganizing the Ottoman Museum's Babylonian collections without fee. Haynes journeyed to Nippur in August 1892 and put himself under the protection of the local sheikhs. Then he built a permanent base near Peters's camp, a mud-brick structure that combined the "features of a castle, a storehouse and a dwelling." In fifteen weeks, his small team of fifty men recovered over eight thousand tablets from a tablet-rich mound near an old canal.

Haynes was about to turn his attention to the complex problems of the ziggurat when a fortunate coincidence put him in touch with a young American architectural graduate student from MIT, who readily agreed to spend a year without salary at Nippur. Joseph Mayer was a skilled draftsman who had had some experience in recording ancient monuments in Egypt and Turkey. Haynes, who had been feeling lonely, found him a congenial companion. His notes, hitherto little more than a chronicle of dangers and frustrations, became a record of the unfolding architecture of the Nippur ziggurat. The laborers toiled at the temple mound all through the summer of 1894 while

Haynes and Mayer recorded every detail with copious sketches, which, for the time, were adequate enough. Unfortunately, Mayer contracted dysentery and malaria in September and insisted on working until his condition was so serious that he was delirious. He died on December 20, leaving Haynes once again alone, miles from the nearest European and without any skilled assistance.

Wisely, Haynes stopped work on the ziggurat, but resumed haphazard digging elsewhere in search of tablets and yet more tablets, the finds that Peters coveted above all others. His progress reports began to dwell on the dangers around him as the solitude of Nippur began to prey on his mind. Cholera was reported at Al-Hillah; the local Arabs fought the Turkish authorities in a hot engagement that killed seventy-one men. The firing could be heard at Nippur, but the excavations continued. Haynes sometimes had difficulty finding workmen to replace his basketmen, who would suddenly drop their tools, seize their weapons with a loud war cry, and prance off to battle. The constant pilfering of cylinder seals, occasional cave-ins and injuries, all the minor irritations produced by a site far from the regular Euphrates and Tigris caravan routes, were too much for Haynes. Nevertheless, he accelerated the pace of excavation in an attempt to remove as many tablets from the site as possible and to give the impression that Nippur was exhausted. Constant rumors of clandestine donkey loads of tablets traveling between the illegal excavations at Telloh and Babylon haunted Haynes almost monthly. It was not until July 1895 that he felt he could stop digging for tablets. By that time he had recovered nearly nineteen thousand tablets in three years of digging.

The lonely Haynes spent the last six months of the campaign working on the northwest side of the ziggurat, often in temperatures of 120 degrees and in the middle of dense sandstorms. By July 1895 the trenches that exposed the temple complex had reached such great depths that the trench walls towered dangerously over the diggers. Furthermore, Peters's huge soil dumps made the walls even higher and would have to be moved if the lower strata of the ziggurat were to be explored at all thoroughly. In August he decided that enough was enough and started to close down the excavations.

Haynes had moved sixty thousand cubic feet of earth before the end of the last season. He had collected a huge mass of valuable antiquities. By this time he was in urgent need of a rest. Throughout his long seasons at Nippur he had declined the help of experts, despite urgings from Philadelphia. The excavation committee finally found two young English architects to work with him and sent them out to Nippur without consulting him. They arrived just as he was closing down the dig. Reluctant to leave two inexperienced foreigners alone with the Arabs, whom he described in a letter as a "defiant, covetous, treacherous, and bloody throng about us," Haynes took the frustrated Englishmen back to Baghdad with him. The architectural details of his last season were never recorded.

Haynes's long excavations were, scientifically speaking, a disaster. They caused increasing concern in Philadelphia, especially among Assyriologists like Hilprecht, who described Haynes's discoveries as "isolated and incoherent." His weekly progress reports gave little clue to the true character of the temple of Bel. Everyone assumed he would bring back detailed daybooks describing every feature of the excavation. It turned out that his letters were all the experts had to go on. Only the work completed with Mayer was of scientific value. Haynes had dug through dozens of mud-brick walls, failed to keep accurate measurements, and shoveled away valuable rooms without any concern for their contents. His excavation methods showed little improvement on Layard, for he dug deep shafts and tunnels that penetrated to the deepest layers without adequately exploring the horizons that lay nearer the surface.

The tablets and inscriptions Haynes had recovered gave Hilprecht many hours of arduous detective work. He gained valuable historical information from fragments discovered in the early strata of the ziggurat, especially a celebrated text of Lugalzaggisi, the king of Uruk, one hundred and thirty-two lines of which he pieced together from eighty-eight fragments of sixty-four different vases. This important historical text shows how a number of minor early Sumerian city-states were constantly quarreling with one another over land and political matters. The more important rulers gave votive offerings at the shine of Bel at Nippur. Names of kings of Uruk, Kish, and Ur, hitherto unknown, reentered the stage of world history.

The fourth American campaign at Nippur was conducted by the University of Pennsylvania in 1898–1900. By this time the University Museum had come into being and had taken over the work of the Exploration Fund. Hermann Hilprecht was appointed scientific director of the excavations, while Haynes was retained as field director, to deal with the practical management of the excavations. Two architects, one English, one American, accompanied the party. By this time there was such bad feeling between Hilprecht and Peters that the trustees of the University set up a special committee to investigate the quarrel, which resulted in Peters severing further connections with the project. So confident did Haynes feel about field conditions that he was allowed to take his wife along. And the sultan of Turkey was so favorably disposed to the Americans that Hilprecht had to wait but two weeks in Constantinople for the firman.

The two-year season was budgeted at $30,000, and clear objectives spelled out. These were to determine the precise character of the temple of Bel and its history, to establish the extent of pre-Babylonian Nippur, to search for city walls and gates, to study burials, and, lastly, to find the temple library. Haynes was given precise instructions about records, notebooks, and photography, and was told how to order his priorities. Hilprecht was to arrive at Nippur later.

In January 1899 sixty-two camels, several mules, and six sailing boats carried the expedition from Babylon to Nippur. A Turkish commissioner, six soldiers, and one hundred fifty workmen accompanied the party. The expedition set itself up in considerable style in the fortresslike house, which had been sealed when Haynes had left. The comfort of the mud-brick fortress — it was nothing else — astonished visitors like Hilprecht, who remembered the primitive camps of earlier seasons. "Though our windows consisted of only spoiled photographic negatives," he wrote, one could almost imagine one's self "transplanted to one of the watering places of the Arab caliphs in the desert." Haynes had taken the precaution of digging wells that were piped into the courtyard of the expedition house, just in case the expedition was besieged. Fortunately, political conditions were quieter than in earlier years, partly because of improved Ottoman administration and some agricultural development work, and also because the regular presence of foreign archaeological expeditions had introduced new ideas to the area. Hilprecht found the Arabs talking with considerable anticipation about the German railroad that was to be built through Mesopotamia.

Haynes started work with two hundred and five men. To the committee's disgust, he quarreled with his architects and went on looking for tablets. It was not until March 1900 that Hilprecht was able to reach Nippur and take over the excavations. Hilprecht stopped all tablet digging, placed the architects under close supervision, and concentrated all efforts on the interpretation of the site. "Every trench cut henceforth — and there were a great many — was cut for the sole purpose of examining and gathering necessary *data* for the history and topography of ancient Nippur. If these trenches yielded tangible museum results at the same time, so much the better; if they did not, I was not troubled by their absence and felt just as well satisfied as if I had packed several thousand tablets, or perhaps even more so."

Hilprecht traced city walls and surveyed all the structures already discovered. He completed the excavation of a Parthian palace, examined over eleven hundred post-Christian burials. The ziggurat was investigated right down to water level, to centuries earlier than those of Sargon I of Agade (2700 B.C.). Hilprecht found a huge Sumerian cemetery around the temple. But the most impressive discovery came from his "tablet hill" of the first season, the exploration of the temple library, which was located near some school buildings. Hilprecht was able to recover the lesson tablets used by pupils learning to write cuneiform, as well as scientific works, king lists, hymns, astronomical records, and so on. The library even owned a complete set of multiplication tables from 1 to at least 1,350. The Sumerian literary tablets were the most interesting of all (they were published in English many years later by Samuel Kramer, a unique contribution to our understanding of Sumerian civilization). Sumerian literature was restricted to myths and epic tales, hymns, lamentations, and occasional essays. The earliest works were probably written down about 2500 B.C., and the literature undoubtedly proliferated in later centuries. The Nippur tablets were so fragmentary that they took years to study. Each fragment had to be copied by hand, then translated and interpreted. But thanks to the devoted work of Hilprecht, Kramer, and others, we know of at least nine Sumerian epic tales, the most famous of which are the epics surrounding the mythical hero Gilgamesh.

It is difficult to overestimate the importance of the American excavations at Nippur. By 1900, Hilprecht had thirty thousand tablets to examine, which, for the most part, recorded commercial and legal transactions. Years of research were to put the Sumerian social and economic structure and king lists on a new and more accurate footing. Hilprecht was wise enough to realize that the study of the Nippur tablets was a long-term cooperative venture, to last far beyond his lifetime. To his credit, these studies are still in progress. The University of Pennsylvania has retained an interest in Nippur to this day.

The Nippur and Telloh excavations were hardly paragons of archaeological virtue. At their worst, they were organized treasure hunting, at their best the first attempts at large-scale scientific investigation of the Sumerian civilization. By excavating over a long period of years, the archaeologists were able to train some skilled workmen, develop a rapport with the local people, and above all, gain some insights into the complexities of excavating mud-brick structures and dissecting occupation levels. Without these skills and the long-term commitments to sites that go with them, no archaeologist could hope to study the Sumerians effectively.

17

Nebuchadnezzar's Babylon

The whole must have conveyed an over-whelming sense of greatness, power, and wealth.

THE GERMAN INTEREST in Assyriology dated back to the days of George Grotefend, who continued to publish cuneiform translations of dubious reliability until his death in 1853. A year after Grotefend died, Kaiser Wilhelm IV had lost a consignment of Assyrian sculptures in the Al-Qurneh disaster. Eventually the Berlin Museum bought some bas reliefs from the Crystal Palace Company in London. This transaction was consummated just as excavations in Mesopotamia entered a twenty-year interregnum. However, the main interest of the few Assyriologists in Germany was in cuneiform and oriental languages. During the remainder of the nineteenth century the distinguished theologian and linguist Eberhard Schrader followed Rawlinson's work closely and studied the Behistun inscriptions himself. Schrader was probably the father of Assyriology in Germany. He accepted Rawlinson's decipherments and used them as a basis for studying the Assyrian text called "Descent of Ishtar into the Underworld." In 1873, he started some private courses in Assyriology in which he dealt with the basic philological principles of the language and discussed the relationship between the Assyrians and the Scriptures. The result was a new and vigorous school of Assyriologists based in Leipzig. Schrader himself earned international recognition for his book on ancient scripts and the Old Testament published in 1876. His students worshipped him. Wallis Budge described him as "a fine example of the old type of German scholar; his modesty was as great as his learning."

Another German Assyriologist, Friedrich Delitzsch, taught himself the cuneiform scripts at an early age and began a precise study of Assyrian grammar and lexicography. He went on to form a class for young Assyriologists and prepared one of the first reading books for students ever published. Delitzsch became the dean of Assyrian scholars in Germany. Never an expert copier, he achieved fame for the quality of his teaching and for the fine students he graduated. It was Delitzsch who was invited to give a series of lectures before Kaiser Wilhelm on the importance of Babylon and Assyria in the context of Biblical studies. In these lectures and his book *Babel and the Bible*, published in 1902, Delitzsch emphasized the parallels between Mesopotamian myths and the Scriptures. Eloquently he urged German participation in Mesopotamian archaeology to clarify these parallels. His views were much criticized by Biblical experts but the Kaiser encouraged his ideas. The German excavations were to change Near Eastern archaeology beyond recognition.

By 1880, the Germans were already digging in other parts of Europe with a precise fervor that reflected both a new concern with scientific reportage and Kaiser Wilhelm's preoccupation with nationalistic prestige. Their revolution in archaeological methods stressed recording of data in the field. When Alexander Conze excavated at Samothrace in 1873 and 1875, he worked with two architects, a photographer, and the assistance of an Austrian warship. The sumptuous report on the excavations was a model of its kind and illustrated with photographs that recorded both architecture and excavation. The German Archaeological Institute came under the Prussian government in 1871. Ernst Curtius and Friedrich Adler worked at Olympia in 1875–1880 with an ample budget and specialist architects in the field. The closing season was financed by Kaiser Wilhelm himself. Even more remarkable, the Germans renounced all claims to the finds and even built a small museum at the site. This precise concern for minute architectural details, small artifacts, and, above all, prompt and orderly reporting of field results contrasted sharply with most current archaeological practice. While the Kaiser wanted to enrich the Berlin Museum, he argued correctly that sumptuous and prestigious academic publications in the tradition of Napoleon's *Description de l'Egypte* reflected favorably on their sponsors.

German interest in Mesopotamia surfaced in the late 1870s, when

Robert Koldewey

the orientalist Ernst Sachan and other scientists visited Assyria and Babylonia in search of likely sites to excavate. Sachan was followed by small parties of excavators who were looking for long-term projects and gaining experience in local conditions. At one point there was a possibility that the Germans would dig at Nippur, but the University of Pennsylvania preempted them. The Royal Prussian Museum of Berlin was also in the field in early 1887, engaged in a preliminary search for promising excavation sites. Bernard Moritz and Robert Koldewey were able to excavate briefly in two huge tells named Surghul and Al-Hiba near Telloh. The mounds were so enormous that they decided to concentrate their efforts on sinking long trenches in order to establish the character of the buildings. They followed mud-brick walls and cleared the contents of chambers, even sectioned deep wells made of terra-cotta rings. The Germans kept their usual careful records and exposed large numbers of mud-brick houses intersected by long narrow streets only about three feet wide. Many of these structures had crumbled so badly that the archaeologists were forced to trace foundations through dark stains in the soil, a technique of almost unheard-of sophistication in the 1880s. The mound deposits were full of burials and occupation debris, but the limited time at Moritz and Koldewey's disposal made extended investigation impossible.

Ten years later, Ernst Sachan was sent out to Mesopotamia again, this time to make specific recommendations for likely sites for long-term excavation. Robert Koldewey accompanied the party. They visited all the excavations in progress, then recommended digs at Babylon and Assur. Koldewey had spent two days at Babylon in June 1887. This time he returned for three more days in December 1897. On each occasion he picked up fragments of enameled bricks that seemed to have formed parts of huge murals. He took the fragments home to Berlin, resolved to return one day to unearth the structures from which they had come. "Mostly works from the period of Nebuchadnezzar will be found," he boldly predicted. The bricks caused considerable interest in Berlin, so much so that the director general of the Royal Prussian Museum applied for a firman to dig Babylon systematically.

Robert Koldewey had a lifelong passion for archaeology. He was born at Blankenburg in 1855 and studied architecture, archaeology, and art history in Berlin, Munich, and Vienna. His early archaeological training came in the field at Assos and Lesbos in Greece. After his preliminary digs at Surgul and Al-Hiba in 1887, he excavated in Syria, Italy, and Sicily while holding a job as an architectural teacher at Görlitz. Koldewey was a lighthearted man with a lively sense of humor. Some of his more single-minded colleagues distrusted his ability to look on the humorous side of his work. When he dug at the Greek city of Selinus in Sicily, he took great delight in describing the gory Carthaginian sieges "in which the ladies of the town took vigorous part." He went on to say: "From this episode, Selinus has not recovered to this day. Because of it, rabbits hop freely through the streets. And because of it, too, I suppose, we have rabbits to eat of an evening now and then."

For all his sense of humor, Koldewey was a precise and thorough scientific archaeologist. Babylon in all its desolation challenged his inquiring mind. Unlike his predecessors on the site, Koldewey was a trained archaeological observer. Babylon, he was certain, could be studied thoroughly by careful digging, precision in recording, and above all, long-term excavation. Koldewey opened his first trenches at Babylon on March 26, 1899, and continued to dig there every year until 1912. "It involves no depreciation of the labors of our predecessors when we say that they are superseded in almost every detail by the results of our many years of excavations, so far as knowledge of the city ruins are concerned," he was to write in 1914.

Koldewey faced a formidable task: "To those accustomed to Greece and its remains, it is a constant surprise to have these mounds pointed out as ruins. Here are no blocks of stone, no columns; even in excavation there is only brickwork." As has been previously mentioned, the Babil mound and the Kasr, the most conspicuous landmarks, had been quarried by brick diggers for centuries. Koldewey stopped the quarrying as much as he could by taking on the brick diggers as laborers, but terrible damage had of course been done. He and his colleagues literally had to develop archaeological technique as they went along. Koldewey set out to train special teams of skilled workmen who did nothing but trace mud-brick walls. The Germans started with the easy fired-brick walls, then gradually turned their attention to sun-dried brickwork, which was harder to trace as it had dissolved faster in antiquity. They were lucky at Babylon, for the stratification of the various buildings was relatively easy to identify, simply because the builders inscribed their bricks with their names.

Koldewey and Walter Andrae, who started at Babylon and then branched out on his own at Assur, realized that Mesopotamian architecture had changed but little over the centuries. The builders of Babylon and Assur had made their mud bricks by dumping tempered clay into a four-sided wooden mold with open top and bottom. The clay was smoothed carefully into place with the side of the hand, the mold was removed, and the brick left to dry in the sun. The endless hot and cloudless days of the dry season baked the bricks to such durable hardness that kiln-fired bricks were deemed unnecessary. Koldewey's predecessors had failed to understand the implications of mud-brick architecture and had dug yards of them away in search of stone foundations or the upright stone slabs that formed the lower parts of palace walls. With the weathering of time, the mud bricks had literally become mud again after the buildings of the city were abandoned. Koldewey realized that the only hope of finding out anything about Babylon was to concentrate on tracing the mud-brick walls.

Season after season, Koldewey's workmen uncovered literally miles and miles of mud-brick walls. They recovered the layout of the royal city with its vast monumental gateways, elaborate fortifications, major streets, and large palaces. Step by step, the archaeologists recorded the architectural finds with meticulous care, for they realized that only the largest and most massive of mud-brick buildings would survive any length of time after the dig.

Eventually, the Germans found that the best technique was to scrape the ground with hoes while looking for wall faces or changes in soil texture that indicated the junction between a mud-brick wall and the filling behind it. Sometimes a clear line of mud plaster came to light on the face of the wall or the pattern of the brickwork could be discerned. Then the expert wall tracer dug carefully into the filling until he had dug a hole large enough to squat in. Then he faced the wall and picked away delicately at the filling until the gentle strokes caused the soil to fall away from the plaster on the wall face. Once the wall face was exposed, the digger simply worked his way round the four walls of the chamber, leaving a layer of filling over the floor and in the center of the room to be removed very carefully later. Thus, the contents of the room could be recorded in place, and evidence for multiple reoccupations of the same structure could be recovered.

Over the many seasons at Assur and Babylon, Koldewey, Andrae, and their assistants developed a comprehensive method of excavation, one that influenced the work of all subsequent archaeologists in Mesopotamia. They started by making a topographical survey of their site, then sunk test pits to obtain a datum baseline for the excavations, a base level, as it were, that provided a yardstick for the untangling of the complicated sequence of cities and buildings. When Koldewey came to investigate the Ishtar Gate at Babylon and the Procession Street that lay behind it, he found that King Nebuchadnezzar had had similar ideas. In order to reach firm soil undisturbed by earlier occupation, his architects had cut the foundations of their great buildings down to clean sand. The foundation walls built into these deep trenches remained undisturbed for Koldewey to uncover: walls decorated with huge reliefs of dragons and bulls that stand thirty feet high even today. The reliefs were protected with a layer of clay plaster — they had never been exposed to view because they formed part of the deep foundations.

The German excavations were a sustained, systematic campaign that was conducted with deliberation and with primarily architectural considerations in mind. The excavators were imbued with an almost fanatical passion for detail, so much so that Koldewey was moved to comment that "the gradual progress of the excavations, important and stimulating as it is for the explorers, appears of less interest to those who take little share in it." Their reports make very dull reading, even for the specialist.

Koldewey started his dig with a general knowledge of the history of the city which he had gleaned from cuneiform tablets. He was faced with the task of filling in the details. He identified the earliest occupation of Babylon as dating to before the fifth millennium B.C. A few scattered flint implements lay below the water table, the baseline for all his work. The first identifiable city belonged to the time of Hammurabi (1790 B.C.). Subsequent settlements followed the street plans laid out in Hammurabi's time. The Assyrian kings maintained and expanded the temples of their predecessors. But it was Nebuchadnezzar (reigned 604–562 B.C.) who rebuilt the entire city, the city cleared by Koldewey and his colleagues. He restored the temple on the citadel and several other shrines, built the first stone bridge over the Euphrates, and completed the southern citadel, which included his own great palace. The Procession Street was enlarged and paved with stone, while the Ishtar Gate was completed and decorated with an enameled frieze of animals. He surrounded the entire city with a huge outer wall. The city reached its greatest magnificence under his rule. Babylon began to decline in Nabonidus's time (556–539 B.C.), and never recovered, even when Alexander the Great tried to restore its prosperity. (Alexander was to die in Babylon before he could complete the restoration.) By the time of the Sassanids (A.D. 226–636), Babylon was a ruin and the site occupied by only a few scattered villages.

Koldewey began by employing his work force of two hundred and fifty men on the clearance of the Procession Street, which extended north to south through the inner city. In April 1899 he wrote that he had been digging for two weeks "and the whole business is a complete success." The secret was a system for wall clearance. Each pickman was armed with two picks: the one a small, pointed implement used for tracing walls; the other a larger pick employed for heavier digging. He was supported by sixteen basketmen, who carried away the soil shoveled into their baskets by three shovelmen. The pickmen advanced in a carefully drawn line, peeling off the soil in sloping layers until the walls emerged from the earth. The basketmen carried their loads to a light railroad car which was used to dump the soil in a place where digging would be unlikely. The 1899 excavations soon turned up the ends of two parallel walls that formed the boundaries of the Procession Street. This street led to the Ishtar Gate, built by Nebuchadnezzar as the processional gate for the temple of Marduk. He had paved the street with huge red-and-white marble flagstones that lay on an asphalt and brick substratum. The flagstones bore Nebuchadnezzar's imprint. He had ordered the Procession Street raised almost forty-two feet above the level of the plain. The walls on either side of the street had been faced with glazed bricks that formed a triple frieze of bulls, lions, dragons, and other animals. The lions were white or yellow with yellow or red manes against a blue background. These walls were defensive in intent and led the traveler toward the Ishtar Gate in seclusion from the fine view of Babylon that now stretches on either side of the great walkway. The excavation of the enameled friezes was a

Reconstruction of the Ishtar Gate at Babylon in the Berlin Museum

long task, for the brickwork behind them had been plundered over the centuries. But Koldewey was able to piece the lions together and to estimate that at least one hundred and twenty animals had once adorned the walls of the street. Each animal was about six and a half feet long.

Koldewey pored over the friezes in an attempt to find out how they had been assembled. He concluded that the sculptors first made a working model, which served as the prototype for clay molds. The model was assembled on a temporary wall, careful attention being paid to the jointing of the bricks. Then burned-clay molds were made for each separate brick. The molds were so shaped and formed that the friezes became an integral part of the wall. The contours of the molded and fired bricks were then outlined with a black, vitreous composition, the different courses filled with colored enamels, and the bricks fired to fuse the enamels in brilliant colors. The bricks, duly numbered in a correct sequence, were now ready for assembly in the frieze. Conditions on the site were so cramped that the brick fragments were shipped back to Berlin for chemical treatment to restore their surfaces. Koldewey insisted that every fragment be numbered so that the friezes could be reassembled later.

This magnificent walkway was but a prelude to Koldewey's most remarkable discovery, Nebuchadnezzar's Ishtar Gate, excavated in 1902. The gate lay at the point where the Procession Street passed through the fortifications of the inner city. Koldewey found that the walls of the gate still stood forty feet high, covered with horizontal rows of bulls and dragons. The double portals of the gate were flanked by two huge towers. The gate was adorned with glazed bricks and figures of at least five hundred and seventy-five bulls and dragons, the latter the sacred animal of Marduk, described by Koldewey as a "walking serpent." One hundred and fifty-two of these figures were still in position on the gate. Koldewey decided to remove them and incorporate them in a full-size reconstruction of the gate in the Berlin Museum. The task of removal went on until 1912, but the six hundred and forty-nine cases of bricks did not leave Iraq until 1926. World War I intervened, the British took over the government of Iraq, and new antiquities laws prevented their release. But eventually the Ishtar Gate went to Berlin in exchange for representative examples of restored panels and two of Koldewey's models of the city of Babylon, which still adorn the Iraq and Babylon museums.

After several seasons of arduous and unspectacular work, Koldewey was able to disentangle the long history of the Kasr, or citadel, of Babylon. He found that Sargon I had built the first buildings on the site. Then came Nabopolassar's mud-brick palace surrounded by an enclosure wall. His son Nebuchadnezzar completely reconstructed the Kasr, erecting the Ishtar Gate, extending the palaces and temples, and enclosing the entire complex with a massive fortification wall. In the northeast corner of the south citadel, Koldewey found a stone-arched structure associated with a well. These vaulted arches were some of the few stone structures in the entire site. Koldewey combed the ancient historical sources and concluded that he had found the supports and water supply for the legendary Hanging Gardens of Babylon, one of the classical Seven Wonders of the World. The Hanging Gardens were much more modest than legend would have had the world believe. Nebuchadnezzar's roof garden was an imposing architectural artifice to be sure, but hardly a spectacular wonder.

The Procession Street passed along the east wall of the temple of E-Temen-Anki, the great ziggurat of Babylon, which, with Birs Nimrod, had been associated time and again with the Biblical Tower of Babel. The ziggurat was surrounded by an enclosure wall and associated buildings, much of them removed by brick robbers. The complex of buildings in the walls was thought to be priests' houses and accommodations for pilgrims.

The ziggurat itself towered over the entire complex, a colossal structure reached by a huge stairway that extended to the summit. Koldewey was confronted with a huge mass of brickwork. Clearly the original temple built by Hammurabi had long since been razed to the ground. King Nabopolassar later built a new ziggurat to commemorate the earlier structure: "At that time Marduk commanded me to build the Tower of Babel, which had become weakened by time and fallen into disrepair. He ordered me to place its base securely on the breast of the underworld, whereas its pinnacles should strain upwards to the skies." His son Nebuchadnezzar boasted that he went even further, raising his temple so that "it might rival heaven." In investigating this stupendous structure, Koldewey had only the base to go on. He studied the foundations and ancient historical records from such authorities as Herodotus, and estimated that the base of the ziggurat was 295 feet square, and at least 165, perhaps 245, feet high. He was almost overwhelmed by the scale of even the ruined structure. "The colossal mass of the tower, which the Jews of the Old Testament regarded as the essence of human presumption," he wrote, "amidst the proud palaces of the priests, the spacious treasuries, the innumerable lodgings for strangers — white walls, bronze doors, mighty fortification walls set round with lofty portals and a forest of 1,000 towers — the whole must have conveyed an overwhelming sense of greatness, power, and wealth, such as could rarely have been found elsewhere in the great Babylonian kingdom." All that was left of the ziggurat was quarried away for bricks after the excavations ended. Nothing remains of the Tower of Babel today except a swamp.

The excavations of the German Oriental Institute at Babylon ran parallel with Walter Andrae's remarkable investigations at Assur in the north, one of the ancient capitals of the Assyrians. Andrae and his colleagues dug into these extensive mounds with great success from 1902 to 1914. Previously, Layard, Place, and Rassam had dug there but had found little. Their hectic scrambles for palaces and bas-reliefs had proved fruitless. Andrae arrived with a season's experience at Babylon behind him, a season when he had been involved in the experiments with wall tracing. He formed specially trained teams of wall diggers, most of them from local villages, surveyed the site with great care, and set out to probe the depths of the early Assyrian city. So successful was this experiment that the villagers became a specialist team of excavators who passed their skills on to the archaeologists of the 1930s and 1940s.

Assur had once perched on a heavily fortified rocky spur washed by the Tigris. At least three ziggurats adorned the summit of the hill, one of them E-hassaq-kurkuma, known as the Great Mountain and House of All Lands. Using Koldewey's techniques and refining them, Andrae traced the city walls and many houses and temple precincts.

The Germans' largest and most important operations were directed at one major structure, the temple of Ishtar, the mythical wife of the city's own god, Assur. Andrae laid out a vertical trench that stripped off successively rebuilt temples, a long succession of at least six earlier buildings, until he reached an archaic Sumerian shrine, with stone statues identical to those in Sumerian temples in the south. Although the Americans had dimly conceived of stratigraphic layers at Nippur, and Koldewey had been able to identify different Babylonian settlements by using inscribed bricks, this was the first time anyone had tried to dissect an entire tell to obtain detailed information on the evolution not only of a temple, but of a civilization as well. Assur was the first site where the Sumerian civilization was found *under* the Assyrian. Gone were the destructive excavations of hasty treasure hunters. Andrae and his colleagues photographed and recorded every building before they removed it, for they realized that the contents of the temples and the rituals associated with them were just as important as the statuary or architecture they recovered.

By their insistence on slow, careful work, Koldewey and his successors revolutionized Mesopotamian archaeology at a time when the amateur archaeologists of Victorian times were being replaced by the first professional scholars to dig for the past. But as good as the German excavations were, Koldewey still overlooked the possible use of pottery for dating. "He was culpably neglectful of pottery, implements, and even graves, to say nothing of human skeletons," wrote the British archaeologist V. Gordon Childe many years later. Future generations of German archaeologists were trained in the study of minutiae, in the ordering and classification of artifacts. Soon they began to use pottery and other finds as a way of developing a chronology for the early centuries of Sumerian civilization. They employed techniques that had been pioneered by the British Egyptologist Flinders Petrie in the Nile Valley. Petrie had developed a technique of sequence dating using Egyptian jars that extended back to pre-Dynastic times, before 3000 B.C. A similar open-ended chronology developed slowly for Mesopotamia in the years immediately before and after World War I, a chronological inquiry that took archaeologists on the first steps toward the discovery of Sumerian origins. This search still continues.

18

Leonard Woolley at Carchemish

*I have decided that you shall be an
archaeologist.*

THE FIRST SCIENTIFIC excavations in Mesopotamia took place against a
backdrop of gradual economic, political, and social change. By the end
of the nineteenth century, Iraq had begun to feel the influence of European capital and of big-power politics. The steamer service between
Baghdad and Basra had been much improved, and in the 1870s telegraph lines had been extended to Baghdad. The Germans would eventually build a railroad from southern Turkey to Baghdad that would
decrease dependence on river transport. But Iraq itself remained a
remote and little-understood province of the Ottoman Empire. Political conditions outside the towns were still those of near anarchy, especially in the lower delta. Although many northern sheikhs were now
involved in town life and local politics and communications for the
traveler were much improved, the tribes of the delta were still in a
state of flux, fighting with the Turkish authorities and with each other.

The solitary traveler still journeyed at his own peril. Robert Koldewey and his Babylon colleagues felt that they were in an oasis amid
the disturbances. The rare Turkish raids against the rebels invariably
ended in futile bloodshed and shooting that often stopped steamer traffic on the river. Swampy terrain, unjust landholding laws imposed by

the Turks, and profound social turmoil made this a deeply troubled
area.

Chaotic as Iraq was, the European powers had their eyes on its future. The Germans and the British were the most aggressive. Besides
Kaiser Wilhelm's personal interest in the German excavations at Babylon and Assur, diplomatic relations were established in 1905, when a
German consul was appointed in Baghdad. The British watched closely.
Numerous British and German visitors now came to Iraq to sightsee, to
trade, to spy out potential military strategies, or to study the archaeological sites.

Many archaeological expeditions visited the country between 1900
and 1915. Most were short-term efforts, like the University of Chicago
expedition to Bismaya, headed by the American consul to Baghdad,
E. J. Banks. The French worked at Kish, also in the south, while
L. W. King reopened Kuyunjik for the British Museum in 1903. King
was a man of great energy and a scholar who loved working out of
doors. He dug down to a depth of sixty-eight feet in the mound, identified three Assyrian levels, and penetrated into a horizon where he
found dark earth that contained stone knife blades and possible pre-
Assyrian occupation. Unfortunately, he died in 1919 before he could
return to continue his work. These and other Mesopotamian excavations were on a small scale compared with the German efforts at
Babylon and Assur. Most of the archaeologists who worked or traveled
in Mesopotamia at the turn of the century wrote popular accounts of
their digs, which fall into the tiresome "I was there" category of anecdotal travelogue. Their books did little to advance scholarship or to
improve public understanding of archaeology. Few excavators are able
to venture successfully beyond the standard travel account or the
dull, scientific monograph. But we are doubly fortunate that one of
the most gifted archaeologists of the twentieth century, who worked
in Mesopotamia for over half a century, could write of it well.

Charles Leonard Woolley not only dug brilliantly but wrote up his
excavations promptly. He was a skilled raconteur who understood the
complicated human problems that went with digging an important site.
His fascinating accounts of Near Eastern excavation three quarters of a
century ago give us unique insights into the day-by-day hurly-burly of
excavation as it was practiced in the days before Arab nationalism
completely changed the climate of archaeological research.

Characteristically, Woolley was fond of telling the tale of the casual
way he became an archaeologist. The year was 1904, Woolley's last
year at New College, Oxford, and he was taking thought of the future.
He had had vague intentions of taking Holy Orders but had changed

his mind. A career as a schoolmaster seemed attractive, a job that Woolley had already enjoyed on a temporary basis. One spring day, he received a summons from the warden of New College. He answered the call with considerable trepidation, at a loss to know why Warden Spooner would want to see him. The conversation took a most unexpected turn.

"Ah, Mr. Woolley," began the Warden. "Quite so. I think that when you came up to Oxford you had every intention of taking Holy Orders?"

Woolley said yes, it was so, but that he had given up the idea. He waited for what was to come.

"And what do you propose to do?" inquired the Warden.

Woolley murmured something about becoming a schoolmaster.

"Oh, yes, a schoolmaster, really," came the reply. "Well, Mr. Woolley, I have decided that you shall be an archaeologist."

"I was not quite sure what an archaeologist was," recalls Woolley. But it was useless to argue with Warden Spooner. Leonard Woolley became an archaeologist and never regretted it.

He began his career as a humble assistant keeper at the Ashmolean Museum in Oxford. The Ashmolean was under the direction of Sir Arthur Evans, then at the height of his triumphant career as the discoverer of the Minoan civilization of Crete. Evans had rescued the Ashmolean from a long and neglected oblivion as a repository of curious oddments. He had enriched it with his own collections and from constant fieldtrips to the Balkans and Mediterranean lands. Evans had long been a thorn in the flesh of Oxford committees as he fought for his precious museum. When the going became difficult, he would take off for the field, leaving his assistant keeper to respond to all queries with the bland reply, "The keeper, sir, is somewhere in Bohemia."

Woolley was soon in the field. He spent five years, from 1907 to 1911, working with various archaeologists on the Eckley B. Coxe Expedition to the Sudan. The Sudan was still a wild and remote territory in those days. Woolley fell in love with the desert, excavated cemeteries, and worked on sites of the mysterious Meroitic civilization. His heart was not in the Sudan — he thought it a remote cultural backwater far from the main pulse of Western civilization — but the unspectacular discoveries were more than compensated for by the interesting people he met on the digs. Some were trained workmen from Egypt who knew all about archaeology and had worked on many excavations. Others were Sudanis, who were less skilled. They had the disadvantage, too, that they loved their native beer. Sometimes, wrote Woolley, "they are rather apt to get out of hand." The Sudanis taught him much about dealing with laborers in remote areas. At the time, the Nile Valley was one of the finest training grounds for a young archaeologist.

As the expedition drew to a close, Woolley was presented with a new opportunity. The British Museum was searching for a director for its recently resumed excavations of the ancient city of Carchemish on the Syrian border. Colleagues recommended the young Egyptologist so strongly that Woolley found himself in charge of a major Near Eastern excavation at the age of thirty-one.

Carchemish was something of a mystery. The ancient city had guarded the main ford of the Euphrates River for centuries. Byzantines and Romans had maintained forts and trading towns on the site. Carchemish was famous from the Scriptures, too. It had been conquered and annexed by Sargon II in 717 B.C. The earlier history of the site was less certain. Egyptologists knew that the pharaoh Tuthmosis III had fought a pitched battle at Carchemish in about 1455 B.C., a conflict that gave him control of the Euphrates crossing. Carchemish itself was known to be a key settlement of the Hittites. But who were the Hittites? Had they ruled over a large area of the Near East and dealt with Assyrians and Egyptians on terms of equality? Over fifty feet of deposits at Carchemish could, conceivably, provide some of the clues. And deep and unknown depths of prehistoric occupation lay below the Hittite, mantling the rocky promontory that gave Carchemish such mastery over the Euphrates.

The British Museum had started operations at Carchemish in 1878. Its deep mounds and extensive fortifications seemed to be a promising treasure-house for fine sculpture and possibly clay tablets. At the instigation of the cuneiform expert George Smith, the British consul at Aleppo was instructed to send a dragoman out to Carchemish to dig up sculptures. Though only a few inscribed fragments reached London, they caused considerable interest, for they were among the first examples of Hittite writing known.

The British consul was farsighted. He thought it wise to use his firman to secure title to the site before any other digging started. He journeyed up from Aleppo in state to purchase the old city in the name of the British government. Carchemish itself was deserted. The local people now lived in the tiny, ramshackle village of Jerablus nearby. The consul found Jerablus flocks grazing on the meadow inside Carchemish's overgrown ramparts. None of the villagers were anxious to claim title to this useless but taxable land except one, a wealthy man who had quietly acquired the title against a rainy day. Ali Agha received the consul courteously, but firmly refused to sell Carchemish to the British Museum. Foreigners could dig in the ruins as much as they liked, but he wanted the land for himself. The consul returned to Aleppo empty-handed.

A few months later, Ali Agha found himself imprisoned in Aleppo, the victim of a sudden arrest on indeterminate charges. His plight was a common but sorry one in Turkish domains, indeed potentially disastrous, for the authorities hardly fed their prisoners. Ali Agha was hungry, without funds for bribery, and desperate. Then he suddenly thought of the British consul. A hasty note brought the consul to his cell. Ali tearfully protested his innocence and begged him to intercede on his behalf. The consul tactfully reminded the prisoner that they had some unfinished business at Carchemish. Ali agreed with alacrity. Within a few hours, he was magically freed from prison, all charges dropped. A quarter share in Carchemish duly changed hands in exchange for an embroidered coat, a pair of blue leather boots, and a revolver.

Carchemish lay silent until 1911, when the British Museum again decided to dig the site. Ali Agha's son honored the long-standing agreement and waived all claims to finds within the city walls. The dig began in March 1911 under the directorship of David Hogarth, an experienced archaeologist who had worked with Arthur Evans on the palace of Knossos. Hogarth was a strong personality, known to his Carchemish workmen as Azrael, the Angel of Death, on account of his crotchety temper before breakfast. His junior assistants were R. Campbell-Thompson, a cuneiform expert, and a young man named T. E. Lawrence. Lawrence was to spend four years at Carchemish, Hogarth only two months. The preliminary work consisted for the most part of shifting the foundations of Roman and other recent buildings, looking for portable antiquities and probing the lower levels of the earthworks. The results were sufficiently promising for the British Museum to embark on a long excavation campaign. There was another good reason, too. Hogarth and Lawrence were keeping a close watch on the German railroad to Baghdad that was being constructed nearby.

The British government was not worried about Baghdad, but about Basra. Baghdad was merely a sleepy provincial town. Basra, on the other hand, posed some threat, for the railway would enable the Germans to control an overland route to the east that bypassed the Suez Canal. British concerns were more strategic, centering on whether Turkey would ally itself with Germany in time of war. Few people were aware of the vast oilfields of Arabia and Iraq. The German railroad led from Constantinople to Ankara, from there to Aleppo, Carchemish, and Mosul, and down the Tigris to Basra. The intelligence work for which Carchemish provided cover was designed to yield information on vulnerable bridges, culverts, and other arteries. Above all, Hogarth told Lawrence (who was equipped with five cameras and even a telephoto lens) to get to know the local people — they were the potential saboteurs of the line. In any event, the intelligence work was futile. The tunnels through the Taurus Mountains were not finished by 1914.

Woolley took over a going concern, an excavation with an active foreman, a team of unruly Arab and Kurdish laborers, and T. E. Lawrence, fresh from Oxford, already a veteran of the diggings. Lawrence was well known for miles around, both for his sympathy with, and understanding of, the local people and also for his impish sense of humor. When Woolley arrived, the workmen were still chortling over the trick Lawrence had played on an officious Turkish soldier. The soldier had jeered at Lawrence and challenged his power and authority. Lawrence quietly smiled. "I'll show you how powerful I am," he said. He produced two glasses filled with water and two packets of Seidlitz powder, one white, the other an imposing blue. The packets looked impressively magical. In fact, Seidlitz, a village in Bavaria, was famous for its carbonated water, the formula for which was often sold in powdered form.

"Take these two glasses, one in each hand," he told the Turk. "Is the water in them hot or cold?" he then asked.

"Cold," replied the soldier.

"Right. You ask what powers I have. Can I make the cold water boil without fire?"

"Of course not," was the reply.

Lawrence passed his hands over the two glasses, quietly poured the powders in them, and muttered strange incantations. "Abracadabra!" he finally pronounced. "Pour the water from one glass to the other."

The Seidlitz powder boiled and bubbled furiously. With a terrified howl, the soldier dropped the glasses and fled.

Woolley never revealed his true feelings about Lawrence, even after Lawrence's exploits in Arabia had made him famous. They came to Carchemish together in a humble cart in March 1912, apparently already on good terms. Lawrence took over photography, sculpture, and pottery, tasks which he seems to have found congenial. But Woolley, although liking him, found his work "curiously erratic." Fortunately, both men shared a penchant for luxurious living after work. Woolley watched Lawrence throw himself into the role of a Great Personage, teaching lessons to young Arabs, treating diseases, and dressing up in elaborate and incongruous costumes. His evening cloak of gold and silver thread weighed sixty pounds and had come — cheap — from a thief in the Aleppo market. Carchemish was an important formative period in Lawrence's life.

Within minutes of arriving at Carchemish on a Sunday, Woolley found his camp besieged by people anxious for work as diggers. When Hogarth left, he had arranged for an official guard to be placed on the site to protect it from looters. The guard commander had done his job well. No one had touched anything. But he now refused to let Woolley start work without the permission of the governor of Birecik, a local official who lived twenty-five miles away. Woolley wrote this gentleman a polite letter, asking for his approval to start work at once, enrolled one hundred and twenty men to begin on Wednesday, and made final preparations for the dig. The next day, the governor flatly refused permission for any digging at all.

"This was a nasty shock," wrote Woolly later. It was also a tricky situation. If the work did not begin on schedule, he would not only waste valuable time but, even more important, he would lose the respect of his men. Respect was the cornerstone of all Woolley's dealings with the local people. Feeling that a few minutes' conversation would correct any misunderstanding, Woolley and Lawrence rode to Birecik the next morning to interview the recalcitrant official. After cooling his heels in the governor's anteroom for a while, Woolley simply walked in on him. He found an "elderly man with grey hair and pointed beard, sly eyes, and flabby figure." The interview got off to a slow start. Woolley produced his firman from the sultan. The governor refused to take any notice of the British Museum until they communicated with him in Turkish. Woolley argued at length, but to no avail. The governor ostentatiously turned over some papers on his desk to indicate that the interview was at an end. Woolley turned to insistence. He pointed out that he had engaged one hundred and twenty men to work on the morrow. "You have only ten men at Jerablus," he told the governor, "and I have a hundred and twenty who want to work." When the governor said he would send more, Woolley lost his temper. "Send all you've got," he said. "I shall still outnumber you and my men are armed." He hoped, he added, that the governor himself would come at the head of his troops. Then he, Woolley, would have great pleasure in shooting him first.

The governor told him he was talking nonsense and refused to budge. Boldly, Woolley called his bluff. He drew his revolver and held it against the governor's left ear. "I will shoot you here and now unless you give me permission to start now," he said with quiet menace. Woolley got his permit that very afternoon and returned to a triumphant welcome from his workmen. Lawrence was deeply impressed. "We are very well amused," he wrote home. These were the days of British arrogance. "There would be a warship in Beyrout if anyone in Birijik only insulted us," he added.

Woolley's first task on site was to examine the wreckage of the Roman city of Europus that stood on the surface. Slowly and deliberately, Woolley removed the Roman city stone by stone. The lower levels under Europus were far more important, so the Romans had to go. Woolley carefully recorded every feature he destroyed. "After all," he remarked, "there are perhaps a hundred sites where Roman towns stand better preserved than at Carchemish."

The removal of the Roman city proved to be the costliest of all the excavations at Carchemish. To his great relief, Woolley was able to give the thousands of tons of Roman stone to the German engineers who were building the track for the Baghdad railway. The Germans began removing the stone at once. But the owner of Carchemish, Ali Agha's son Hassan Agha, protested that Woolley had given away the stone when the laborers could have made a profit from it. When Woolley told him the engineers would never pay, the story reached the ears of the governor of Birecik. A few days later, a summons from the governor's court arrived for Lawrence. He was to stand trial for stealing stone from Hassan Agha.

The summons was highly illegal. No British subject could be tried in a Turkish court without adequate representation. Furthermore, the court concerned administered Islamic law, which applied to Moslems only. Nevertheless, Lawrence attended the preliminary hearing. The governor promptly confiscated all the papers relating to the site, then adjourned the case.

A few days later, some soldiers arrived to stop the stone removal. They held up the contractors' carts until Woolley hit on the brilliant strategy of employing the workmen on the Germans' behalf. Then he walked proudly up to the guards at the head of his men. When the guard commander tried to stop him, Woolley asked him what he would do if force was used. "Go ahead," replied the Turk amicably, "for that will clear me with the governor." So Woolley drew his revolver and marched the guard commander to the German dump. The two men quietly smoked cigarettes as several loads of stone arrived safely. Once again, the governor was stymied. He retaliated by fining Woolley thirty pounds. Woolley tore to shreds the paper demanding the fine.

Woolley himself accompanied Lawrence to the next hearing, only to find that the case had again been postponed. Woolley told the governor to convene the court at once, which he did. When the court was assembled, Woolley immediately challenged its legal validity. The prosecution applied for another remand and the archaeologists were asked to sign a lengthy document in Turkish. Woolley firmly informed the judge that the case was over and demanded his papers back.

Leonard Woolley at Ur of the Chaldees

The magistrate refused. When Woolley demanded the presence of the governor, that worthy official refused to attend.

"I'm not going to leave until I get the papers," stated Woolley.

"In that case," replied the magistrate, "you won't leave till next week."

Everyone laughed except Woolley, who got up and leveled a revolver at the magistrate. "You will not leave the room alive unless I get those papers," he shouted. Woolley's foreman also drew his two revolvers. The court trembled in silence. Lawrence was sent to waylay the governor and to obtain the missing papers. A few minutes later, the permits were back in Woolley's pocket. He pocketed his revolver as well, and left in triumph surrounded by salaaming officials.

A few weeks later, the British consul in Aleppo received a visit from a high local official. "Those English of yours at Jerablus are doing irresponsible things," he complained. "They tried to shoot the governor."

"Did they really shoot him?" inquired the consul.

"Well, they *threatened* to, but they did not actually kill him."

"What a pity," the consul remarked quietly.

And that was almost the end of the matter. When Woolley next called on the British ambassador in Constantinople, he received a somewhat frosty reception. Turkey, he was informed, was a civilized country.

Woolley's acts were, to put it mildly, high-handed. He preferred to brazen his way rather than use finesse. Local conditions were such that he felt he had to be firm. The moment the excavations were bogged down in bureaucracy they were dead. One is reminded of Claudius James Rich's terse comment in the early nineteenth century: "Nothing but the most decisive conduct will do." In the context of Woolley's time, Rich was again right. Fortunately for Woolley, an Englishman's word was still law, even to the Turks.

Woolley's predecessor, David Hogarth, had suffered under a series of incompetent and corrupt Turkish archaeological commissioners, none of whom had done anything to settle the constant disputes between the archaeologists and local officialdom. Woolley found himself saddled with Fuad Bey, an Arab from Baghdad who had trained as a civil servant in Constantinople.

Fuad was a puny little man, city-bred, who was convinced that the local tribesmen would cut his throat at the slightest provocation. He distrusted Woolley, too, certain that the archaeologists were out to steal everything. At first he insisted that an armed guard sleep outside his tent and tried to set traps for Woolley by leaving antiquities lying around for him to steal. But this time he had met his match. Woolley was ruthless and, we may surmise, set out to reform the commissioner. Quite what methods he used, we do not know. He seems to have given Fuad a short but intensive course on field archaeology in general and on Carchemish in particular, and on British customs into the bargain. Within a few months Fuad Bey was working enthusiastically in the laboratories, talking freely to the villagers, and being thoroughly cooperative. "I had reproved him more than once," wrote Woolley. One wonders what sort of rebukes Woolley used, for Fuad was unswerving in his loyalty to the expedition. Woolley must also have used his full powers of persuasion along with coercion, as he did so often with petty officialdom. One exasperated bureaucrat who had given trouble over permits admitted defeat when Fuad interceded on Woolley's behalf. "I don't know what you have done to Fuad," he remarked to Woolley, "but he is greatly changed; he seems to be becoming quite English!"

Woolley settled in for a long stay. He organized the labor force into teams of four men. A shoveler and two basketmen supported every pickman. The basketmen carried the discarded soil out of the dig and dumped it in the nearby Euphrates. Everyone wanted to be a pickman, the person who loosened the soil and had the greatest chance of finding new discoveries that were rewarded with a small payment.

Discoveries brought not only money but considerable personal prestige as well, especially if a basketman found an object overlooked by his superiors. Lawrence and the foreman worked out a system whereby really magnificent discoveries were greeted with a ceremonial volley from the foreman's revolver. The workmen would summon the foreman, who would assess the number of cartridges the find was worth. The resulting salvo announced to the world that another important discovery had come to light. "The whole thing may sound childish," Woolley remarked, "but in fact it is such things that make the work go well, and when digging at Jerablus ceases to be a great game and becomes, as in Egypt, a mere business, it will be a bad thing." Judging from the chronicle of difficulties that confronted the archaeologists, the game must have become a considerable strain at times.

The truly great Near Eastern archaeologists almost invariably got on well with their workmen. Leonard Woolley was no exception. He commanded quite extraordinary loyalty from the local people, and he and Lawrence lived like kings among them. They built a fine excavation house for seventy-five pounds that suited Woolley's style. It boasted, as Lawrence wrote, "mosaic floors and beaten copper fittings. . . . Woolley fancies himself in the bathroom: a gleaming mosaic floor reflecting his shining body against the contrast of the red-stuccoed walls." A copper bathtub, a large fireplace, many carvings, and thick sheepskin rugs completed the imposing decor. The excavation house was always full of visitors, both Arab and European, gossiping, arguing, engaged in the constant political intrigue that was an integral part of the Carchemish dig. Visitors were often served coffee in Hittite clay cups. "If I drop it," said Lawrence once, "the British Museum will be glad to have the pieces."

Hogarth had brought a Cypriot foreman named Gregori to Carchemish in 1911, a veteran of Knossos and other digs. Gregori needed a local man to work with him. He chose a redheaded pickman as his new assistant, one Mohammed ibn Sheikh Ibrahim, known to generations of archaeologists as Hamoudi. A tall and gaunt man with a powerful figure and a fiery temper, Hamoudi worked with Leonard Woolley from 1912 to 1946. No Woolley dig was complete without him. He taught himself to read and write, served as Woolley's political assistant in World War I, and became a close family friend. Hamoudi ruled the workmen with a firm hand, but always with a sense of fun and proportion that made any Woolley excavation a formidable opponent for officialdom. Many evenings Hamoudi would brew coffee for Woolley and himself. They would smoke and chat until dinner was announced. Woolley could have written a book about these sessions.

"Yes," said Hamoudi one evening many years later, "there have been two passions in my life, archaeology and violence."

Woolley's wife Katherine laughed at him. "You wicked old murderer," she exclaimed.

Hamoudi was horrified. "Murderer?" he cried. "I have never in all my life killed a man for money, only for fun!"

This remarkable man had started life as a bandit and an outlaw. His four sons followed in his footsteps and became part of a highly effective team that ran Woolley's later excavations at Ur of the Chaldees like clockwork. Hamoudi and Woolley understood each other perfectly. Each was a compulsive worker and had a lively sense of humor. Perhaps Hamoudi described it best: "We have broken much bread together."

Woolley's house foreman was just as formidable a character. Haj Wahid and Hamoudi hated each other. A large, handsome man, the Haj had spent many years as a courier in the British consulate in Aleppo. Unfortunately, he was devoted to strong drink and to firearms. After a heavy bout with the bottle, the Haj would lie down on his flat rooftop with a rifle and fire ineffectually on passersby through the Aleppo city gate that lay below him. Consular couriers had diplomatic immunity, so the Haj could shoot at the feet of camel drivers with relative impunity. Traffic inevitably ground to a standstill until he tired of his game.

Even Haj Wahid could go too far. His flirtations with the daughter of a prominent family so enraged her male relatives that they seized swords and revolvers and set on him one dark night. Haj flailed around him with his official courier's scimitar and discharged his revolver wildly. A few moments later, four of his assailants lay dead at his feet, another was badly wounded. He himself was found unconscious next day and arrested. As the British consul said, a murder or two could be overlooked, but not four in a single night. The Haj served two years of a life sentence, but managed, by some nefarious means, to have his term commuted. There was no way the British consul could rehire such a turbulent man. So he recommended him to the Carchemish expedition as a servant. Although some of the Haj's ways were described by Woolley as "peculiar," especially his habit of cooking meals with a rifle over his shoulder, he became a loyal protector of Woolley's, and the British Museum's, interests.

Woolley was to spend most of his time at Carchemish digging the Hittite city under the Roman settlement. The Hittites were a shadowy people in 1912. In 1878, an English scholar named A. J. Sayce had published a memorable paper in which he declared that the Biblical "Hittites" had ruled over a large empire in northern Syria and Turkey. The Hittites were, Sayce argued, a third major political force in the Near East over three thousand years ago, and were treated with respect by both Assyrians and Egyptians. The Assyrians referred to the Hittites as the "people of Hatti." Carchemish was one of the small city-states into which the Hittites were organized.

Sayce's arguments aroused considerable controversy until Wallis Budge bought the Tell el-Amarna tablets for the British Museum in 1887. These cuneiform archives contained frequent references to Hittite raids on the Egyptians' Syrian domains, to proposed marital alliances between Egyptian and Hittite royalty, and to a long history of diplomatic intercourse between two empires that regarded each other as equals. After the German Assyriologist Hugo Winckler dug into the fortress mound of Boghazkoy in central Turkey in 1906–1907, he worked out a list of Hittite rulers. Among others he identified the king Suppiluliumas, who, we now know, created the Hittite Empire from many smaller city-states by bold military campaigns after 1370 B.C. Suppiluliumas captured the fortress of Carchemish in 1354 B.C. and gained control of the Euphrates crossing. Carchemish remained a Hittite city for six hundred years, until its capture by Sargon II of Assyria in 717 B.C.

As the diggers began to uncover the Hittite levels of the city, they found abundant evidence that Carchemish had once been a powerful Hittite settlement. They came across a great wall facing the Euphrates. Its black basalt facing gave way to a massive water gate with intricate carving that led to the Hittite citadel. A broad roadway extended west from the gate to an open space in front of the citadel, which protected the palaces and temple. As the excavators cleared the road, they came across some collapsed sculptured figures, which Woolley replaced in their original positions. They formed a long procession of foot soldiers marching in pairs and following chariots and horses tread-were shooting down their fleeing foes, as the army marched toward the goddess Ishtar and her temple. From the square at the end of the roadway a wide flight of steps led up to the entrance door of the citadel. The door was flanked by basalt lions.

Another palace lay on the south side of the square. Lively sculptures of strange and mythical figures, demons, and legendary events adorned its walls. The Hittite sculptors depicted a conquering army marching in triumph to receive the thanks of the seated king and his family. The victorious host bear their shields in ceremonial order, helmets in place, bow or javelin at the ready. The captains lead their men and bear an olive branch of peace and victory. Musicians and priests parade on the entry walls, watched by an awesome god seated in a lion-drawn chariot. Inside the palace walls lions and stags pranced in relief, pursued by eternal hunters living in a world of easy pleasure.

Unfortunately, neither Woolley nor his colleagues could relax for a moment and enjoy the luxury of archaeology without distractions. Many of the workmen were Kurdish nomads, fiercely proud and independent, from different tribes that were in a constant state of barely suppressed warfare. Everyone, including the archaeologists, carried a firearm. Woolley had to behave like a king, a political equal among the nomad sheikhs who lived across the Euphrates. The Kurds hated the Turks, tolerated the Arabs, and adored Woolley's direct dealings. He was constantly receiving Kurdish visitors and mediating disputes.

Woolley was trusted on all sides, but the excavation was far from secure. His Kurdish neighbors were perfectly capable of raiding his camp, although they never did so. Carchemish commanded the critical ford that raiding parties had to cross should they decide to attack Aleppo. The local sheikh told Woolley he would provide a guard of two thousand men for the excavations if the attack took place!

The diplomatic visits with the Kurds took valuable hours away from the excavations. Such niceties could never be ignored, for even a small lapse of etiquette could trigger a major dispute. His particular friend Sheikh Busrawi was fond of strong liquor, something forbidden all Moslems. "We Kurds like drink," Busrawi stated when rebuked. "We are Kurds first and Mohammedans afterward." Woolley, who provided drink, was soon known as "the elder brother of Busrawi." They retained close ties for years.

Second to the Kurds' hatred of the Turks was their loathing for the Baghdad railway that was about to cross their territory. The original German engineer in charge of the construction work hated Woolley into the bargain. On more than one occasion, the archaeologists had to keep the peace between German and Kurd. Several times Busrawi eagerly threatened to cut the throats of every engineer. Matters came to a head in 1912, when the Germans asked if they could dig away part of the city walls of Carchemish for a railway embankment. Woolley firmly refused and the chief engineer left in a fury. When the excavations closed down for the summer, the Germans quietly moved in and started recruiting men to dig away the walls. Word of the German duplicity came to Haj Wahid, who went at once to see the chief engineer and on Woolley's behalf forbade him to start work. His effort was useless. So the next morning the Haj took a rifle and two revolvers and lay down on the threatened wall. When the Germans and three hundred workmen approached, Haj Wahid told them to keep their distance or he would open fire. The standoff continued for three days while Lawrence, warned by telegraph, summoned up the authorities, who stopped the work at once.

If that was not enough, the workmen employed by the Germans would always ally themselves with Woolley and his men rather than with their own employers. The trouble was that the Germans were incapable of handling the locals, indeed they made no effort to understand them. Some months after the Haj's one-man standoff, Woolley found himself mediating a serious wage dispute between the Kurdish workmen and the Germans. By the time he came on the scene, shots were being exchanged between a handful of Germans and three hundred furious laborers. The Germans even shot at Lawrence and Woolley. One bullet struck between Woolley's feet. It took two hectic hours and some desperate force before Woolley, Lawrence, Hamoudi, and Haj Wahid could restore order. Even so, one man was killed, which started talk of a blood feud. The whole incident ended with the comic-opera arrival of the Aleppo Volunteer Fire Brigade, brass helmets and all, closely followed by two hundred troops. It was a tribute to Woolley's diplomatic skill that he was asked to act as official mediator, a task that took days of patient negotiation before peace was restored.

The Carchemish dig ended with the outbreak of World War I. Woolley went on to become an intelligence officer and spent two years after the siege of Al-Kut as a Turkish prisoner of war. Lawrence left his full and intense life at Carchemish with deep insights into the Arab character that were to lead him to immortality as "Lawrence of Arabia." He never returned to the dig, but Woolley resumed work in 1919 under even trickier conditions than before. A garrison of French soldiers was quartered on the site while Woolley tried to work out the complicated ancient defenses of the town. The wily Busrawi was forever stirring up trouble between the various factions that passed through Jerablus. Woolley again found himself mediating peace and war, this time between the French and the Kurds. The excavation house came under fire when the Kurds decided to pressure the French to accept the terms of a peace agreement worked out by Woolley. Busrawi asked Woolley when the French ate dinner and quietly scheduled the mock attack for that very hour. For three days the Kurds kept the soldiers busy while their soup got cold. Woolley quietly enjoyed his dinner in the next room as the bullets flew overhead. But the dig continued without interruption.

The busy world of the dig must have seemed a haven of peace after all these constant complications. Woolley felt deeply moved by Carchemish. Its very position by the main ford of the Euphrates ensured the city a lasting place in history. Prehistoric farmers, Hittite kings, Assyrians, Egyptians, and Romans had passed this way. Byzantine officials crossed the Euphrates by the city walls. Modern travelers paused at the Carchemish dig all the time. French soldiers now guarded the same ford. Woolley dug the city just as the Baghdad railway bridge was thrown across the Euphrates nearby. It was, he realized, the final chapter in pages and pages of history. He could stand among the sculptures eyeing the stately figures of marching soldiers and magnificent kings and imagine himself back two thousand years and more in the past. The bases of the cedar pillars of the palace worked in elegant bronze would come to life. He could imagine the dry spring dust blowing over the bustling city, the echo of innumerable footsteps on the worn cobblestones. Twenty-five hundred years ago, he remembered, the sculptures glistened with bright colors and cedar panels covered the dark brick.

Then the image would fade, to be replaced by deserted ruins and the gossip of idle workmen at their lunch break. But the place had a subtle charm of its own, one that could come to life as itinerant musicians would pipe for the dancing workmen. "No background more fitting could be found," Woolley wrote years afterward. "The tumbled stones, the steps rising like a theatre set for their outdoor play, the row of sculptured chariots showing off their life against its frozen age."

Carchemish was far more than an excavation. The comfortable images of the past, the regal excavation house, the workmen, the constant tumult of political intrigue and petty conflict, all were part of the Carchemish dig as they were of other Near Eastern excavations of the time. This tumultuous and perhaps naive world seems as remote today as the Hittites themselves.

V

SCIENCE AND NATIONALISM

19

Gertrude Bell and the New Iraq

*The credit of the country requires proper
provision for a department of antiquities.*

THE ARCHAEOLOGISTS who worked in Mesopotamia just before World
War I were dimly aware that major political changes were in the of-
fing. Some of them, like David Hogarth and Leonard Woolley, knew
that their excavations provided convenient bases for discreet observation of big-power strategies at work in the Ottoman Empire. Before
the 1870s, Britain had sought to bolster the sultan and his empire against
aggressors, the objective being to protect British trade and strategic
communications. The last decades of the nineteenth century saw a
change in big-power policy toward the Turks. European nations became less tolerant of Ottoman inertia and gave high priority to economic expansion in the Near East. Concession seeker after concession
seeker had persuaded the Turks to mortgage their finances in the hope
that railways, new factories, banks, mines, and other industrial developments would lead to prosperity. In the event, the Ottoman Empire sank
deeper and deeper into debt, and its outlying possessions evaporated.
The 1890s saw civil war in Turkish Crete. The Balkans loosened Ottoman ties early in the new century. The Ottoman Empire was widely
known as the "sick man of Europe." Every great power was keenly in-

terested in the political outcome of the final collapse of the sultan's rule.

The progressive weakening of Ottoman authority that climaxed in the Turkish Revolution of 1908 had little effect on the day-to-day governance of Iraq. The newly formed Committee of Union and Progress that ruled Turkey from 1909 to the outbreak of World War I governed the obscure province of Iraq substantially as before. Some improvements in the standard of government were made in the last six years of Turkish rule. The Germans were encouraged to extend their railway as far as the vicinity of Baghdad. The British irrigation expert Sir William Willcox headed up efforts to carry out some large-scale flood-control projects in the delta. Gertrude Bell described him as "a twentieth-century Don Quixote, erratic, elusive, maddening, and entirely lovable." But the Iraqis themselves were beginning to demand a greater say in their own affairs. Some Iraqis had attained high office in the Ottoman bureaucracy of Baghdad. They were in touch with Arab émigrés in Paris who dreamed of nationhood and a new Iraq. The years between 1908 and 1914 saw a gradual emergence of new ideals among thinking Iraqis, ideas of Arab nationalism, separatism, and local autonomy. Local politicians were far more aware of the outside world, of international trends and the strategic importance of their own country. Baghdad's newspapers advocated pro-Islam movements, Arab unity. Some brave souls even displayed anti-Turkish placards in the streets at night. These muted protests were beginning to increase in number and volume when World War I broke out in 1914, by which time Arabs and Turks found little to agree upon. Most foreigners in Mesopotamia, though sympathetic to the Arab's plight, felt that their aspirations were premature. They held no brief for Turkish rule, but they distrusted the Arabs' ability to govern themselves. Iraq was a morass of complex political problems, of anti-Turkish movements, and of tribal and religious conflicts. The tribal communities of the countryside hated the townspeople, different Moslem sects quarreled constantly, and the Kurdish border areas were in a state of perennial ferment.

All of these stirrings had little effect on foreign archaeologists, who continued to work much as they always had, exporting most of their finds and dealing with their laborers and officialdom in an arbitrary, high-handed manner. Only a few archaeologists were aware of the new pulse of excitement in tent and bazaar. One was the English archaeologist and traveler Gertrude Bell, who had journeyed widely in the Near East in the years before World War I. Bell was fluent in Arabic and gained profound insights into the attitudes and customs of the local people wherever she went. She captured these feelings in one memorable passage:

"For the first time in all the turbulent centuries to which those desolate regions bear witness, a potent word had gone forth, and those who caught it listened in amazement, asking one another for an explanation of its meaning. Liberty — what is liberty? I think the question which rang so perpetually through the black tents would have received no better solution in the royal pavilions which once spread their glories over the plain. Idly though it fell from the lips of the Bedouin it foretold change."

The nascent political aspirations of the Iraqis came to an abrupt halt on November 5, 1914, when Turkey entered World War I on the side of the central powers. The British government had long made contingency plans to protect their new, vital oil interests at Abadan, installations they could ill afford to lose. On November 6, a brigade of British troops landed there and secured both the oil facilities and Basra in the face of feeble Turkish opposition. Basra became a British-occupied enclave. The British wondered timidly whether they should advance on Baghdad as well. An abortive campaign up the Tigris in 1915 ended in the disastrous 140-day siege of Al-Kut and the surrender of British forces in April of the following year. Bloody but unbowed, the British spent the rest of 1916 consolidating their Basra bridgehead and setting up a network of roads and service facilities for mechanized transport. They also built airstrips and employed thousands of Arabs in building light military railways and canals. Communications in southern Iraq were revolutionized in a few short months. Major General Stanley Maude led a successful campaign to recover lost ground up the Tigris in February 1917. On March 11, 1917, British troops entered Baghdad. By the 1918 armistice, they occupied almost all of Iraq, as far north as Mosul.

The Iraqis found the British a startling contrast to the Turks. Only a short time after Maude occupied Baghdad, he made a famous speech in which he announced the British government's support of the "aspirations of their Race." Meanwhile, the British were faced with the task of setting up a viable and efficient civilian administration from the ruins of Turkish rule. This burden fell on the head of Sir Percy Cox, an Indian political officer of vast experience, who soon became known to the Iraqis as "Cokkus." He found Baghdad in chaos, sanitary conditions shocking, and no experienced bureaucrats to run Iraq. So he created a British-run administrative service from scratch, one that was designed to be as cheap and efficient as possible. The question of the political status of Iraq had to hang fire until Britain and Turkey made peace.

Nationalist sentiment began to run high as international discussions on Iraq's future began. The Conference of San Remo, held in Italy on

April 24, 1920, settled her fate. France was granted Syria, and Iraq was mandated to Britain. In July 1920 a serious anti-British insurrection involving tribal rivalries broke out in southern Iraq. It took massive reinforcements from India to put down the revolt, which dragged on for eight months. Sir Percy Cox was recalled from a post he had taken in Tehran and was appointed British high commissioner in Baghdad. He found himself confronted with an intricate maze of political maneuvering and mediation.

Once the rebellion was quashed, Cox set up a provisional government of Iraq under the leadership of the naqib of Baghdad. This caretaker administration gave the British time to search for a national leader. A conference in Cairo in 1921 chose Prince Feisal, the son of King Hussein of the Hijaz, the sharif of Mecca, as the ruler of Iraq. On August 23, 1921, King Feisal was duly proclaimed the elected sovereign. The British tried to cope with the growing tide of Arab nationalism by concluding a compromise treaty with Feisal's new government in 1922. The treaty softened the mandate relationship by giving Iraq limited control of its own affairs. This covenant covered constitutional procedure, guaranteed freedom of religion, education, and missionary enterprise. While Iraq was to become self-defending within four years, the rights of foreigners were safeguarded. Adequate antiquities legislation was to be implemented under the treaty. Feisal was to rule for twelve years, during which the treaty was renegotiated three times. Britain agreed to terminate the mandate in 1929. On October 3, 1932, Iraq was admitted to the League of Nations and became the first fully independent Arab state.

Iraq was also one of the first places where the British had to face the fact that they could not rule as an imperial power. The transition to independence was achieved with remarkably little disruption or bitterness, considering that the changeover from stagnant Ottoman rule to British imperial governance, and then to direct Iraqi control, took barely fifteen years. Without question much of the credit for this remarkable transition must lie with Sir Percy Cox and the small team of administrators and military officers who organized the effective administration of a chaotic Turkish province from the ground up in a few short years. One of his key advisers was Gertrude Bell, by now an extraordinary expert on the Arab world and an accomplished archaeologist. She was the only female official in Cox's all-male administration. In the course of her administrative career, she was to set the archaeology of Iraq on a radically new course.

Gertrude Bell was born in County Durham, England, on July 14, 1868, the daughter of a well-to-do north country family. After private schooling, she went up to Oxford in 1886, at a time when few women undergraduates attended the university. Gertrude achieved a brilliant modern history degree in two years. At the same time, "she swam, she rowed, she played tennis, and hockey, she acted, she danced, she spoke in debates," wrote an admiring contemporary. She emerged from the university with an "Oxfordy" manner, an insatiable appetite for travel, and an honesty and independence of judgment that tended to disconcert her elders. Her travels began in 1892, with a trip to Tehran. The following year she went to Switzerland, Italy, and Algiers. She then traveled around the world and took up mountaineering. After a few seasons, she was recognized as one of the foremost female climbers of her generation. She was, remembered one well-known male climber, an effort to follow.

In November of 1899, Bell set out for a seven-month stay in Jerusalem. By this time she had published a travel book on Persia and a volume of her translations of Persian poems. She went to Jerusalem to improve her Arabic and to travel in the desert as far afield as Petra and Palmyra. This was her first experience of the discomforts of desert travel: "tents with earwigs and black beetles and muddy water to drink." But she chattered away in Arabic to sheikhs and storekeepers, and fell in love with the East. "One doesn't keep away from the East when one has got into it this far," she wrote prophetically. It was during this stay that she developed an interest in archaeology. She took over six hundred photographs of ancient monuments near Jerusalem, then spent the next few years alternately traveling in Europe, Morocco, and Egypt and studying archaeology in Rome and Paris.

Bell worked on excavations in western Turkey in 1902 and studied Byzantine monuments in northern Syria and Cilicia in 1905. This latter trip resulted in her second travel book *The Desert and the Sown* (1907). In 1909, she published a major work on Byzantine Anatolia, a study of the Thousand and One Churches at Birbinkilise, which is a unique record of a series of sites that virtually no longer exist. Byzantine ruins were not her first love. In 1907 she wrote, "I shall go back to Arabia, to the desert." She now toyed with the idea of a trip through the central Arabian desert to the town of Ha'il. Sir Percy Cox, the British resident in the Persian Gulf, managed to dissuade her from trying this trip in 1909, for the desert tribes were in a state of great political unrest. So she set off from Aleppo for a journey across the desert to the Euphrates and to the territory of the Deleim Arabs, who were notoriously dangerous. Her objective was the walled Abbasid palace of Ukhaidir, a huge castle with a fortified enclosure. She spent four days planning and photographing the site, which no one had ever described in detail before. Her soldier escort refused to set their rifles aside for a moment, so they tumbled all over them as they held her measuring tapes. "I can't persuade them to lay down the damnable things for an instant," she complained. Ukhaidir cast a profound spell on Gertrude Bell. She first described it in the most famous of her books, *Amurath to Amurath*, which appeared in 1911. It was in this book that she first hinted at the rising tide of Arab nationalism that she came across in her travels.

In 1911 Bell took a caravan across the desert in February in bitter cold. "Nor was my toilette very complicated as I had gone to bed in my clothes," she wrote. She was undeterred by the chill of their early morning departures. "Can you picture the singular beauty of these moonlit departures?" she wrote home. "The frail Arab tents falling one by one, leaving the camp fires blazing into the night; the dark masses of the kneeling camels; the shrouded figures binding up the loads, shaking the ice from the waterskins, or crouched over the hearth for a moment's warmth before mounting." She wrote later: "While I wonder and rejoice to look upon this primeval existence, it does not seem to be a new thing; it is familiar, it is part of inherited memory."

Bell found time to make a short cut to her beloved Ukhaidir and found that some of the German archaeologists at Babylon had visited the palace in her absence. They were preparing a volume on the site. Her own study, based on her surveys and on the German work, appeared in 1914. She dedicated it to Walter Andrae. "A subject so enchanting and so suggestive as the Palace of Ukhaidir is not likely to present itself more than once in a lifetime," she wrote. "I call to mind the amazement with which I first gazed upon its formidable walls; the romance of my first sojourn within its precincts; the pleasure undiminished by familiarity of my return; and the regret with which I sent back across the sun-drenched plain a last greeting to its distant presence."

From Ukhaidir she journeyed to Babylon and then Baghdad, which she reached safely in late March 1911. She was greeted at both places with the deference due an experienced traveler who enjoyed the confidence of the locals. Everywhere she went she received a steady stream of local sheikhs and dignitaries for ceremonial coffee drinking. One of her contemporaries drew a cartoon of her at such a function and appended a pithy verse:

> *From Trebizond to Tripolis*
> *She rolls the Pashas flat*
> *And tells them what to think of this*
> *And what to think of that.*

On her way north, Bell spent three days at Assur with Walter Andrae and his colleague Conrad Preusser. Andrae was enchanted with his expert visitor and took her over every detail of the excavations. The Germans taught her how to take flashlight photographs, a useful technique for recording dark church interiors. She admired Andrae's "brilliant and comprehensive" views and left with a heavy heart for Hatra, where the entire Turkish detachment paraded in her honor.

On her way home, she stopped at Carchemish in the hope of catching David Hogarth. He had already gone home and R. Campbell-Thompson and T. E. Lawrence were digging away by themselves. She spent a day at the excavations and later remarked that Lawrence "is going to make a traveler." The visit started badly when she told them that their methods were "prehistoric" compared with those of the Germans. So Campbell-Thompson and Lawrence counterattacked, we are told by the latter, with "a display of erudition": "She was taken (in five minutes) over Byzantine, Crusader, Roman, Hittite and French architecture (my part)." Then Campbell-Thompson talked about Greek folklore and Mesopotamian archaeology until Lawrence barged in with "prehistoric pottery and telephoto lenses, Bronze Age metal technique, Meredith, Anatole France, and the Octobrists." Campbell-Thompson ended this tour de force with a dissertation on "German methods of excavation with the Baghdad railway." It was not the most cordial of meetings. "Gerty has gone back to her tents," Lawrence wrote to Hogarth with glee.

Neither the British nor the Ottoman authorities approved of her next exploit, a desert journey in 1913 through Jordan and central Arabia to Ha'il, the stronghold of the Rashid Arabs. She was locked up on her arrival and firmly told to leave for Baghdad at once. She did so, but only after some forthright protestations. Two months before World War I, she returned to England and gave the British intelligence services much new information on Arabia that was to prove of the greatest value. In 1915, she was called out to Cairo to serve in the Arab Intelligence Bureau, where her unrivaled knowledge of central Arabia proved exceedingly valuable.

In the spring of 1916, she was posted to intelligence headquarters in Basra to study tribal politics from the Mesopotamian end. The military authorities found a woman rather an embarrassment, so they offered her to Sir Percy Cox as a chief political officer, a line of work she was to pursue for the rest of her life. Bell found herself in a position of considerable importance. She had to see that agreements made with sheikhs and tribal leaders were actually carried through. When Cox took over as civil commissioner in Baghdad, he arranged for her to be posted there as a member of his new secretariat. She proved useful as a filter between the harassed Cox and the dozens of Iraqi visitors, often of great prestige, that called on him. She flattered, interviewed, gave presents, briefed her boss on the points he should mention. Within a few months the Arabs regarded her as the pro-Arab member of the administration, a reputation she resolutely denied, although she wrote that she was sometimes overcome "with the sense of being as much an Asiatic as a European." Certainly she enjoyed her constant meetings with the desert sheikhs, from whom she got most of her news. "They are to me an endless romance," she wrote. "They come and go through the wilderness as if it were a high road, and they all, most politely, treat me as a colleague, because I too have been in Arcadia. When they talk of tribes or sheikhs, or watering places, I don't need to ask who and where they are. I know; and as they talk, I see again the wide Arabian horizon."

Gertrude Bell lived a hectic but extremely lonely life, which she recorded in a series of letters home to her family. She was a woman full of enthusiasm for all sorts of interests — archaeology, dogs, photography, mountains, languages, and, above all, people. Her intense fascination with the Arabs stemmed at least in part from her sympathy with the fierce loyalties and friendships of the desert. She became a champion of Arab independence, at her best when the government of Iraq was a makeshift affair and personal contacts rather than impersonal memoranda ran the affairs of state.

One of the first problems the new government had to face was that of antiquities legislation. Foreign expeditions were eager to take advantage of the new political conditions and to dig on a large scale at sites like Eridu and Ur of the Chaldees. The Germans were pressing for approval to export the crates containing the remains of the Ishtar Gate from Babylon. Clearly something had to be done to improve the antiquated legislation of the Ottoman Empire, especially to control the flow of important national antiquities overseas. Within a few months, all archaeological matters were referred to Gertrude Bell. With characteristic enthusiasm, she sat down to organize a department of antiquities, new excavation legislation, and an Iraq museum in which to house artifacts.

King Feisal had just appointed Bell honorary director of antiquities. She had been lobbying the king for months. "Today the King ordered me to tea and we had two hours of most excellent talk," she had written the July before. "He undertook to push the law through the government. . . . He's perfectly sound about archaeology, having been trained by T. E. Lawrence," she wrote. The debates over the new antiquities law were surprisingly acrimonious, for many Iraqis were anxious to protect their country's interests as much as possible and felt that a fifty-percent division of finds was too generous to foreigners.

The new antiquities law was Gertude Bell's cherished project, made more urgent by pressure from the British Museum to begin fieldwork in Iraq again. In June and October of 1919, the director of the University of Pennsylvania Museum, George Byron Gordon, had called on Sir Frederick Kenyon, his opposite member at the British Museum. Pennsylvania was also anxious to return to Iraq to follow up its campaigns at Nippur with a major effort at the same or another location. The two directors agreed to cooperate, for the costs of large-scale excavation were now such that neither could afford to excavate a big tell by themselves. A long correspondence ensued. Meanwhile, the British Museum was influential in obtaining a rider to the peace treaty that obligated Britain to create an antiquities law for Iraq.

Excavations had actually begun in Iraq on a small scale before the end of the war. R. Campbell-Thompson, who had worked at Carchemish and then spent three years on war service in Mesopotamia, started digging at Eridu in 1918, using Indian soldiers. Eridu had long had a reputation for being an extremely ancient city, largely because the Babylonian creation legends stated that "all the lands were sea; then Eridu was born." Eridu was the home of the Sumerian god Enki. A platform some three hundred yards square and forty feet high, with the ruins of a ziggurat at the north end, the site lies fourteen miles south of Ur of the Chaldees in a desolate landscape. "From the ziggurat, as far as the eye can see, there is naught but awful solitude," Campbell-Thompson wrote. "You look down on sombre desert which encircles you for miles." This dust-filled landscape was swept by winds that made excavation a misery. Campbell-Thompson covered the site with small trial pits about two yards square, which he excavated with the greatest care. He was frustrated, for the trial pits yielded quantities of loose sand, then accumulations of incomprehensible mud brick. He lacked the facilities to reach the mud-brick structures beneath the overburden. His trial-pit method helped but little in locating the early city of Eridu, which had been abandoned in about 2400 B.C. Campbell-Thompson also made small soundings at nearby Ur, excavations so promising that they encouraged the British Museum to work at this hitherto almost untouched site.

The first British Museum excavations at Ur were on a very limited scale. H. R. Hall took charge of the work. He was later to become keeper of the Department of Egyptian and Assyrian Antiquities in the museum. He opened trenches at Ur, Eridu, and a small mound near the former named Al-ʿUbaid. While excavating the Sumerian temple he found there, Hall noticed an unfamiliar type of light-green, black-painted pottery on another part of the mound. He could not afford to open up a larger area of the site, nor of Ur, so contented himself with describing his interesting new pottery in his report.

The correspondence between London and Pennsylvania began with Kenyon telling Gordon that no excavations would now be permitted in Iraq until a peace treaty in Turkey was signed and the Iraqi government could afford the expense of administering excavations. "The credit of the country requires proper provision for a department of antiquities," he wrote, and added, "It is desirable to impress on the Indian Office the fact that the civilized world expects facilities for archaeological explorations."

In March 1921, Kenyon told Gordon that the Colonial Office had taken over Iraq and that archaeology would be headed by Colonel T. E. Lawrence, "who was digging for us at Carchemish before the war." Gordon and Lawrence met in London in the fall, by which time Gordon knew that Leonard Woolley might be available to dig for a joint expedition because the country around Carchemish was too unsettled for excavations.

In January 1922, Lawrence wrote unofficially to Gordon and told him to apply for a permit. "We are going to be a little particular about the quality of these excavations," he informed him. All permits would be vetted by a committee in London.

The Americans were eager for a survey expedition, but Kenyon wrote that it would be difficult for the museum to join. "Our funds available for an expedition are funds for the acquisition of objects for the Museum. . . . Without a certainty of adequate return, we could not use our money simply for a survey." However, negotiations went ahead so well that on June 12, 1922, Kenyon was able to write to Philadelphia and agree to a joint expedition to Ur of the Chaldees under the direction of Leonard Woolley.

When Woolley arrived in Baghdad on October 29, 1922, he met Gertrude Bell and was told that the new antiquities law was about to be passed. Meanwhile, he was to work under a temporary permit. "In Miss Bell we shall of course have a most sympathetic director," he wrote to Gordon. Gertrude was not so enthusiastic. "He's a tiresome little man," she told her father, "but a first class digger and an archaeologist after my own heart, i.e., he entirely backs me up in the way I'm conducting the Department."

After the passage of the antiquities law, Bell began to work on a proposal for an Iraq museum. She started by keeping artifacts on a shelf in her home. A year later she wrote her father: "I've been spending most of the morning at the Ministry of Works where we are starting — what do you think? The Iraq Museum! It will be a modest beginning, but it is a beginning." For some months the artifacts she had collected and her new finds had been housed in a few humble rooms near the palace.

Both Leonard Woolley and an Oxford University expedition were working in southern Mesopotamia, at Ur and Kish respectively. Bell not only supervised the permits but visited the excavations at the end of the season to divide the finds between the Iraq Museum and the excavators. "It took us the whole day to do the division [at Ur] but it was extremely interesting and Mr. Woolley was an angel," she wrote home in March 1923. "We had to claim the best things for ourselves but we did our best to make it up to him and I don't think he was much displeased." Her visits were always traumatic for Woolley, who had to fight hard for his beloved finds. She always took an impartial referee with her to arbitrate over tricky points. On one occasion, in 1926, Woolley lost a hard-fought argument over a statuette of the goddess Bau. The referee supported him, but she insisted on keeping the find. The poor referee was quietly addressed as "the traitor" for several days afterward as she carried off the find in triumph. But she was very fair. "Actually in the division we did very well and have no cause for complaint — though I would not say that to Miss Bell," wrote Woolley after the second season in 1924.

Bell arrived at Kish to find the Oxford University Expedition directed by Professor Stephen Langdon and Ernest McKay sunk in gloom, expecting her to shut them down within an hour. They were relieved to discover that she was only interested in their finds. "Who decides if we disagree?" asked Langdon. "I replied that I did, but he needn't be afraid for he would find me eager to oblige," she wrote. Her museum was growing daily and she spent more and more time cataloguing and labeling the new finds.

In March 1926 the government gave the Iraq Museum a more permanent home, "a real museum, rather like the British Museum only a little smaller. I am ordering long shallow drawers in chests to hold the pottery fragments, so that you will pull out a drawer and look at Sumerian bits," Bell wrote. When she started on the listing of all the Kish and Ur finds, as well as settling the matter of the Babylon finds with the Germans, Woolley helped her design the display cases.

Toward the end of her career in Baghdad, Bell was politically discredited. She had swept aside the British high commissioner's warnings that there would be trouble in the countryside. The troubles duly arrived and she found herself increasingly isolated from the corridors of power. She was depressed and mortified, and buried herself deeper and deeper in archaeological matters. Her emotional involvement with Iraq was such that she felt an obligation to shoulder the increasing workload of the museum and the department of antiquities. The more overseas universities applied for permits, the harder she worked. King Feisal opened the first room of the museum in June 1926. Although her health was deteriorating rapidly in the debilitating summer heat, she

Gertrude Bell at Ur of the Chaldees during the excavations. Max Mallowan is in the background, right

preferred not to resign. "It isn't merely a responsibility to the Iraqis but to archaeology in general. . . . I work as hard at it as I can, but it's a gigantic task," she wrote home to her father.

Run down, worried about her health and her future, Gertrude Bell took an overdose of sleeping pills and died on July 12, 1926, at the age of fifty-eight. The whole of Baghdad attended her funeral, including the desert sheikhs, who were perhaps the people with whom she was most comfortable. Three years later the British School of Archaeology in Iraq was founded in her memory. A bust of Gertrude Bell occupied a proud position in the newly opened Iraq Museum.

Bell was a vivid personality. Max Mallowan, who was to work with Woolley at Ur, remembered her as "of striking appearance, always smartly dressed." Her intelligence was legendary, her learning prodigious. Gertrude never suffered fools gladly and fought long and hard both for her adopted country and for archaeology. She made many enemies, often people who could not keep up with her. Her reputation in Iraq is somewhat tarnished today, for many Iraqis consider that she gave away too much to foreign excavators. She was often in an agonizingly difficult position, having to balance the needs of Iraq and the very limited conservation facilities at her disposal with the necessity of satisfying foreign expeditions' backers and making sure she obtained the best possible preservation conditions for unique artifacts. Bell the scholar tended to put the interests of science above national goals. This is something difficult for Iraqi nationalists to understand. No one can deny her legacy to Iraq and to the wider world of archaeology, for the museum she struggled to organize is now one of the finest repositories of antiquities in the world.

20

Ur of the Chaldees

Well, of course, it's the Flood.

E XPEDITION STARTING OUT," cabled Leonard Woolley to Gordon in Philadelphia on October 26, 1922. With this terse message, Woolley embarked on one of the most ambitious and spectacular Mesopotamian excavations ever conducted. He was to work at Ur of the Chaldees for twelve seasons, from 1922 until 1934.

Woolley was not only the unanimous choice of both museum boards for the directorship, but ideal for the job. "He was a man of slight stature and no commanding appearance," a contemporary wrote many years later. "But presence, yes! — and even a blind man would have known what manner of man he was." Woolley was by now an archaeologist of international reputation, single-minded of purpose and totally wrapped up in his work. He was an exacting taskmaster, who ran huge excavations with the smallest of European staffs, relying heavily on the loyalty and sound training of his foreman Sheikh Hamoudi and Hamoudi's three sons.

Few people had the energy to keep up with Woolley's breakneck work pace. The excavations began each day at dawn and, for the European staff, rarely ended before midnight. Woolley himself would often work until two or three o'clock in the morning. Anyone working with him was forewarned to expect hard work and somewhat authoritarian direction. His best-known archaeological assistant was Max Mallowan. Mallowan came to Iraq with a general interest in Greek sculpture and a classical degree but no formal archaeological training. David Hogarth, then keeper of the Ashmolean Museum in Oxford, recommended him to Woolley, who took him after a brief interview: "Partly, I suspect, because as always Woolley was in a hurry, and partly because twenty-one years earlier, in 1903, Warden Spooner of New College had likewise ordered him into archaeology." It was a fortunate choice. Mallowan thrived on the hard work and on Woolley's style of training: dropping the apprentice pell-mell into the dig and letting him direct the work. Mallowan was warned what to expect. Sir Frederick Kenyon told him: "You will have your own thoughts: keep them to yourself." Mallowan did so and went on to became a famous Assyriologist himself.

Woolley was regarded as the ideal archaeologist for Ur. He could unravel complicated architectural sequences from masses of mud brick with uncanny skill and with far more imagination than the Germans at Babylon and Assur displayed. He was a digger of infinite skill, who could dissect the most complicated of temple sequences, and with equal facility recover the remains of a fragile wooden harp from the hole left in the ground by its perished case. He had a genius, Mallowan tells us, for finding what he set out to look for, and the patience to know when to wait. One of his 1922 trial trenches revealed gold objects, possibly from a cemetery. Woolley waited four whole years before digging it, knowing the task would stretch his technical abilities to the limit. He simply felt that he was too inexperienced to tackle it. Iraqi archaeology was in its scientific infancy and few of the objects in the cemetery could be dated accurately. His aim, he wrote, "was to get history, not to fill museum cases with miscellaneous curios, and history could not be got unless both we and our men were duly trained."

Above all, Woolley was a gifted writer with a fluent literary style and the kind of lively imagination that could capture the attention of his readers. To him, Ur was not a dead city but a thronged settlement with busy streets. He would lead his visitors down winding alleys and into abandoned four-thousand-year-old brick houses. He actually knew the names of many of the individual owners from cuneiform tablets found inside. He would point out the details of the roof design, drainage contrivances, even the height of the steps. He had an enthusiasm for the past that brought Ur alive in ways few archaeologists could have done. His preliminary reports were invariably published only a few months after the season's work was completed. He had a natural flair for publicity, too, so the Ur excavations were followed by a far wider audience than usual. But while his readers would read of royal treasures almost as splendid as those of Tutankhamun and of the discovery of the Biblical Flood, his professional colleagues could appreciate Woolley's ultimate technical purpose — to discover the origins of Sumerian civilization.

Hamoudi organized the unruly mob of workmen into the traditional gangs of pickmen, spademen, and four or more basketmen, depending on the distance they had to carry soil to the light railway. He ruled the work gangs with a hand of iron. A master of invective, he was at once sensitive to trouble, happiness, and genuine fatigue. In a moment of genius, he hired a tall, singing boatman who used his spade to paddle an imaginary canoe through imaginary reeds to a lilting song as the men shifted piles of heavy soil. Hamoudi's philosophy was simple: "Work was provided by Allah to prevent men from thinking." Both Hamoudi and Woolley were rarely at a loss however difficult the situation. The workmen enjoyed Woolley's humor, respected his strength, and dreaded his anger. On one occasion, a workman named Zuwair was dismissed for some misdemeanor. He promptly started to cut his throat in public. Woolley rose to the occasion and pardoned him.

The Ur archaeological team was always a small one. Inevitably there were tensions. Mallowan recalls that Woolley would train his apprentices by putting them in charge of a part of the work, then making them read their field notes to him after several days. Invariably they were subjected to devastating criticism, but with a patience and understanding that not only gave a sound training, but made the dawn-to-dusk hours bearable. Many of the tensions revolved round Katherine Keeling, who first visited Ur as an unpaid volunteer in 1925. She drew artifacts for the site catalogue and took charge of showing visitors around for two seasons. She became Woolley's wife in 1927. Katherine Woolley was, wrote Mallowan, "a dominating and powerful personality," a woman of great gifts. Gertrude Bell described her as "a dangerous woman." She was an artist of considerable talent with the gift of interesting the public in the excavations. Her skill at public relations brought much-needed funds to the expedition coffers. But the staff lived in fear of her. She could be alternately charming and rude to the point of insolence. The laborers showed her great respect. On one occasion her sudden appearance at the scene of a bloody tribal squabble was enough to separate the antagonists immediately.

Even today, half a century after the dig, few people can speak of Katherine Woolley dispassionately, although they all agree she was a fascinating companion on a remote excavation. She relished the role of being the only woman on the dig. The Woolleys were careful to allow no other females at Ur. The excavations were immensely enriched by this talented woman, who was to die at an early age of the ill health that dogged her entire life.

The Ur experience was by no means all hard work or personal conflicts. Father Leon Legrain, the American epigrapher in 1925–1926, remembered more congenial moments, such as "our Christmas dinner in good English style with one turkey, one goose, four ducks, two plum puddings, six bottles of champagne, one of gold sherry, two of vermouth, and no end of whiskey." He added in his letter to Gordon, "Don't print that in the *Museum Journal* please. I like to have them under the impression of our hardships." The detective novelist Agatha Christie, who visited the Ur excavations and later married Max Mallowan, is thought to have used the personalities at the dig as a basis for her *Murder in Mesopotamia*.

The excavations began inauspiciously. Woolley was awakened abruptly by the sound of rifle fire only a few nights after his arrival. Crouching to avoid the bullets that were flying through the tent walls, he peered out to see six riflemen firing at the camp from only thirty yards away. By the time the robbers had escaped with some cash and a handsome haul of personal belongings, a camp guard was dead and the tented compound like a battlefield. Woolley sent his men in pursuit of the marauders and mobilized the local authorities. Four of the gunmen were captured and much of their loot recovered. The excavations were delayed while Woolley hastened to build a fourteen-room excavation house made of bricks from the ruins at a cost of two hundred pounds. The expenditure was worth it in savings on guards' wages alone. In the event, there was no more trouble. It was typical of Woolley that he insisted on employing the convicted robbers as diggers once they had served two years in jail.

Woolley realized that it would take years to dig the site, for Ur was enormous. Even working at high pressure and at times employing up to four hundred men, he could not hope to clear even a small portion of the city. The earlier levels were buried deep under many feet of later occupation debris, levels it was essential to investigate since they would throw light on the earliest stages of Sumerian civilization. Woolley had very little information to go on. Taylor and Hall's preliminary investigations at Ur and Al-ʿUbaid had shown some promising results. Sumerian tablets suggested that the archaeologists would find evidence of kings as early as Ur-Nammu, the founder of the Third Dynasty. Although it was known that Sumerian cities went back much earlier than Ur-Nammu and the names of the earlier kings were known from inscriptions, no one knew when they had reigned, despite Sumerian king lists that extended back over 241,200 years, a period that covered the reigns of only eight rulers! Did earlier Sumerian history have any basis in fact? It was hoped that Ur would provide some answers.

Woolley started off by digging trial trenches over the site to gain some idea of the layout of the city. Nebuchadnezzar, that indefatigable builder, had erected a great wall enclosing Ur. Its limits would provide some guidance for the excavations. The trial trench sunk to locate this wall was sited by sheer guesswork, for there were no surface indications to guide the excavation. Woolley, expert at mud-brick walls, found that most of his trench in fact lay inside the walls. The late Babylonian finds were scanty, so he deepened his cutting and immediately unearthed plentiful finds—pottery, small bronze objects, and large quantities of glass and stone beads. Whenever the foreman or one of the staff dug in the trench, he found gold beads as well. The workmen never found any. Woolley rightly surmised that the gold beads were being sold to dealers at the weekend. One Saturday, he boldly announced that the work gangs in the area would be paid a large bonus every time Hamoudi or a European found a gold bead. The bonus was three times the dealers' price. The chagrined workmen promptly bought back the beads they had sold to the dealers and produced a veritable harvest of gold on Monday.

As part of his chronological studies, Woolley turned his attention to the small Al-ʿUbaid mound four miles north of Ur. Hall had dug the mound in 1919 and uncovered the remains of a First Dynasty Sumerian temple, a find so important that excavation on a much larger scale was called for. When Woolley returned to Al-ʿUbaid, he dug into another low mound some sixty yards from the temple ruins. The mound was only six feet high and was littered with a greenish-colored, black-painted pottery of a type already found at Eridu. Everyone had labeled this pottery "prehistoric" and left it at that. Woolley was astonished to find that the mound was easy to excavate. A layer of light dust covered a three-foot layer of hard mud mixed with painted potsherds, flint and obsidian tools, and the remains of matting houses. He found that this small village had been built on a low hill of clean river silt that had once risen above the marshy plain. A few traces of Sumerian buildings lay in the upper levels, structures contemporary with the First Dynasty temple nearby. So, Woolley concluded, this small village had been abandoned before the Sumerians had built Ur.

The ʿUbaid people turned out to have no metals. Their finest products were their painted pots, which Woolley compared to pottery recovered at faraway Susa. He wondered whether the ʿUbaid people had been the first farmers to settle in southern Iraq, bringing their fine pottery and simple stone hoes with them. Was this simple culture the ultimate ancestor of all later human settlement in the delta? How did Al-ʿUbaid relate to Eridu and to Ur? What was the connection between these simple farmer folk and the earliest stages of Sumerian civilization?

Woolley looked for these connections in the Sumerian temple nearby. The First Dynasty temple at Al-ʿUbaid had been overthrown in antiquity. The brick walls had been undermined and then pushed over from the inside, so that huge lumps of mud brick with friezes attached to them had to be uncovered and pieced together to obtain a plan of the shrine. The structure turned out to have been a solid mass of brick on a platform approached by a flight of steps. Only the substructure remained. The temple itself was gone. One day, a workman handed Woolley a tablet which G. J. Gadd, his epigrapher, joyfully translated: "A-anni-pad-da, king of Ur, son of Mes-anni-pad-da, king of Ur, has built this for his lady Nin-kharsag." This foundation stone identified the temple as the work of the son of the first king of the First Dynasty of Ur. It took weeks to dissect the remains of the temple, especially a great copper relief of an eagle and stags. The building challenged Woolley's architectural skills. He described it as "very gay and fanciful, the gold and color of its decorations vivid against the white walls." He admired the way the Sumerian architects had graded the decorations and reliefs from ground level up to form an imposing shrine. At the time of its discovery, the Al-ʿUbaid temple was the oldest building yet found in Iraq. Woolley concluded, rightly, that the equivalent structure at Ur was completely buried inside Ur-Nammu's ziggurat, which still stood.

After four seasons of excavation, Woolley finally felt competent enough to tackle the mysterious cemetery by Nebuchadnezzar's wall. Here, he argued, he might find the links between Al-ʿUbaid and the early Sumerians. He soon found that he was dealing not with one cemetery, but with two, the later dating to the time of Sargon I of Agade (c. 2370 B.C.). The earlier cemetery had been dug into deep mounds of rubbish. It turned out to be a "holocaust of treasure which revealed to us the wealth and splendor of archaic Sumer beyond our wildest dreams."

The scale of Woolley's cemetery clearance simply boggles the mind. He cleared no less than two thousand graves of common people and sixteen royal burials in four years. He pegged out the limits of the cemetery very carefully, setting up base marks for plotting the position of each grave. The workmen were watched by the staff like hawks. They were trained to stop at once whenever they came upon the fine deposit that marked a grave. Then paintbrushes and knives took over and another burial was recorded and cleared. It was dull work, for the graves were monotonously similar. At least two thirds of them had been plundered or destroyed in antiquity by people reusing the same cemetery or by grave robbers.

The graves of the common people were little more than rectangular shafts from four to twelve feet dug deep into the tell. Each corpse was wrapped in matting or placed in a coffin of basketwork, wood, or clay. The body was laid on its side with the legs flexed at hip and knee, the hands in front of the breast. A few personal effects accompanied the dead — a handful of beads, perhaps a dagger or a pin. Some food and drink offerings in pots, and some weapons or tools, were deposited in the matting-lined grave. The filled-in sepulcher was almost unnoticeable to the excavators, who had little more to go on than a "paper-thin wavy line of white powder," the remains of the decayed matting that had lined the grave. The wood and matting survived as impressions, or casts, in the earth that, when photographed, looked like the real thing.

The first royal tomb came to light on the very last day of the 1926–1927 season. The workmen found a mass of bronze weapons apparently unassociated with any burial, then a magnificent gold-bladed dagger with a hilt of blue lapis lazuli adorned with gold studs. The gold sheath was worked with a network design in imitation of plaited grass. So unusual was this find that one expert considered the dagger and a gold toilet outfit found nearby to be Arab work of the thirteenth century A.D. The local sheikh guarded the rich grave closely until the following autumn. Then Woolley uncovered a brilliant masterpiece, Prince Mes-kalam-shar's gold helmet in the form of a wig, with the individual locks of hair hammered in relief. This grave made him realize that he was dealing with a very early cemetery indeed.

The same season they came across five bodies lying alongside one another in a sloping trench, none of them richly adorned. They lay above a layer of matting, which led the archaeologists to a group of ten women, all wearing elaborate headdresses and necklaces, and carefully arranged in two rows. Close to these skeletons Woolley spotted a hole in the ground, then a second one. Suspecting some unusual feature, he poured plaster of Paris into the holes. Carefully he dug round the edges of the cast and was able to recover a decayed wooden harp, complete with its copper bull's head and the shell plaque that had once decorated it.

These finds turned out to be lying at the entrance to a royal tomb-chamber containing the remains of a male ruler of uncertain identity. A second stone chamber was built up against it, that of a woman named Pu-abi, possibly his wife. The queen had been buried later. The Sumerian workmen who had worked on her sepulchre had quietly quarried into the king's tomb, removed some of the treasures, and then hid their tunnel behind a great clothes chest. After many months of backbreaking and meticulous excavation, Woolley was able to reconstruct not only the tombs and their contents, but the burial rites as well.

The royal tomb-chambers lay at the bottom of a forty-five by thirty-foot shaft some thirty feet deep. A steeply sloping passage led from ground level to the chamber on one side of the shaft. The walls of each burial chamber were of stone and the vaulted roof of brick. Once the mausoleum was ready, the priests had carried the royal corpse into the chamber and laid it out in all its finery, along with food offerings in gold and silver vessels. Two or three personal attendants then crouched by the coffin or bier, and were killed or drugged before the chamber was walled up forever. This completed the first phase of the funeral.

A long procession of soldiers, courtiers, and male and female servants now filed into the mat-lined burial pit, all of them brilliantly decked out in their uniforms and finest ornaments. The musicians bore their harps, the royal chariots were driven into the pit, animals led by grooms, drivers in their places. The entrance was guarded by a detachment of soldiers. Everyone carried a small cup in his hand. As music played, each member of the court drank poison from his cup, then lay down in his assigned place. Finally, someone came down and killed the oxen and asses that drew the chariots — the animals' bodies lay on top of those of their grooms. The same functionary checked that everything was in order before the earth fill covered the royal court forever.

The burial pits were filled in stages, the first covering the burial chamber and the courtiers. Woolley reconstructed the later ceremonies from another royal tomb nearby, where he was able to remove the upper levels of the burial shaft stage by stage. He found that a funerary feast had been held at the site of the burial chamber. Then an offering to the god or gods of the underworld had been laid out and covered with a clay bowl before a mud-brick structure was erected over the site. This, in turn, was filled with layers of clay, each covered with offerings and the body of a sacrificial victim. The building also contained the coffin of an important personage who was a special sacrifice and was completely buried in the earth fill of the shaft. Presumably some form of funerary chapel marked the site of the grave, but no trace of it remained. The elaborate rituals must have extended over a considerable period of time, and to judge from the more or less identical finds in several Ur tombs, were conducted at many royal funerals.

The excavation of these death pits, crowded as they were with delicate objects, challenged every archaeological skill Woolley possessed. Hamoudi and his sons supervised the removal of the soil in the pits bit by bit until the skeletons were almost exposed, covered only by fragments of brick that had been used as the filling of the shaft. Then the skilled staff moved in, marking out the pit in squares and excavating each skeleton in turn, recording the ornaments and objects in place before removing them.

"It was slow work, and especially so in those cases where we decided to remove the entire skull with all its ornaments in position on it," wrote Woolley. They removed them by clearing away the soil and then pouring liquid paraffin wax over the bones and gold. Then waxed cloth was pressed carefully over the specimen before the whole lump was removed from the soil for later examination. Queen Pu-abi's body, for example, lay on a wooden bier with a golden cup near her head. The upper part of her body was hidden by a mass of gold, silver, and semiprecious-stone ornaments. Her elaborate, wiglike gold headdress was crushed by the earth and hid the skull. Fortunately, its parts were so well preserved that Woolley was able to reconstruct the entire piece. It was exhibited in London on a plaster cast of a contemporary skull, which the talented Katherine Woolley had carefully modeled in wax with the features of a Sumerian woman. The headdress was reassembled on the skull using glued wire and paper and gave a remarkably accurate impression of the royal queen's appearance.

The preservation of the more delicate objects in the royal cemetery was almost as formidable a task as their excavation. The Iraq Museum had no conservation facilities so everything was exported to London, where the experts restored some of the most spectacular finds. One was a wooden model of a he-goat with his front legs on branches of a thicket. When Woolley found the statue, it was in a sorry state. The wooden head had decayed to nothing, the animal was a mere silhouette, the shell and lapis-lazuli inlay lay in the earth around the decayed wood. All he could do was pour paraffin wax onto the remains, lift the statue intact, and then restore it in the laboratory. The wax was melted, the earth inside the body removed, the legs straightened and strengthened. Then the gold leaf of the head was unfolded and reshaped, a "jigsaw in three dimensions," said Woolley. Eventually the statue was restored to as close its original state as was possible. "In dealing with the antiquities from Ur, we have preferred a restoration which implied the least possible interference with the object to a restoration that may give a better appearance but depends more on the modern hand," said Woolley.

He applied the same principle to the celebrated Standard of Ur, a panel of wood carved on both sides and inlaid with a lapis-lazuli and shell mosaic. This fragile object, perhaps the remains of a lyre box, had decayed almost completely. By the time Woolley found it, the wood had long since rotted away and only the thousands of tiny shell and lapis-lazuli fragments were left. Fortunately, they were lying in place in the ground. Woolley cleared them of dirt inch by inch and poured

The famous ram from Ur of the Chaldees, an offering stand of gold, silver, and lapis lazuli, reconstructed from fragments by Leonard Woolley

wax on each section. Now came the tricky part: to separate the mosaics on one side of the standard from those on the other. The two mosaics were lifted as one unit. Woolley then affixed waxed cloth to the exposed parts of the inlays on each side of the lump of soil and mosaic fragments. Each side was in turn placed faced downward on glass, and the protective cloth removed by warming the wax. By peering up underneath the glass, Woolley was able to check the design as he removed surplus bitumen and earth. Once the design on each side was restored, the thousands of fragments, now moved together, were given a new and permanent backing. The standard turned out to consist of two rectangular panels depicting peace and war, the king feasting and judging captives, his chariots at war. The standard was designed to be carried in procession and was not only a remarkable art object but a useful historical document. It chronicled the formidable military armory that enabled the Sumerians to expand their city-states into an empire of international importance.

All these, and other finds from the royal cemetery at Ur, are now among the most prized possessions of the British Museum and the University Museum in Philadelphia. The export of some of them under Gertrude Bell's successors caused considerable local resentment and undoubtedly contributed to the difficulties foreign excavators were to have after Iraq achieved independence in 1932.

The excavation of the royal cemetery created a sensation almost rivaling that caused by the discovery of the tomb of Tutankhamun in 1922. Woolley established the date of the royal graves by using seal impressions and tablets in the rubbish that overlay and underlay the tombs. The levels above the royal graves date to the First Dynasty of Ur, like the Al-'Ubaid cemetery. Those underneath are now dated to between 2000 and 2500 B.C., the earliest period of Iraqi history yielding written records. Though they throw some light on Sumerian society and on the people actually buried in the royal graves, they are, unfortunately, highly incomplete and the experts have been unable to puzzle out the names of several of the rulers. They have also been unable to explain the elaborate rituals in which entire royal households accompanied the ruler in death. Did such mass self-immolation take place at every royal funeral or were such rituals reserved for certain kings who enjoyed divine status? Were the women actual queens? Or were they priestesses who held some special position in the Ur temple hierarchy at some point in their lives? The answers can only come from the study of the thousands of Sumerian tablets that still await decipherment and interpretation, a task that may take decades to complete.

Although Woolley's dating and interpretation of the royal cemetery have, naturally, been subjected to some reinterpretation in the past half century, no one has challenged the excavation records and precise deductions made from them in the field. The royal cemetery is still unique in Iraqi archaeology.

The royal cemetery excavations also revealed Woolley's genius as an organizer. Every item in the excavation had to be plotted in position, recorded in the catalogue, given emergency restoration, and packed for shipment. The storerooms at the dig were overflowing. "There was gold scattered under our beds," remembered Max Mallowan. One of the exposed royal tombs looked like "a golden carpet ornamented with the beech leaf headdresses of the ladies of the court, and overlaid by the gold and silver harps and lyres."

Woolley's work did not end with the excavations. Archaeology enthusiasts in dozens of countries followed the royal cemetery excavations with bated breath. Here we see Woolley at his worst. By nature a loner, he relied but little on discussion with his staff in interpreting the details of the excavations. Eager to show that the Sumerian civilization was older than the Egyptian, he tended to date the Ur cemetery earlier than his colleagues would have, and overstated his findings in popular books to dramatize his story. Sometimes his own staff were surprised to find him announcing conclusions about their own trenches, conclusions he had never discussed with them. Sometimes even his fellow excavators were in the dark, carrying out their own limited tasks without receiving the confidence of Woolley's wider hypotheses about the season's work. Sometimes they even read about their discoveries in the newspapers.

Woolley continued to puzzle over the connections between Ur and Al-'Ubaid until the royal cemetery was completely excavated. By this time he was convinced that the spectacular royal burials came from a time earlier than the First Dynasty temple, and that they belonged to a highly civilized society, one whose ancestry lay in the lowest levels of the Ur tell. In 1929 he decided on a test excavation into the lowest levels of the mound. His first trench was only five feet square, a cutting size determined by limited funds and shortage of time. The pickmen cut through three feet of occupation debris. Then the finds abruptly ceased and he was digging in sterile river mud. When the workman reported the sterile level, Woolley agreed that he should work elsewhere. But wisely he checked the mud horizon against his site levels and found that the mud was too high. Woolley had never assumed that Ur was built on a hill above the plain, merely on a low ridge. On a hunch, he told the workman to keep digging, despite the latter's eloquent protests. Eight feet lower down, his spade revealed flint implements and 'Ubaid painted pottery.

Woolley leaped into the pit, and after examining the thick zone of

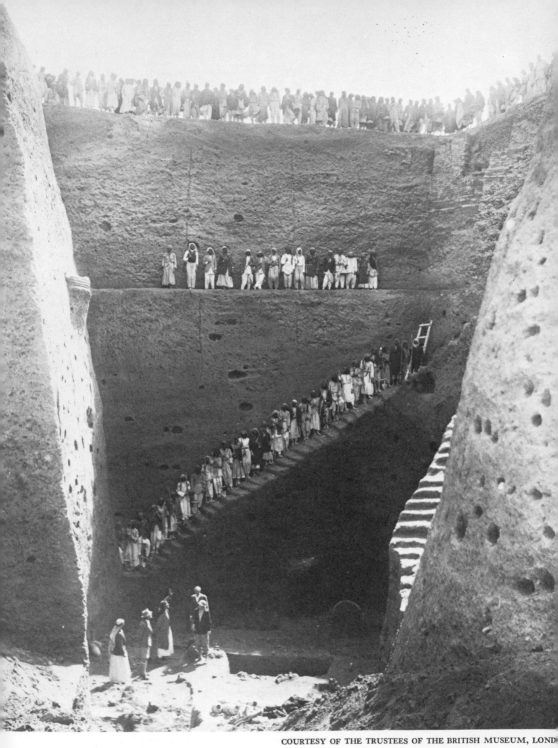

The great Flood Pit at Ur. The base of the pit dates to
c. 2900–2800 B.C. *The rectangular hole at the base of the steps*
leads into the flood deposit

mud, wrote hastily in his notebook: "I . . . was . . . quite convinced of what it all meant." But he asked his staff what they thought. They were nonplussed until Katherine Woolley came by, glanced at the trench, and remarked casually, "Well, of course, it's the Flood!" That was the very conclusion Woolley himself had reached, but "one could scarcely argue for the Deluge on the strength of a pit a yard square."

Next year they laid out a huge trench seventy-five feet by sixty that ended up going down sixty-four feet to bedrock. Almost as soon as the workmen starting digging, they came across eight levels of houses, the earliest of which were built of mud brick. Eighteen feet of broken pottery lay underneath the houses, the remains of a pottery factory with the kilns among the sherds. The fragments came from "seconds," vessels that were cracked or distorted. So the potters smashed them and simply built their kilns on top. The character of the potsherds changed through time, from wares like those found in the houses to a characteristic greenish pottery painted with red and black designs.

As he examined the red and black sherds, Woolley recalled Langdon's recent excavations at Kish eight miles east of Babylon. During the excavation Langdon had been shown a low mound named Jemdet Nasr, eighteen miles northeast of Kish, which he excavated in 1926 and 1928. It turned out to be an early town which yielded not only some extremely primitive clay tablets but thousands of black-, yellow-, and red-painted vessels adorned with lattice and check designs. The Kish excavations were continued under the direction of a French archaeologist named Watelin, who dug a pit right through the tell and found Jemdet Nasr pottery under early Sumerian levels. The Jemdet Nasr and Kish finds gave Woolley a useful chronological check for his deep pit.

The Ur potters' workshop had continued in use for centuries as pottery styles had changed. Below the Jemdet Nasr vessels were accumulations of plain red pots of a type also found in the lower levels at Uruk. Arnold Noldeke and Julius Jordan dug at the site from 1928 to 1939. When they cut a deep shaft through the tell, they found plain red vessels in the lower levels of the site immediately overlying ʿUbaid occupation on virgin soil.

At Ur, Woolley found that some ʿUbaid burials had been dug into the clean and sterile river silt that underlay the centuries-old potters' workshop. The silt itself was eleven feet deep, a uniform, water-laid deposit of Euphrates mud. And again, human occupation lay beneath the silt: three superimposed floor levels of mud-brick and reed houses associated with ʿUbaid pottery identical to that from the original Al-ʿUbaid site. The basal huts had been built on a stiff, green clay, in which "all traces of human activity ceased and we were at the bottom of Mesopotamia." This green clay was once a swampy marsh, Woolley conjectured. The first occupants of Ur had tipped their rubbish into the marsh and had gradually built up a low mound that formed the core of the later city.

The Ur dig took Sumerian civilization and its predecessors down to a baseline of sterile soil. Once the German trenches at Uruk were completed, Woolley could define a series of cultural stages that documented southern Mesopotamian society: what began as simple peasant villages became a complex urban civilization.

The excavation of the so-called Flood Pit at Ur gave Woolley a unique chance to exercise his fluent pen. Here, he claimed, was not only evidence of a great flood in the area popularly associated with the Garden of Eden, but also archaeological confirmation of the great deluge described in Assyrian and Sumerian epics. To Woolley, the ʿUbaid people of pre-Flood times had not been obliterated by the deluge but had survived the waters to plant the seeds of Sumerian civilization. "And among the things they handed down to their successors was the story of the Flood; that must have been so, for none but they could have been responsible for it." Woolley pointed out that Noah's Flood was not a Hebrew story, but a Sumerian one, taken over by the Hebrews with some modification. Even much of the phrasing was identical, he claimed. The evidence at Ur suggested a huge flood, an inundation unparalleled in Iraqi history. Even the Sumerian king lists spoke of rulers who reigned before and after the Flood.

Woolley traced the extent of the silt deposit by putting down test pits all round the Ur site. He found that the silt was deepest against the north slope of the mound, where the city's deposits had broken the force of the water. Elsewhere the Euphrates scoured away the flood silt, which, estimated Woolley, must have covered an area at least three hundred miles long and a hundred across, destroyed hundreds of villages and most settlements except for the oldest cities that were safe on their ancient tells. "It was not a universal deluge," wrote Woolley, "it was a vast flood in the valley of the Tigris and Euphrates which drowned the whole of the habitable land between the mountains and the desert; for the people who lived there that was all the world." Only a few people survived the disaster, he continued. "No wonder that they saw in this disaster the gods' punishment of a sinful generation and described it as such in a religious poem."

Woolley's lucid and dramatic description of the Flood had more impact on the general public than on his colleagues, most of whom were more interested in the ʿUbaid settlement that lay under the thick layer of mud. This, they realized, was a possible baseline for

Sumerian civilization, one that was to be identified as a widespread and prosperous culture in later excavations. As to Woolley's Flood, it was just a more catastrophic example of flooding in an area that was an endemic flood region. In retrospect, the Ur flood deposits are indeed the remains of a great inundation, but one that was too early to be associated with the Biblical Flood. Max Mallowan believes the latter to be associated with a Sumerian king of Shuruppak, mentioned in the *Epic of Gilgamesh*, who reigned about 2900 B.C., far later than the early silt deposits at Ur. In fact, traces of this later flood have been located not only at Kish but also much higher in the Flood Pit at Ur.

Season after season, extraordinary archaeological discoveries continued to come from the ancient city. Woolley's workmen cleared the great ziggurat of Ur-Nammu, which had been little more than a sandy hill up which British cavalrymen had ridden their horses in 1915. He worked on Nebuchadnezzar's city and uncovered dozens of crowded Sumerian dwellings. Innumerable artifacts of diverse types came from the digs, including thousands of cuneiform tablets from all periods of Iraqi history. Eight hundred of these tablets are inscribed with Sumerian literary texts, which have enabled George Gadd, Samuel Kramer, and other cuneiform experts to restore many Sumerian myths, epic tales, and other literary masterpieces. The Ur campaigns continued until 1934, when both changing political conditions and a feeling that a period of study and publication was needed caused the two museums to shut down the diggings. Woolley wrote most of the ten massive volumes that report on the excavation. It has taken half a century for all of them to appear. The epigraphers have published eight volumes of Ur texts so far. Leonard Woolley never worked at Ur of the Chaldees again. He died in 1960 after a long and distinguished career of excavation elsewhere in the Near East. His achievement at Ur can only be described as prodigious. Few archaeologists have ever matched his pace of work and flair for brilliant, scientific discovery.

21

Nationalism and Archaeology

The like of it had never been done before.

THE ENDING OF Leonard Woolley's excavations at Ur of the Chaldees marks the end of a heroic era in archaeology, one that saw unlicensed treasure hunting replaced by scientific digging to solve specific historical problems. The Ur excavations were almost the last dig of their kind, a massive operation conducted almost single-handed by a lone archaeologist who relied on a few assistants to help him with supervision of the trenches. Woolley employed huge numbers of laborers and moved prodigious quantities of earth with dramatic results. But his excavations, like those of many of his similarly inclined contemporaries, skimped on record keeping and detail. By 1930, excavation on the grand scale was on the way out. Woolley and his contemporaries had trained a whole generation of specialist archaeologists who were to refine their digging methods and make the excavation of Sumerian and Assyrian cities a highly specialized craft. The study of cuneiform had advanced to the point where the linguistic skill needed to make a serious contribution to decipherment and interpretation took years to acquire.

The closing chapter of our history is perhaps the most important of all. It sees the dawning of the age of the specialist, a period when smaller-scale excavations became the rule of the day and conclusions were based on meticulously researched data. Where gifted amateurs had worked on excavations and clay tablets, fully qualified professional scholars now took over, people whose interests in cuneiform or some other special subject were an academic career. As more and more data came from the new excavations, so did specializations become more and more narrow and esoteric to the layman. This natural fragmentation of specialties was the only logical response to large bodies of new information. As specialization developed so did a recognized need for team excavations, in which an archaeologist worked in the field with architects, epigraphers, and other experts in residence on the site. These new teams tended to work much more slowly than their predecessors. They were forced to rely on much less extensive excavations whose size was determined by the limited budgets of the Depression and the inflationary pressures of more recent decades.

The discoveries of the specialists are necessarily not as spectacular as those of the pioneers. Many of them are little known outside archaeological textbooks or journals. But the range of archaeological inquiry has been extraordinary. The specialists have dated the beginnings of farming in Mesopotamia to over ten thousand years ago, dug into the very lowest levels of the great Kuyunjik mound, and excavated the earliest settlements of the delta. Teams of experts have surveyed thousands of miles of ancient field and irrigation systems, reconstructed Sumerian temples from almost invisible mud-brick foundations, and discovered an astonishing diversity of Sumerian literature from archives excavated over fifty years ago. The incomplete archaeological vignettes of the early archaeologists have been replaced with a flowing narrative of Mesopotamian history that is rich in detail and still full of unanswered questions. The story of the specialists is no anticlimax, rather the logical and exciting culmination of over a century of intensive archaeological research.

The settled political conditions in Iraq during the late 1920s and early 1930s gave great impetus to the development of specialist excavation. Perhaps the most famous was the German expedition to Uruk, which had been probed by Walter Andrae in 1912. Andrae himself was behind the expedition but the actual fieldwork was in the hands of Julius Jordan and Arnold Noldeke. The Germans followed the meticulous principles laid down by their predecessors in an excavation campaign that lasted from 1928 to 1939. William Kennet Loftus, it will be recalled, had worked at Uruk in 1854 and recovered Parthian slipper coffins as well as some Sumerian cone mosaic fragments. The Germans had arrived at the site with much more background information at their disposal. Andrae had noticed in 1912 that the early levels did outcrop near the surface on some eroded portions of the site. These were the areas the new expedition concentrated on. Ever since the days of Koldewey's work at Babylon, the Germans had paid close attention to architecture. They spent years excavating two large temple complexes. As Andrae had done at Assur, the excavators dissected the two ceremonial complexes brick by brick. One complex, known as Eanna, contained a succession of large structures that had been demolished to make room for their successors. The other, Kullaba, consisted of a high terrace upon which stood the so-called White Temple, a building with a long central chamber and rooms arranged symmetrically on either side. The terrace itself contained the remains of earlier shrines, which, unlike those in Eanna, had not been demolished to make way for later buildings. The unraveling of the complicated sequences of architectural events in these two building complexes turned out to be the most demanding feat of excavation ever carried out in Iraq. The Germans found abundant pottery fragments similar to those found at Jemdet Nasr by the British and the Americans. At the time the Jemdet Nasr vessels were in use, the two ceremonial precincts at Uruk were merged into a single religious center, the predecessors of the large Sumerian temples of later times.

Walter Andrae had pioneered the excavation of a deep pit into the heart of a tell at Assur. Other excavators followed his example. The Anglo-American expedition at Kish in 1926–1928 had dug a sounding to bedrock that had yielded Jemdet Nasr pottery. Leonard Woolley's Flood Pit at Ur had revealed evidence not only of ʿUbaid pottery, but of what he had thought was the Flood as well. Now, in 1930–1931, the Germans put a deep trench into Uruk. They uncovered Jemdet Nasr ware and under it levels containing plain, wheel-made potsherds, which they named Uruk pottery. At the base of Uruk, they found characteristic ʿUbaid pot fragments, similar to those at the bottom of Ur.

The Ur and Uruk discoveries served to focus academic attention on the origins of the Sumerians. In 1929, a conference of archaeologists in Baghdad agreed that the ʿUbaid period was the earliest human settlement in southern Iraq, that it was followed by the Uruk and Jemdet Nasr periods, and then by the Early Dynastic period of Sumerian civilization. Two years later the Eighteenth International Conference of Orientalists held in Leiden dated the ʿUbaid from 4000 to 3500 B.C., Uruk from 3500 to 3000 B.C., and Jemdet Nasr from 3200 to 2800 B.C. The orientalist Henri Frankfort argued that the ʿUbaid people had been the original ancestors of the Sumerians, a hypothesis that still finds many supporters today. The German archaeologist Julius Jordan argued, on the other hand, that the Uruk people were the Sumerians and that they had displaced the ʿUbaid people. At the time little was known of the ʿUbaid people and their achievements. More recent ex-

*Life-sized head in bronze of an Akkadian king, perhaps Sargon I.
Found by Campbell-Thompson and Mallowan at Nineveh*

cavations at Eridu have demonstrated the great degree of cultural continuity between Uruk and 'Ubaid.

The search for the origins of Mesopotamian society now shifted northward to Assyria. Walter Andrae had found pre-Sumerian occupation at Assur, thirty miles downstream of Nineveh. How far north had Sumerian civilization and its predecessors extended? Were the origins of the 'Ubaid people to be found in Assyria? In 1930 Campbell-Thompson and Mallowan came to Kuyunjik to make a sounding to the base of the great mound that had been ransacked by Layard and Rassam, and been tunneled and undermined by dozens of treasure hunters later in the nineteenth century. Campbell-Thompson had dug briefly at the site with only ten men in 1927–1928, completing the excavation of the temple of Tabu, work that had been started in 1905, and digging further in Ashur-bani-pal's palace. He found the region much changed. Mosul had expanded and now boasted plenty of automobiles and a second Bridge of Boats. Many traditional customs, such as the veil, were less prevalent. Nebi Yunus had a new mosque. Campbell-Taylor paid his workmen tenpence a day (Rassam had paid fourpence), tolerated some stealing of small antiquities, and controlled his quarrelsome men by letting it be known that "instant dismissal (temporary) is certain for brawlers." He even had a truck to transport his finds. The mound had been fortified by the Turks in World War I. Campbell-Thompson had a moment of excitement when he submitted a sample of a waxlike substance, which he labeled a "curious mineral" from a sulphur spring near Kuyunjik, to an expert in England for analysis. "This is not Assyrian at all," came the reply. "It is nitroglycerine and still explosive!"

Max Mallowan was in charge of the vertical pit that the expedition sank into the lower, pre-Assyrian levels of the mound in front of the Ishtar temple. He laid out a trench seventy-five by fifty feet, on the assumption that he would have to dig a very deep cutting indeed. The workmen reached the base of the Assyrian levels at fourteen feet, then dug down for another seventy-two feet of prehistoric occupation. The vertical trench was difficult to dig, for earth removal was laborious and tricky. At first the earth was removed by a spiral staircase. But the upper levels were so soft that the walls had to be sloped to avoid slippage. Eventually the baskets of earth were passed from hand to hand by a chain of men standing on wall steps. Mallowan reached bedrock at ninety feet below the surface, using a tiny, twelve-foot square cutting.

The trench passed through thick Akkadian levels, where Mallowan was lucky enough to recover a magnificent bronze head of an Akkadian king, possibly Sargon I of Agade himself (c. 2370 B.C.). This head is one of the great art treasures of Iraq, depicting the king as an aquiline-nosed ruler of great authority. Below the Akkadian levels came traces of a prosperous settlement that was contemporary with the Early Dynastic period of the south. Deep Uruk levels underlay this occupation, themselves preceded by 'Ubaid ware, and beneath that a horizon containing highly characteristic painted pottery, known from the site of Tell Halaf on the Khabur River. Below the Halaf levels was a scatter of potsherds of a type found in 1912–1914 at Samarra on the Tigris upstream of Baghdad. In the tiny twelve-foot square at the very base of the mound, Mallowan recovered eleven incised potsherds, of a hitherto-unknown type. Kuyunjik had been not only a flourishing Sumerian city but a town for centuries before that, probably as long as some of the oldest settlements in southern Iraq. For twelve years the earliest inhabitants of Nineveh were known only from these eleven potsherds.

The Tell Halaf–like potsherds recovered from immediately under the 'Ubaid levels caused particular interest. In 1911–1914 and in 1929, Baron Max von Oppenheim had excavated the Tell Halaf mound, and in digging an Iron Age palace there, he came across earlier levels containing brilliant, polychrome pottery. The potsherds had been brought to the surface by the Iron Age people who had dug the foundations of the palace. No one could date this "Halafian" ware until Mallowan found it at Kuyunjik and estimated it to be as early as 5000 B.C.

The deep trench at Kuyunjik was an extraordinary piece of excavation. "The like of it had never been done before, and is not likely to be done again," wrote Mallowan many years later. Campbell-Taylor was so economical a digger that the entire operation cost only seventeen hundred pounds. He solemnly returned the unexpended balance of the grant to the private sponsor — elevenpence in stamps.

Campbell-Thompson had noticed Halafian pottery on the surface of a small mound named Arpachiyah, four miles east of Nineveh. In 1932 Max Mallowan spent a season on the site under the aegis of the British School of Archaeology in Iraq. He had no difficulty obtaining a permit from the Iraq Department of Antiquities, then headed by the German archaeologist Julius Jordan. (Jordan was an accomplished musician, and, we are told, a fervent Nazi.) Arpachiyah was only some two and a half acres in area. After a slow start, Mallowan uncovered four levels of 'Ubaid houses and a contemporary cemetery underlain by eleven earlier settlements of circular, domed clay houses built on stone foundations. Some of the buildings may have been shrines associated with burials. He also uncovered caches of painted pottery and numerous figurines of bulls and women. Some traces of Halafian and early Nineveh occupations came from the lowest levels. Again, these lowermost discoveries were too scanty for anyone to establish their precise relationship to later occupations. But Mallowan had reason to be well satisfied with his excavations. He had revealed a highly distinctive prehistoric culture in the north that had flourished before the 'Ubaid and that had been preceded by even earlier farming cultures known from a few potsherds at Kuyunjik and Arpachiyah.

The division of finds from the site proved to be very troublesome. Jordan and Mallowan negotiated for three days in 106-degree heat, with the lion's share of the finds going to Iraq. The government was now enforcing the antiquities law far more strictly than before. It took five months and a vote of the cabinet for Mallowan to be given permission to export his finds. His was the last expedition to be treated so generously.

While Mallowan was working at Kuyunjik and Arpachiyah, the Americans were working in several other areas of Iraq. From the 1930s onward, the University of Pennsylvania dug at the mound of Tepe Gawra, ten miles northeast of Nineveh near the Zagros foothills. E. A. Speiser embarked on an ambitious excavation to dig the entire seventy-two feet of the mound but soon revised his plans when funds ran low. The expedition found twenty levels of occupation. The earliest, the Halafian, was followed by 'Ubaid and Uruk phases with a series of elaborate temple structures. Speiser traced the development of a small country town that flourished for over four thousand years, from the second to sixth millennia B.C. The excavations showed that the northern plains had been the home of a prosperous culture in the fourth millennium B.C., a culture that was just as vigorous as those to the south.

Also attracted to Iraq was the Oriental Institute of the University of Chicago, which had been founded by John D. Rockefeller, Jr., in 1919, under the directorship of James H. Breasted, an eminent Egyptologist. After many seasons of work in Egypt, the institute extended its operations to Asia Minor and Mesopotamia. In 1927–1928, an initial expedition to Khorsabad found the site looted and neglected. A head of King Sargon II was being used as a chopping block in a local village. This, Edward Chiera, the leader, described as "irritating to say the least." The Oriental Institute archaeologists had worked in Egypt on undemanding sites and had to learn the techniques of mud-brick wall tracing from scratch. Serious work at Khorsabad began in 1930, lasted three years, and resulted in the clearance of a temple complex at the foot of the palace mound exploited by Botta and Place.

The Oriental Institute expeditions were exceptionally well financed and split into several groups. One of these teams was diverted to the

Diyala Valley, where they dug at Tell Asmar and Khafaje, using elderly but skilled workmen from the German dig at Assur to train younger men in wall tracing. The Oriental Institute refined German methods, set up a permanent base in the valley, and to achieve better understanding of Sumerian architecture, studied the modern building techniques used by the native Iraqis in the area. Pierre Delougaz, the director of the Khafaje excavations, succeeded in uncovering an oval Sumerian temple by using compressed air to clear mud-brick walls and pavements, some bearing the footprints of sacrificial sheep in the dried mud. He even found the mesh of a priest's fishing net in the residential quarters of the temple. By the end of the excavations, Delougaz had recovered not only the oval temple but the remains of ten successive rebuildings of the same structure over a depth of thirty feet of successive foundations. All this had been achieved while working around the depredations of illicit diggers. Fortunately, the very irregularity of their tunnelings made the task of reconstruction rather easier than it would have been had the excavation been completed by a scientific expedition interested in "total" excavation.

While the Oriental Institute was reopening Victor Place's excavations at Khorsabad and examining mounds in the Diyala Valley, the French had returned to Sarzec's Telloh, the Sumerian city-state of Lagash. Telloh had been the center of an archaeological scandal in 1924, when an illegally exported collection of statues of Gudea appeared on the European and American markets and were snapped up rapidly by collectors. The French government decided to apply for permission to reopen the site and provided a subsidy and a warship to support the expedition. For four seasons, from 1929 to 1933, Abbé de Genouillac, André Parrot, and others excavated where Sarzec had left off. They searched for royal tombs, recovered a large number of artifacts, and found traces of Uruk and ʿUbaid occupation in the lower horizons. Compared with the excavations of the Germans and the Americans, the French excavations were not so rigorous, but theirs was a team effort nevertheless, with an architect and epigrapher regularly on site.

After digging at Telloh, the French turned their attention to Larsa, southeast of Uruk, a site tested by Loftus in 1853–1854 and by Andrae in 1903. In subsequent years, tomb robbers had tunneled into Larsa in search of sculptures and portable artifacts. So brazen did the illegal excavators become that the Department of Antiquities arranged for British RAF planes to disperse them. Officially, the site was put under guard, but the looting continued right up to the beginning of the French excavations in 1933. The site looked like a battlefield. But preliminary diggings were promising and soon yielded a rich harvest

Statue of Gudea in diorite, now in the Louvre

of architectural information and over two hundred cuneiform tablets. Just as the 1934 season was about to begin, changing political conditions caused many foreign expeditions to abandon Iraq for a while and direct their attention to Syria or Turkey, where conditions for excavation were still more liberal.

On October 3, 1932, Iraq became the first fully independent Arab state. King Feisal died in September of the following year and was succeeded by Prince Ghazi, a young and inexperienced ruler. A group known as Iha al'-Watana (the National Brotherhood Party) took control of the government and embarked on a more nationalistic course. The impact on antiquities legislation and archaeology was immediate. A new antiquities law was passed in 1934 which placed severe restrictions on the export of antiquities. The new legislation was preceded by a propaganda campaign alleging that Iraq had been robbed of its antiquities by foreign expeditions operating under the previous, more liberal, law. Leonard Woolley attacked the new restrictions in no uncertain terms and pointed out that eleven expeditions had worked in Iraq in 1933, whereas only three returned in 1935, all of them long-term projects. He defended the export of the Standard of Ur and the two goat figures from the royal cemetery on the grounds that they could not have been restored successfully with local facilities at the time. If, he wrote, there are no concessions, there will be no foreign excavations in Iraq.

During the 1920s and 1930s, the Iraq Department of Antiquities had made important progress and had developed its own photographic and conservation laboratories. The Iraq Museum was now housed in a large building and had developed important collections of its own. Increasingly, the Iraqis themselves were taking on the responsibility of archaeological research in their country. By the late 1930s the level of foreign activity had dropped sharply. Only some long-term excavations by the Oriental Institute of the University of Chicago and the University of Pennsylvania Museum, and by the Germans at Uruk, were still in progress. Even these were shut down as the clouds of World War II gathered on the horizon.

By this time, the Iraq Department of Antiquities was no longer purely an administrative organization but had begun to excavate on its own. At first the Iraqis were hampered by a lack of trained scholars. The shortage was alleviated in 1939, when two Iraqi students returned from training at the Oriental Institute in Chicago. Since the department had at its command a growing number of locally trained inspectors and excavators who had been assigned to foreign expeditions over the years, fieldwork could now be undertaken. The department was headed by an

Iraqi, Saty Beg al-Hasri, instead of by Julius Jordan, who now became an expert adviser.

When Jordan was recalled home, the Iraqis sought British assistance instead. Seton Lloyd was appointed adviser in 1939. He was present at the department's first large-scale excavations in 1940, at Tell 'Uqair, fifty miles south of Baghdad. Tell 'Uqair is a small mound — a temple platform and its associated settlement. The Iraqis scraped the surface of the platform clean and on its summit uncovered the walls of the temple, which were still standing intact to a height of six feet. They also found that the inner walls were decorated with frescoes and ornaments of mosaic cone bricks. The feet and legs of men and animals could be discerned, but the wall tracers discovered that the temple had been filled with mud brick to form the platform for a later structure. The precious frescoes were sticking to the later brick. World War II was on and no European experts could advise the Iraqis what to do. So the archaeologists had to devise special techniques on the spot. They reduced the fill to a narrow layer, then picked it away in tiny fragments to expose the frescoes underneath. Experiences like this made the Iraqis increasingly self-reliant and expert in their own right.

The Antiquities Department embarked on an even more ambitious scheme later in the war. At that time, the government was carrying out a systematic survey of land ownership throughout the country. So the department arranged for one of its inspectors to accompany each of the survey parties. The inspectors claimed each newly discovered site as state property under law, collected a bag of surface pottery, and plotted the position of the settlement on official maps. In ten years, over five thousand tells had been located, given numbers, and dated from surface finds, providing a massive data base of new information.

In 1942 the department received a bag of potsherds from a mound called Hassuna, twenty miles from Mosul. The archaeologists who examined the fragments were astonished to find that they bore incised decoration similar to that of the eleven sherds Mallowan had found at the very base of Kuyunjik. Hassuna proved to be a tiny mound, barely fifteen feet high and a hundred yards across. Large-scale excavations were relatively easy on such a shallow mound, with a good chance that the true identity of the earliest inhabitants of Kuyunjik might be discovered. Fuad Safar and Seton Lloyd excavated this remarkable settlement soon afterward. The site lay in unadministered tribal territory on the very edge of the desert. The locals, remembers Lloyd, had "most liberal ideas about private ownership, and there was usually a good deal of shooting during the night." Car tires were worth at least a hundred pounds each in wartime, so everything had to be kept chained down. The excavations continued under these difficult conditions, concentrating on the eastern side of the settlement.

The lowest levels contained the remains of a tiny, temporary encampment. All that remained were transitory hearths, storage jars, and sickles with flint teeth set in bitumen. This temporary village had been followed by a larger, more permanent settlement of simple, puddled clay houses that formed the nucleus of a tiny farming community. The levels of this village sealed the deposits of the temporary camp at the base of the mound. They were littered with hundreds of incised sherds and fine vessels. A Halafian settlement overlay parts of the Hassuna occupation, confirming the sequence of human cultures found at Kuyunjik and elsewhere. Safar and Lloyd were able to date Hassuna only in general terms, to about 5100 B.C.

The Iraqis continued to excavate other sites during and after the war, selecting settlements from all periods of local history so that their personnel could obtain training in a wide range of archaeological problems. In 1947–1949 the department carried out excavations at Eridu in the south. Fuad Safar and Seton Lloyd dug into the corner of the ziggurat and uncovered a sequence of prehistoric temples and nineteen distinct occupation levels that extended back to about 5000 B.C., to early ʿUbaid times. The sequence of occupation was far longer than that at Ur or Uruk. Gradual changes in pottery styles and in temple architecture were documented from each layer, with the result that the ancestry of the Sumerians among the ʿUbaid and Uruk people was established beyond reasonable doubt. The Eridu people had worshipped at the location, on a precinct that is known to have been scared to Enki, the Sumerian god of water. Truly, Eridu was one of the oldest cities in the world, as the Sumerians themselves had believed.

As the origins of Iraqi society extended further and further back into prehistory, archaeologists began to search not only for early evidence of Sumerian civilization but for the beginnings of agriculture and animal domestication. Until the 1940s most people assumed that agriculture had been invented in the Near East and more specifically in Egypt. No one had any idea when the first farmers had lived in the area, or how agriculture had been developed. Scholars thought vaguely of a great genius who had conceived the brilliant idea of growing his food rather than gathering it. The first attempt at a comprehensive synthesis of the problem came from the well-known prehistoric archaeologist Vere Gordon Childe in 1934. He surveyed the new data from Egypt and Iraq, and placed it in a new conceptual framework. Childe envisaged two great revolutions in prehistory, the "Neolithic," or Agricultural, Revolution, and the "Urban" Revolution, when cities and civilization had emerged. He considered the origins of food production and of civilization two great watersheds in the human experience, both of them sparked by technological and economic innovations resulting from the beginnings of the domestication of plants and animals. Childe's hypotheses, which, he fully admitted, were based on inadequate archaeological evidence, led to a great deal of hard thinking about the origins of agriculture.

When foreign expeditions returned to the Near East after World War II, they came with specific research objectives in mind. One such objective, formulated by Robert J. Braidwood of the University of Chicago, was a systematic investigation of the origins of food production in the Near East. He led an Oriental Institute expedition to northern Iraq and the Zagros Mountains in 1948, the first institute expedition to visit the area since 1937. The team of specialists studied not only pottery and architecture, but animal bones, seeds, and other food remains. Botanists and geologists examined the ancient environment; zoologists, the evidence for early animal domestication among the fragmentary animal bones from the excavations. Braidwood concentrated his efforts on the hilly flanks of the Zagros Mountains that overlooked the lowlands of Mesopotamia, where wild species of goats, sheep, and cereal crops were to be found. The sites the team examined were small village settlements, many of them little more than transitory camps that had been occupied for short periods of time. The Braidwood team came with a battery of new archaeological techniques developed in Europe and the United States for the recovery of fragile objects. Of special relevance were methods for recovering minute plant remains from the occupation deposits for long-abandoned tells.

The most important site was Qal'at Jarmo, a small village that was occupied for over four thousand years. The village was never more than a cluster of twenty or so houses separated by small alleys and courtyards, but the experts were able to demonstrate that its inhabitants had domesticated barley and wheat, sheep and goats. Nearby lay an even earlier settlement named Karim Shahir, a temporary camp where the inhabitants were probably still hunters and gatherers.

In later years Braidwood and his students extended the surveys into Turkey, and in the same period the British archaeologist Kathleen Kenyon discovered early farming settlements at the very base of the great mound at the Biblical city of Jericho. The Braidwood projects were of vital importance not only for their discoveries of far earlier farming villages than had ever been excavated before but because the research opportunities in his well-financed expeditions stimulated a whole generation of young archaeologists and natural scientists to expand his pioneer researches all over the Near East.

Braidwood was one of the first archaeologists to make use of a new, revolutionary dating technique, radiocarbon dating. This method was developed by Willard Libby and J. R. Arnold in 1950, from wartime research in atomic physics, and measures the amount of decay of the radioactive isotope carbon 14 in organic remains like charcoal and burned bone found in archaeological sites. Radiocarbon dates are, in fact, little more than statistical approximations of the date of an object, but are far more accurate than the guesses of earlier generations. The new technique provided Braidwood with a method of dating archaeological sites older than the five thousand years of historical civilization in Mesopotamia. His samples from Jarmo were dated to 6700 B.C. and even earlier, while an early farming settlement at Jerico was radiocarbon-dated to 7800 B.C. These and other dating experiments extended the origins of agriculture in the Near East back at least ten thousand years from the present, if not earlier. The ultimate antecedents of Mesopotamian civilization were in hundreds of tiny, pioneer farming villages that dotted much of the lowland plains of Iraq as well as the highlands. Unfortunately, many of the lowland villages are buried under many feet of river alluvium or lie in areas currently inaccessible to archaeologists because of political conditions.

The Oriental Institute also sponsored surveys of changing settlement patterns in Iraq. The first survey began in the Diyala Valley under Thorkild Jacobsen in 1935 and was completed in 1957. Robert Adams and other American scholars conducted many more. These experts had realized that an understanding of changing regional settlement patterns through time was essential to amplify the chronological sequences and architectural details from large-scale excavations. Their comprehensive studies of early irrigation in Iraq showed how the modest schemes of early Sumerian times became the elaborate flood-control and irrigation projects directed by the Babylonian state and the states that followed it. The surveys were conducted with agricultural techniques in mind, so successfully that the archaeologists were able to document an accumulation of silt some thirty-three feet thick, laid down since the arrival of the first farmer at the northern edge of the southern plains. Increased salinity, silt accumulation, and social change all contributed to the progressive deterioration of irrigation and of the cultivation of wheat and barley. But by the time the Iraqis could no longer grow barley on a large scale, their strain of barley had become a staple crop all over the Old World.

The Oriental Institute expeditions were by no means the only systematically planned research of the 1950s, 1960s, and 1970s. Max Mallowan was able to work at Nimrud from 1949 to 1960, expanding Layard's excavations and those of his immediate successors. He also recovered a superb series of Assyrian ivories from the North West Palace of Ashur-nasir-pal, a stela recording the city buildings in the king's time, and even some cuneiform inscriptions on wax. His workmen cleared three wells, which yielded magnificent ivory carvings, including a head of a young girl and a plaque depicting a black man being mauled by a lioness in a thicket of papyrus. This fine piece once formed part of Sargon II's throne before he moved to Khorsabad. Agatha (Christie) Mallowan played an important role in the preservation of the damp ivories as they emerged from the deep wells. The huge palace and military precinct of Shalmaneser III yielded yet more superb ivories, its excavation the culminating achievement of the combined efforts of twelve experts. Mallowan used third-generation wall tracers from the Assur area on the dig. The Iraq Antiquities Department then restored part of the North West Palace for posterity.

David and Joan Oates worked in central Iraq looking for the earliest occupation of the area by the makers of Samarra pottery and for the origins of irrigation agriculture in the region. An understanding of early irrigation was, they realized, essential to any study of the origins of human settlement in the delta. Concentrating their survey efforts on the eastern rim of the plains where the alluvial deposits are thinner, they found mounds with Samarra and 'Ubaid pottery on them and excavated the mound of Choga Mami. There they uncovered seeds that had almost certainly been cultivated by irrigation techniques and the cross-sections of canals and watercourses that had once flowed near the tell.

The archaeological researches of the postwar years, for all their smallness of scale and the economic problems caused by rising costs, have provided tantalizing insights into the origins of agriculture and the beginnings of Mesopotamian civilization. The archaeologist of today looks out over a complicated landscape of village and city sites that provides enough information for us to be certain that Gordon Childe's Neolithic and Urban revolutions were but convenient labels for a long process of cultural change that began at least twelve thousand years ago and culminated in the pragmatic and innovative civilization of the Sumerians. The archaeological researches of the future will not yield such dramatic results as those of earlier generations, but they should gradually fill in gaps and give a new understanding of the most fascinating periods in human history.

The character of foreign archaeological research in Iraq has changed in recent years. The British, the French, and the Germans have now been joined by archaeologists from many other countries, some of whom, like the Canadians, have never worked in Iraq before. Excavation permits have become harder to come by as successive governments have fostered a new sense of national identity in Iraq. Some involvement in rescue archaeology — survey and excavation designed to save sites in advance of large-scale irrigation or dam schemes — is now considered compulsory for all foreign excavators, whatever the primary academic objective of their work. The Iraq Museum is now internationally famous and the country's own archaeologists are deeply engaged in excavations and survey work all over the country. The goals of archaeological research are enmeshed with national objectives. To what extent foreign archaeologists will be involved in future large-scale work in the area is unclear. But for the first time, this research, should it take place, will be wholly on Iraq's terms and in accordance with the government's wishes and needs. The archaeological wheel has come full circle, from exploitation to scientific excavation, and from wholesale plundering and export, to partial and then almost total local control of archaeological finds. Only time will tell whether this control will benefit the scholarly world at large, as it should.

Sources

The research for this book covered not only a bewilderingly diverse archaeological literature, but the work of scholars in many other disciplines as well. I relied heavily on contemporary travelers' accounts and nineteenth-century archaeologists' writings. Published works were amplified with archival sources whenever this was possible, desirable, or practicable. Rather than burden the reader with a mass of detailed references, I have listed the main sources for each chapter in case anyone wishes to read further into the literature. The illustrations for the book were derived from contemporary lithographs and photographs, or are of modern origin.

Chapter 1

An excellent and concise account of the geography of Mesopotamia can be found in the Great Britain Naval Intelligence Division Handbook *Iraq and the Persian Gulf* (H. M. Stationery Office, London, 1944). The archaeology of Iraq is admirably summarized in a number of readily available volumes, including David and Joan Oates's *The Rise of Civilization* (Phaidon, London, 1976) and Nicholas Postgate's *The First Empires* (Phaidon, London, 1977), Max Mallowan's *Early Mesopotamia and Iran* (McGraw-Hill, New York, 1965), and Seton Lloyd's *The Archaeology of Mesopotamia* (Thames and Hudson, London, 1978). Seton Lloyd's *Twin Rivers* (Oxford University Press, London, 1943) is an admirable account of Mesopotamia that is very useful for the later, historical periods. David Oates's *Studies in the Ancient History of Northern Iraq* (Oxford University Press, London, 1968) is a basic source on prehistoric cultures and later developments in Assyria.

The classic source on the Arabs and the rise of Islam is Philip K. Hitti's *History of the Arabs* (St. Martin's, New York, 10th ed., 1970). This wonderful synthesis of Arab culture can be combined with Guy Le Strange's *The Land of the Eastern Caliphate* (Cambridge University Press, Cambridge, 1905), which is excellent on the Arab scholars. Translations of the Arab geographers' works can be found in most large university and college libraries.

Chapters 2 and 3

At this point we introduce the reader to Seton Lloyd's *Foundations in the Dust* (Oxford University Press, London, 1947), an entertaining and literate account of early Mesopotamian archaeology that carries the story up to 1945. Lloyd is good on the early travelers, and should be read in conjunction with Marcus Nathan Adler's *The Itinerary of Benjamin of Tudela* (Phillipp Feldheim, New York, 1965). Karl Dannenfelt's *Leonhard Rauwolf* (Harvard University Press, Cambridge, 1968) describes this remarkable traveler, while Carsten Niebuhr is engagingly treated by Thorkild Hansen in *Arabia Felix*, translated by James and Kathleen MacFarlane (Harper and Row, New York, 1964). Leonard Cottrell's *Land of Shinar* (Souvenir Press, London, 1955) is useful for this period. Sarah Searight's *The British in the Near East* (Weidenfeld and Nicholson, London, 1969) is a mine of information on the Ottoman Empire and on early travelers.

Chapters 4 and 5

Most unfortunately, Claudius Rich's papers were lost and the only sources on this fascinating man are his *Collected Memoirs*, edited by his wife (John Murray, London, 1833), and Constance Alexander's enchanting *Baghdad in Bygone Days* (John Murray, London, 1928), which was based on the family papers. Mary Rich also published her husband's *Narrative of a Residence in Koordistan* (John Murray, London, 1836), which contains an account of their visit to Nineveh. Sir Robert Ker Porter's *Travels in Georgia, Persia, Armenia, and Ancient Babylon* (Longmans, London, 1821) contains some references to Rich, but is fascinating on Behistun and other sites. James Silk Buckingham's *Travels in Assyria, Media, and Persia* (2 vols.; Henry Coburn, London, 1829) is probably the most entertaining Mesopotamian travel book of the period. It contains charming vignettes of Baghdad and desert travel.

Chapter 6

James Baillie-Fraser's *Travels to Koordistan, Mesopotamia, etc.* (2 vols.; Longmans, London, 1840) is rather tiresome except for its vivid descriptions of the plague in Baghdad. The Euphrates Expedition is best described by

William Ainsworth, the expedition surgeon, whose *A Personal Narrative of the Euphrates Expedition* (Kegan Paul and Trench, London, 1888) is full of evocative description and local color. Colonel Chesney's tomes are heavy going, but his *Narrative of the Euphrates Expedition* (Longmans, London, 1868) is rather easier to read than his two-volume report, published in 1890. Take a look at the folio of maps produced by the expedition surveyors. They are exquisite.

Chapter 7

The decipherment of cuneiform is an often-told tale. For writing in general and cuneiform as well, try David Diringer's *Writing* (Praeger, London, 1962). Samuel Kramer's *The Sumerians* (University of Chicago Press, Chicago, 1963) is the best source for understanding the significance of cuneiform texts and contains some information on decipherment. Wallis Budge, *By Nile and Tigris* (2 vols.; John Murray, London, 1920), gives useful insights into the early cuneiform experts. Edward Hincks was biographized by E. F. Davidson (Oxford University Press, Oxford, 1933). Surprisingly enough, there is as yet no biography of Henry Rawlinson, except George Rawlinson's *Memoir of Major General Sir Henry Rawlinson* (Longmans, Green, London, 1898). Having read many of Henry Rawlinson's letters in the British Museum, I am hardly amazed. In legibility his writing resembles the cuneiform scripts that he deciphered in all their complexity! Wallis Budge's *The Rise and Progress of Assyriology* (Hopkinson, London, 1925) contains valuable data on early cuneiform experts from all over Europe and from the United States.

Chapter 8

Seton Lloyd's *Foundations* is a useful source on Paul Botta, while some hours spent looking at Botta and Flandin's *Monuments de Ninive* (Paris, 1849) is a joyful experience. Be warned that this is a rare book and obtainable only in reprint form or in special collections of large libraries. The text of this work was our major source for this chapter.

Chapters 9 and 10

Austen Henry Layard has been covered in almost embarrassing detail in the archaeological literature. By far the best biography is Gordon Waterfield's definitive *Layard of Nineveh* (John Murray, London, 1963). The discerning reader need go no further, except to Layard's own writings. These are *Early Adventures in Persia, Susiana, and Babylonia* (John Murray, London, 1887), *Nineveh and Its Remains* (John Murray, London, 1849), and *Discoveries in the Ruins of Nineveh and Babylon* (John Murray, London, 1853). Arnold Brackman's *The Luck of Nineveh* deals with Layard, but was not available when I wrote this work (McGraw-Hill, New York, 1978). Our account of Layard's exploits is largely based on his correspondence, preserved in the British Museum. See also C. J. Gadd, *The Stones of Assyria* (Chatto and Windus, London, 1936).

Chapter 11

The best source on early excavations in the south is Hermann Hilprecht's *The Excavations in Assyria and Babylonia* (Holman, Philadelphia, 1904), which is almost too thorough in its blow-by-blow descriptions of the pioneer digs. William Kennet Loftus's *Travels and Researches in Chaldea and Susiana* (Nisbet, London, 1857) is saved from being pedestrian by its lively accounts of early excavations at Uruk. For the French scientific expedition, see M. Pillet, *L'Expédition scientifique et artistique de Mésopotamie et de Médie, 1851–1855* (Paris, 1922).

Chapter 12

Hormuzd Rassam's papers appear to be lost, so we are forced to rely on his *Asshur and the Land of Nimrod* (Eaton and Mains, New York, 1897), which at best can be described as a self-serving document. Victor Place remains a rather shadowy figure, except for M. Pillet's biographical sketch, *Un Pionnier de l'Assyriologie* (Cahiers du Société Asiatique, Paris, 1960), a study which includes some fascinating early photographs of the Khorsabad dig. Place's three-volume *Ninive et l'Assyrie* (Paris, 1869) is a description of Sargon's palace. It is, quite simply, grandiose.

Chapter 13

George Smith's *The Chaldean Account of Genesis* (Scribner's, New York, 1876) is a good starting point. For the best account of the significance of his discoveries, try to locate a copy of Edmond Sollberger, *The Babylonian Legend of the Flood* (British Museum, London, 1971). This is sold by the museum and is designed for the general public. Samuel Kramer's *The Sumerians* (University of Chicago Press, Chicago, 1963) gives a broad account of the antecedents and significance of the deluge epics. Kramer's article in *Ancient Near Eastern Texts Relating to the Old Testament*, edited by J. B. Pritchard (Princeton University Press, Princeton, 1969), gives recent translations of the Sumerian flood epic.

Chapters 14 and 15

For Rassam, I used the sources listed above, amplifying them with archival materials in the British Museum, especially correspondence with Layard and the trustees that was preserved in the Layard archives. An atmosphere of low comedy always seems to surround Wallis Budge in my mind, although I realize this is unfair. One source on his activities is *By Nile and Tigris*, already mentioned, a book best described as a gossipy compendium of information on his trips to Mesopotamia and on academic doings in Assyriology in the closing decades of the nineteenth century. The same author's *Rise and Progress of Assyriology* is also useful for filling in details.

Chapter 16

Hermann Hilprecht's *Explorations in Biblical Lands* (A. J. Holman, Philadelphia, 1903) is a useful source of information on the events which led to the excavations at Telloh and on the Nippur digs. Peters's *Nippur, or Explorations and Adventures on the Euphrates* is rather prosaic compared with Hilprecht's book and adds little to his expert account. A. Parrot, *Archéologie mésopotamienne* (vol. 1; Michel, Paris, 1946) is informative on Telloh and the early French excavations. Sarzec and Heuzey's *Découvertes en Chaldée* (Paris, 1884–1912) is the basic source on the earliest work on the Sumerian city. For the Sumerians in general, read Samuel Kramer, *The Sumerians* (University of Chicago Press, Chicago, 1963).

Chapter 17

The Germans were reticent in writing about their work for the general public, but Robert Koldewey's *The Excavations at Babylon* (Macmillan, London, 1914) gives an outline, and a rather dull description, of the many campaigns at the site. This can be amplified by Seton Lloyd's *Foundations in the Dust* (Oxford University Press, London, 1947), an admirable account of local digging conditions in the early years of this century. See also Walter Andrae's *Das Wiedererstandene Assur* (Leipzig, 1938).

Chapter 18

Leonard Woolley always wrote up his excavations thoroughly, both for the specialist and for the general public. His most entertaining books were anecdotal, especially *Dead Cities and Living Men* (Philosophical Library, New York, 1956), in which he describes the lighthearted side of Carchemish. The stories he tells seem historically accurate, even if T. E. Lawrence was upset by their first publication. Two excellent biographies of Lawrence have appeared recently: John E. Mack's *A Prince of Our Disorder* (Little, Brown, Boston, 1976) and Desmond Stewart's *T. E. Lawrence: A New Biography* (Harper and Row, New York, 1977). For the Hittites, see T. O. Gurney, *The Hittites* (Pelican Books, Baltimore, 1961).

Chapter 19

Accounts of the political developments of 1905 to 1932 are legion, but the most widely consulted is Stephen Longrigg's *Iraq, 1900 to 1950* (Oxford University Press, London, 1953). The same author's *Four Centuries of Modern Iraq* (Clarendon Press, Oxford, 1925) is widely admired by experts. H. V. F. Winstone's *Gertrude Bell* (Jonathan Cape, London, 1978) is a recent biography. Bell's writings still give pleasure, especially *The Desert and the Sown* (Heinemann, London, 1907) and *Amurath to Amurath* (Heinemann, London, 1911). Her letters were published by her mother in heavily expurgated form. See Lady Bell, *The Letters of Gertrude Bell* (2 vols.;

Boni and Liveright, New York, 1927). The correspondence between the
University of Philadelphia and the British Museum was published by Robert
Dyson in *Expedition* for 1977. Full publication of the Bell archives in the
University of Newcastle and of the Pennsylvania files will reveal a mass of
new material on this period.

Chapter 20

Every popular writer on archaeology covers Ur at some point or other. By
far the best source is still Loenard Woolley himself. I used the expedition
monographs and preliminary reports as well as Woolley's summary *Excavations at Ur* (Barnes and Noble, New York, 1954). Sir Max Mallowan's
autobiography *Mallowan's Memoirs* (Dodd, Mead, New York, 1977) is not
particularly entertaining, but contains useful memories of the Ur excavations. Further historical material on Ur can be found in *Iraq* (1960), a
volume of that academic journal offered in tribute to Woolley and published soon after his death. Agatha Christie's *An Autobiography* (Collins,
London, 1977) is a delightful vignette of the archaeological and literary life,
while her *Come Tell Me How You Live* (Collins, London, 1943) tells of
digging in the Near East after Ur.

Chapter 21

This chapter was written from a plethora of sources, including Seton Lloyd's
Mounds of the Near East (Aldine, Chicago, 1963) and David and Joan
Oates's *The Rise of Civilization*, also cited for Chapter 1. The autobiographi-
cal sketches mentioned in Chapter 20 were also of use here. Max Mallowan's
Nimrud and Its Remains (2 vols.; Collins, London, 1966) is a magnificent
account of his remarkable ivory discoveries at Nimrud and of work since
Layard's day. Robert Braidwood and Bruce Howe, *Excavations in Iraqi
Kurdistan* (Oriental Institute, Chicago, 1960), summarizes the team approach
that resulted in the excavation of Jarmo and other sites. Robert Adams,
Land Behind Baghdad (University of Chicago Press, Chicago, 1965), and
The Uruk Countryside (University of Chicago Press, Chicago, 1972) sum-
marize the results of the Oriental Institute irrigation surveys. Thorkild
Jacobsen's *The Treasures of Darkness* (Yale University Press, New Haven,
1976) is a superb account of Mesopotamian religion that places the Biblical
legends and Sumerian, as well as later, beliefs in a broad perspective.

Index